D1195468

Psychosemantics

Explorations in Cognitive Science
Margaret A. Boden, general editor

1. *Mental Processes: Studies in Cognitive Science*
   H. Christopher Longuet-Higgins

2. *Psychosemantics: The Problem of Meaning in the Philosophy of Mind*
   Jerry A. Fodor

3. *Consciousness and the Computational Mind*
   Ray Jackendoff

Psychosemantics

The Problem of Meaning in the Philosophy of Mind

Jerry A. Fodor

A Bradford Book
Published in cooperation with
The British Psychological Society

The MIT Press
Cambridge, Massachusetts
London, England

This book was set in Palatino by Achorn Graphic Services and printed and bound by Halliday Lithograph in the United States of America.

Library of Congress Cataloging-in-Publication Data

Fodor, Jerry A.
 Psychosemantics: the problem of meaning in the philosophy of mind.

 (Explorations in cognitive science)
 "A Bradford book."
 Bibliography: p.
 Includes index.
 1. Psychology—Philosophy.   2. Representation (Philosophy)   3. Causation.
 4. Human behavior.   I. Title.   II. Series.   [DNLM: 1. Cognition.   2. Philosophy.
 3. Psychology.   BF 311 F653p]
 BF38.F63   1987   128'.4   86-33173
 ISBN 0-262-06106-6

For Ned Block and Georges Rey; old cronies

Contents

Preface   ix

Chapter 1
Introduction: The Persistence of the Attitudes   1

Chapter 2
Individualism and Supervenience   27

Chapter 3
Meaning Holism   55

Chapter 4
Meaning and the World Order   97

Epilogue
Creation Myth   129

Appendix
Why There Still Has to Be a Language of Thought   135

Notes   155
References   169
Author Index   173

We have not that Science yet perfect,
'tis one of the Desiderata.

John Aubrey (on astrology)

Preface

I have, as it happens, a strikingly intelligent cat. Here are some of the behaviors in which his intelligence is manifest:

In the morning, at his usual feeding time, Greycat prowls the area of the kitchen near his food bowl. When breakfast appears, he positions himself with respect to the bowl in a manner that facilitates ingestion.

When the house is cold, Greycat often sleeps before the fireplace. But he does this only if there's a fire on the hearth, and he never gets close enough to singe his hair.

When his foot encounters a sharp object, Greycat withdraws it. In similar spirit, he maintains an appreciable distance between himself and the nearest aggressive dog.

He occasionally traps and disembowels small rodents.

In saying that these behaviors manifest striking intelligence, I do not mean to imply that Greycat is at an intellectual advantage with respect to *other cats*. On the contrary, many cat owners have similar anecdotes to report. I allow for the hyperbole that their infatuation prompts, but by and large I believe them.

No, my point is that Greycat is strikingly intelligent in comparison with, for example, *rocks, trees, worms, and spiral nebulae*. Rocks, trees, worms, and spiral nebulae are, each in its own way, quite complicated objects. Each has claimed the attention of some of our best scientific minds, and there are, no doubt, many things about them that we still don't understand. Yet none of their behaviors seems remotely as clever as Greycat's. In fact, they don't—excepting, maybe, grossly metaphorically—*behave* at all. Oh, mice have died, and worms have eaten them; but no rock, and no spiral nebula—and no worm, for that matter—has ever *chased* a mouse, let alone caught one. (Mousetraps catch mice, of course; but that manifests *our* intelligence, not theirs.)

It seems to me to want explaining, this impressive difference between Greycat's behavioral capacities and those of, say, the spiral nebula in Andromeda. I have, as it happens, a strikingly intelligent theory.

The theory is that Greycat—unlike rocks, worms, nebulae, and the rest—has, and acts out of, beliefs and desires. The reason, for example, that Greycat patrols his food bowl in the morning is that he wants food and believes—has come to believe on the basis of earlier feedings—that his food bowl is the place to find it. The reason that Greycat avoids aggressive dogs is that he is afraid of them. The reason that Greycat scratches at the door is that he wants out. And so forth. Whereas, by contrast, rocks and the like do not have beliefs and desires. Their 'behaviors' are different from Greycat's because they are, in this respect, differently caused.

I have no serious doubt that this theory (what I call 'commonsense belief/desire psychology') is pretty close to being true. My reason for believing this—set out at length in chapter 1—is that commonsense belief/desire psychology explains vastly more of the facts about behavior than any of the alternative theories available. It could hardly fail to do so: there *are* no alternative theories available.

Still, I'm prepared to admit that commonsense belief/desire psychology is, in philosophically interesting ways, problematic. The problems I have in mind aren't the old ontological and epistemological worries: *Could beliefs and desires be material? Could they be immaterial? How do I know that Greycat has any?* Fascinating though these questions have sometimes seemed, I find that I have grown bored with them; perhaps because the answers are so obvious. (The answer to the first question is 'yes,' because whatever has causal powers is ipso facto material; the answer to the second question is 'no,' for the same reason; and I told you the answer to the third question a paragraph back.) The really interesting problems about commonsense belief/desire psychology—or so it seems to me—are the ones that center around the phenomena of intentionality.

There's quite a lot of Greycat's behavior that I want to explain by adverting to the way that Greycat *takes the world to be*; how he represents things. For example: It's part of *my* story about why Greycat turns up in the kitchen in the morning that *Greycat* has a story about his bowl; and that, in Greycat's story, the bowl figures as—it's represented as being—a likely locus of food. Since I believe my story about Greycat to be true, and since attributions to Greycat of representational states are intrinsic to it, I am under some obligation to take such attributions seriously; to do my best, in fact, to make sense of them. Because believing and desiring are representational states, Realism about belief/desire explanations leads one, by a short route, to worry about representation.

Mental states like believing and desiring aren't, however, the only things that represent. The other obvious candidates are *symbols*. So, I write (or utter): 'Greycat is prowling in the kitchen,' thereby producing a 'discursive symbol'; a token of a linguistic expression. What I've written (or uttered) represents the world as being a certain way—as being such that Greycat is prowling in the kitchen—just as my thought does when the thought that Greycat is prowling in the kitchen occurs to me.

To a first approximation, symbols and mental states both have representational *content*. And nothing else does that belongs to the causal order: not rocks, or worms or trees or spiral nebulae. It would, therefore, be no great surprise if the theory of mind and the theory of symbols were some day to converge. In fact, something of the sort now seems to be happening. Every time a philosopher of language turns a corner, he runs into a philosopher of mind who is pounding the same beat.

It appears increasingly that the main joint business of the philosophy of language and the philosophy of mind is the problem of representation itself: the metaphysical question of the place of meaning in the world order. How can anything manage to be *about* anything; and why is it that only thoughts and symbols succeed? It's good news that philosophers, tired of the ontology and epistemology of mind, have turned to considering this question. The bad news is that—so far—the tenor of their inquiry has been mainly skeptical.

There are, beyond the slightest doubt, deep and difficult problems about understanding representation. "Very well, then," one might reasonably say, "let us try, in a spirit of gradual and cumulative research, to solve these deep and difficult problems." But that has not, by and large, been the philosophical response. What a surprising number of philosophers of language have said instead is: "If there are deep and difficult problems about representation, then *we won't have any* representation." And what an equally surprising number of philosophers of mind have added is: "If no representation means no belief/desire psychology, then *we* won't have any of *that*." Chorus: "We all keep a respectable ontology; troublemakers not allowed."

Considered as a research strategy, this strikes me as frivolous, not to say petulant. There are various things that you can usefully do when your car gets a ping in its cylinders; but declining to quantify over the engine is not among them. You need a story about the engine to explain how the car behaves; you need commonsense belief/desire psychology to explain how Greycat behaves. Rational strategy is the same in both cases: if you are having trouble with the thing, get it fixed.

That, then, is what this book is about. I propose to look at some of the semantical problems that have recently been raised as hard cases for belief/desire psychology: proposed inferences from premises in the philosophy of language to skeptical conclusions in the philosophy of mind. I don't, by any means, have solutions for all of these problems. But I do have suggestions for some of them, and I expect that there are other and better suggestions just waiting to be made. On even the most optimistic estimate, it's a long way from the intuitive belief/desire explanations that common sense gives us to the rigorous and explicit intentional psychology that is our scientific goal. This book is not, therefore, intended to *conclude* the philosophy of mind; just to mitigate the panic that has lately tended to predominate. The main moral is supposed to be that we have, as things now stand, no decisive reason to doubt that very many commonsense belief/desire explanations are—literally—true.

Which is just as well, because if commonsense intentional psychology really were to collapse, that would be, beyond comparison, the greatest intellectual catastrophe in the history of our species; if we're that wrong about the mind, then that's the wrongest we've ever been about anything. The collapse of the supernatural, for example, didn't compare; theism never came close to being as intimately involved in our thought and our practice—especially our practice—as belief/desire explanation is. Nothing except, perhaps, our commonsense physics—our intuitive commitment to a world of observer-independent, middle-sized objects—comes as near our cognitive core as intentional explanation does. We'll be in deep, deep trouble if we have to give it up.

I'm dubious, in fact, that we *can* give it up; that our intellects are so constituted that doing without it (I mean *really* doing without it; not just philosophical loose talk) is a biologically viable option. But be of good cheer; everything is going to be all right. Or so I hope presently to persuade you.

This book is mostly a defense of belief/desire psychology, and it is mostly written for philosophers. However, though other versions of Intentional Realism are no doubt conceivable, I'm much inclined to bet on a species called the Language of Thought Hypothesis (LOT) (or, alternatively, the Representational Theory of Mind (RTM)). Cognitive scientists who aren't philosophers will perhaps be more interested in the status of LOT than in Intentional Realism per se. An outline argument for LOT is therefore presented in chapter 1; and I've added an Appendix in which LOT is discussed at length. Language-of-thought freaks may wish to consider skipping the rest of the book and just reading the Appendix.

Various versions of various pieces of this manuscript have been floating around, in published and unpublished form, for the last couple of years. Chapter 2 differs only in details from the paper of the same title that appears in the *Proceedings of the Aristotelian Society* for 1986; and the paper "Banish DisContent" (also 1986) gave a sort of preliminary overview of the positions adopted in chapters 2 and 3. A very long manuscript called "Psychosemantics," and a somewhat shorter one called "Narrow Content and Meaning Holism," served as first approaches to the problems discussed in chapters 3 and 4. These are both now defunct; the treatments they proposed were quite different from the ones given here, and, I think, very much less satisfactory.

I owe a lot of this work to other philosophers; especially to the faculty and graduate students of the philosophy departments at the University of Michigan (Ann Arbor) and Princeton University, where substantial portions of this book were presented in two series of lectures early in 1986. The leaks they sprang I have subsequently attempted to patch. An early version of the Appendix was read as an invited address at the Sydney meetings of the Australian Philosophical Association in the summer of 1985. I'm indebted to Peter Slezak both for his hospitality and for some useful philosophical points.

Among other philosophers whose conversation, correspondence, and marginalia have helped shape this text—but who nevertheless refuse to be blamed for it—the following have been particularly helpful: Jon Barwise, Ned Block, Sylvain Bromberger, Tyler Burge, Martin Davies, Dan Dennett, Michael Devitt, Fred Dretske, James Higgenbotham, David Israel, Ron McClamrock, John Perry, Georges Rey, Dennis Stampe, Kim Sterelney, Steven Stich, and Scott Weinstein. I am especially indebted to Gabe Segal both for philosophical conversation and for working up the bibliography.

Psychosemantics

1

Introduction: The Persistence of the Attitudes

A Midsummer Night's Dream, act 3, scene 2.
Enter Demetrius and Hermia.

Dem. O, why rebuke you him that loves you so?
Lay breath so bitter on your bitter foe.

Herm. Now I but chide, but I should use thee worse;
For thou, I fear, hast given me cause to curse.
If thou hast slain Lysander in his sleep,
Being o'er shoes in blood, plunge in the deep,
And kill me too.
The sun was not so true unto the day
As he to me: would he have stol'n away
From sleeping Hermia? I'll believe as soon
This whole earth may be bor'd; and that the moon
May through the centre creep, and so displease
Her brother's noontide with the antipodes.
It cannot be but thou hast murder'd him;
So should a murderer look; so dead, so grim.

Very nice. And also very *plausible*; a convincing (though informal) piece of implicit, nondemonstrative, theoretical inference.

Here, leaving out a lot of lemmas, is how the inference must have gone: Hermia has reason to believe herself beloved of Lysander. (Lysander has told her that he loves her—repeatedly and in elegant iambics—and inferences from how people say they feel to how they do feel are reliable, ceteris paribus.) But if Lysander does indeed love Hermia, then, a fortiori, Lysander wishes Hermia well. But if Lysander wishes Hermia well, then Lysander does not voluntarily desert Hermia at night in a darkling wood. (There may be lions. "There is not a more fearful wild-fowl than your lion living.") But Hermia was, in fact, so deserted by Lysander. Therefore not voluntarily. Therefore *involuntarily*. Therefore it is plausible that Lysander has come to harm. At whose hands? Plausibly at Demetrius's hands. For Demetrius is Lysander's rival for the love of Hermia, and the presumption is that rivals in love do *not* wish one another well. Specifically, Hermia believes that Demetrius believes that a live Lysander is an impediment to the success of his (Demetrius's) wooing of her (Hermia). Moreover, Hermia believes (correctly) that if x wants that P, and x believes that not-P unless Q, and x believes that x can bring it about that Q, then (ceteris paribus) x tries to bring it about that Q. Moreover, Hermia believes (again correctly) that, by and large, people succeed in bringing about what they try to bring about. *So*: Knowing and believing all this, Hermia infers that perhaps Demetrius has killed Lysander. And we, the audience, who know what Hermia knows and believes and who share, more or less, her views about the psychology of lovers and rivals, understand how she has come to draw this inference. We sympathize.

In fact, Hermia has it all wrong. Demetrius is innocent and Lysander lives. The intricate theory that connects beliefs, desires, and actions—the implicit theory that Hermia relies on to make sense of what Lysander did and what Demetrius may have done; and that *we* rely on to make sense of Hermia's inferring what she does; and that Shakespeare relies on to predict and manipulate our sympathies ('*deconstruction' my foot*, by the way)—this theory makes no provision for nocturnal interventions by mischievous fairies. Unbeknownst to Hermia, a peripatetic sprite has sprung the ceteris paribus clause and made her plausible inference go awry. ''Reason and love keep little company together now-a-days: the more the pity that some honest neighbours will not make them friends.''

Granting, however, that the theory fails from time to time—and not just when fairies intervene—I nevertheless want to emphasize *(1) how often it goes right, (2) how deep it is, and (3) how much we do depend upon it*. Commonsense belief/desire psychology has recently come under a lot of philosophical pressure, and it's possible to doubt whether it can be saved in face of the sorts of problems that its critics have raised. There is, however, a prior question: whether it's worth the effort of trying to save it. That's the issue I propose to start with.

1. How Often It Works

Hermia got it wrong; her lover was less constant than she had supposed. Applications of commonsense psychology mediate our relations with one another, and when its predictions fail these relations break down. The resulting disarray is likely to happen in public and to be highly noticeable.

Herm. Since night you lov'd me; yet since night you left me;
      Why, then, you left me,—O, the gods forbid!—
      In earnest, shall I say?
Lys. Ay, by my life;
      And never did desire to see thee more.
      Therefore be out of hope. . . .

This sort of thing makes excellent theater; the *successes* of common-sense psychology, by contrast, are ubiquitous and—for that very reason—practically invisible.

Commonsense psychology works so well it disappears. It's like those mythical Rolls Royce cars whose engines are sealed when they leave the factory; only it's better because it isn't mythical. Someone I don't know phones me at my office in New York from—as it might be—Arizona. 'Would you like to lecture here next Tuesday?' are the words that he utters. 'Yes, thank you. I'll be at your airport on the 3 p.m. flight' are the words that I reply. That's *all* that happens, but it's more than enough; the rest of the burden of predicting behavior—of bridging the gap between utterances and actions—is routinely taken up by theory. And the theory works so well that several days later (or weeks later, or months later, or years later; you can vary the example to taste) and several thousand miles away, there I am at the airport, and there he is to meet me. Or if I *don't* turn up, it's less likely that the theory has failed than that something went wrong with the airline. It's not possible to say, in quantitative terms, just how successfully commonsense psychology allows us to coordinate our behaviors. But I have the impression that we manage pretty well with one another; often rather better than we cope with less complex machines.

The point—to repeat—is that the theory from which we get this extraordinary predictive power is just good old commonsense belief/desire psychology. That's what tells us, for example, how to infer people's intentions from the sounds they make (if someone utters the form of words ('I'll be at your airport on the 3 p.m. flight,' then, ceteris paribus, he intends to be at your airport on the 3 p.m. flight) and how to infer people's behavior from their intentions (if someone intends to be at your airport on the 3 p.m. flight, then, ceteris paribus, he will produce behavior of a sort which will eventuate in his arriving at that place at that time, barring mechanical failures and acts of God). And all this works not just with people whose psychology you know intimately: your closest friends, say, or the spouse of your bosom. It works with *absolute strangers;* people you wouldn't know if you bumped into them. And it works not just in laboratory conditions—where you can control the interacting variables—but also, indeed preeminently, in field conditions where all you know about the sources of variance is what commonsense psychology tells you about them. Remarkable. If we could do that well with predicting the weather, no one would ever get his feet wet; and yet the etiology of the weather must surely be child's play compared with the causes of behavior.

Yes, but what about all those ceteris paribuses? I commence to digress:

Philosophers sometimes argue that the appearance of predictive adequacy that accrues to the generalizations of commonsense psychology is spurious. For, they say, as soon as you try to make these generalizations explicit, you see that they have to be hedged about with ceteris paribus clauses; hedged about in ways that make them *trivially* incapable of disconfirmation. "False or vacuous" is the charge.

Consider the defeasibility of 'if someone utters the form of words "I'll be at your airport on the 3 p.m. flight," then he intends to be at your airport on the 3 p.m. flight.' This generalization does *not* hold if, for example, the speaker is lying; or if the speaker is using the utterance as an example (of a false sentence, say); or if he is a monolingual speaker of Urdu who happens to have uttered the sentence by accident; or if the speaker is talking in his sleep; or . . . whatever. You can, of course, defend the generalization in the usual way; you can say that '*all else being equal*, if someone utters the form of words "I'll be at your airport on the 3 p.m. flight," then he intends to be at your airport on the 3 p.m. flight.' But perhaps this last means nothing more than: 'if someone says that he intends to be there, then he does intend to be there—unless he doesn't.' That, of course, is predictively adequate for sure; nothing that happens will disconfirm it; nothing that happens could.

A lot of philosophers seem to be moved by this sort of argument; yet, even at first blush, it would be surprising if it were any good. After all, we do use commonsense psychological generalizations to predict one another's behavior; and the predictions do—very often—come out true. But how could that be so if the generalizations that we base the predictions on are *empty*?

I'm inclined to think that what is alleged about the implicit reliance of commonsense psychology on uncashed ceteris paribus clauses is in fact a perfectly general property of the *explicit* generalizations in *all* the special sciences; in all empirical explanatory schemes, that is to say, other than basic physics. Consider the following modest truth of geology: A meandering river erodes its outside bank. "False or vacuous"; so a philosopher might argue. "Take it straight—as a strictly universal generalization—and it is surely false. Think of the case where the weather changes and the river freezes; or the world comes to an end; or somebody builds a dam; or somebody builds a concrete wall on the outside bank; or the rains stop and the river dries up . . . or whatever. You can, of course, defend the generalization in the usual way—by appending a ceteris paribus clause: '*All else being equal, a meandering river erodes its outside bank.*' But perhaps this last means nothing more than: 'A meandering river erodes its outside bank—unless it doesn't.' That, of course, is predictively adequate for sure. Nothing that happens will disconfirm it; nothing that happens could.''

Patently, something has gone wrong. For 'All else being equal, a meandering river erodes its outside bank' is neither false nor vacuous, and it doesn't mean 'A meandering river erodes its outside bank—unless it doesn't.' It is, I expect, a long story how the generalizations of the special sciences manage to be both hedged and informative (or, if you like, how they manage to support counterfactuals even though they have exceptions). Telling that story is part of making clear why we have special sciences at all; why we don't just have basic physics (see Fodor, *SS*). It is also part of making clear how idealization works in science. For surely 'Ceteris paribus, a meandering river erodes its outside bank' means something like 'A meandering river erodes its outside bank in any nomologically possible world where the operative idealizations of geology are satisfied.' That this is, in general, stronger than '*P* in any world where not not-*P*' is certain. So if, as it would appear, commonsense psychology relies upon its ceteris paribus clauses, so too does geology.

There is, then, a face similarity between the way implicit generalizations work in commonsense psychology and the way explicit generalizations work in the special sciences. But maybe this similarity is *merely* superficial. Donald Davidson is famous for having argued that the generalizations of real science, unlike those that underlie commonsense belief/desire explanations, are "perfectible." In the real, but not the intentional, sciences we can (in principle, anyhow) get rid of the ceteris paribus clauses by actually enumerating the conditions under which the generalizations are supposed to hold.

By this criterion, however, the only real science is basic physics. For it simply isn't true that we can, even in principle, specify the conditions under which—say—geological generalizations hold *so long as we stick to the vocabulary of geology.* Or, to put it less in the formal mode, the causes of exceptions to geological generalizations are, quite typically, not themselves *geological* events. Try it and see: 'A meandering river erodes its outer banks unless, for example, the weather changes and the river dries up.' But 'weather' isn't a term in *geology;* nor are 'the world comes to an end,' 'somebody builds a dam,' and indefinitely many other·descriptors required to specify the sorts of things that can go wrong. All you can say that's any use is: If the generalization failed to hold, then the operative idealizations must somehow have failed to be satisfied. But so, too, in commonsense psychology: If he didn't turn up when he intended to, then something must have gone wrong.

Exceptions to the generalizations of a special science are typically *inexplicable* from the point of view of (that is, in the vocabulary of) that science. That's one of the things that makes it a *special* science. But, of course, it may nevertheless be perfectly possible to explain the exceptions *in the vocabulary of some other science.* In the most familiar case, you go 'down' one or more levels and use the vocabulary of a more 'basic' science. (The current failed to run through the circuit because the terminals were oxidized; he no longer recognizes familiar objects because of a cerebral accident. And so forth.) The availability of this strategy is one of the things that the hierarchical arrangement of our sciences buys for us. Anyhow, to put the point succinctly, the same pattern that holds for the special sciences seems to hold for commonsense psychology as well. On the one hand, its ceteris paribus clauses are ineliminable from the point of view of its proprietary conceptual resources. But, on the other hand, we have—so far at least—no reason to doubt that they can be discharged in the vocabulary of some lower-level science (neurology, say, or biochemistry; at worst, physics).

If the world is describable as a closed causal system at all, it is so only in the vocabulary of our most basic science. From this nothing follows that a psychologist (or a geologist) needs to worry about.

I cease to digress. The moral so far is that the predictive adequacy of commonsense psychology is beyond rational dispute; nor is there any reason to suppose that it's obtained by cheating. If you want to know where my physical body will be next Thursday, mechanics— our best science of middle-sized objects after all, and reputed to be pretty good in its field—is *no use to you at all.* Far the best way to find out (usually, in practice, the *only* way to find out) is: *ask me!*

2. *The Depth of the Theory*

It's tempting to think of commonsense psychology as merely a budget of such truisms as one learns at Granny's knee: that the burnt child fears the fire, that all the world loves a lover, that money can't buy happiness, that reinforcement affects response rate, and that the way to a man's heart is through his stomach. None of these, I agree, is worth saving. However, as even the simple example sketched above serves to make clear, subsumption under platitudes is *not* the typical form of commonsense psychological explanation. Rather, when such explanations are made explicit, they are frequently seen to exhibit the 'deductive structure' that is so characteristic of explanation in real science. There are two parts to this: the theory's underlying generalizations are defined over unobservables, and they lead to its predictions by iterating and interacting rather than by being directly instantiated.

Hermia, for example, is no fool and no behaviorist; she is perfectly aware both that Demetrius's behavior is caused by his mental states and that the pattern of such causation is typically intricate. There are, in particular, no plausible and counterfactual-supporting generalizations of the form $(x) (y) (x$ *is a rival of y*$) \rightarrow (x$ *kills y*$)$. Nothing like that is remotely true; not even ceteris paribus. Rather, the generalization Hermia takes to be operative—the one that *is* true and counterfactual-supporting—must be something like *If x is y's rival, then x prefers y's discomfiture, all else being equal.* This principle, however, doesn't so much as mention behavior; it leads to behavioral predictions, but only via a lot of further assumptions about how people's preferences may affect their actions in given situations. Or rather, since there probably are no generalizations which connect preferences to actions irrespective of beliefs, what Hermia must be relying on is an implicit theory of how beliefs, preferences, and behaviors interact; an implicit decision theory, no less.

It is a deep fact about the world that the most powerful etiological generalizations hold of unobservable causes. Such facts shape our science (they'd better!). It is thus a test of the depth of a theory that many of its generalizations subsume interactions among unobservables. By this test, our implicit, commonsense *meteorology* is presumably *not* a deep theory, since it consists largely of rule-of-thumb generalizations of the "red at night, sailor's delight" variety. Correspondingly, the reasoning that mediates applications of commonsense meteorology probably involves not a lot more than instantiation and modus ponens. (All this being so, it is perhaps not surprising that commonsense meteorology doesn't work very well.) Commonsense psychology, by contrast, passes the test. It takes for granted that overt behavior comes at the end of a causal chain whose links are mental events—hence unobservable—and which may be arbitrarily long (and arbitrarily kinky). Like Hermia, we are all—quite literally, I expect—born mentalists and Realists; and we stay that way until common sense is driven out by bad philosophy.

3. Its Indispensability

We have, in practice, no alternative to the vocabulary of common-sense psychological explanation; we have no other way of describing our behaviors and their causes if we want our behaviors and their causes to be subsumed by any counterfactual-supporting generalizations that we know about. This is, again, hard to see because it's so close.

For example, a few paragraphs back, I spoke of the commonsense psychological generalization *people generally do what they say that they will do* as bridging the gap between an exchange of utterances ("Will you come and lecture . . . ," "I'll be at your airport on Thursday . . .") and the consequent behaviors of the speakers (my arriving at the airport, his being there to meet me). But this understates the case for the indispensability of commonsense psychology, since without it we can't even describe the utterances as forms of words (to say nothing of describing the ensuing behaviors as kinds of acts). *Word* is a *psychological* category. (It is, indeed, *irreducibly* psychological, so far as anybody knows; there are, for example, no acoustic properties that all and only tokens of the same word type must share. In fact, surprisingly, there are no acoustic properties that all and only *fully intelligible* tokens of the same word type must share. Which is why our best technology is currently unable to build a typewriter that you can dictate to.)

As things now stand—to spell it out—we have *no* vocabulary for specifying event types that meets the following four conditions:

1. My behavior in uttering 'I'll be there on Thursday . . .' counts as an event of type T_i.
2. My arriving there on Thursday counts as an event of Type T_j.
3. 'Events of type T_j are consequent upon events of type T_i' is even roughly true and counterfactual supporting.
4. Categories T_i and T_j are other than irreducibly psychological.

For the only known taxonomies that meet conditions 1–3 acknowledge such event types as uttering the *form of words* 'I'll be there on Thursday', or *saying that* one will be there on Thursday, or *performing the act* of meeting someone at the airport; so they fail condition 4.

Philosophers and psychologists used to dream of an alternative conceptual apparatus, one in which the commonsense inventory of types of *behavior* is replaced by an inventory of types of *movements;* the counterfactual-supporting generalizations of psychology would then exhibit the contingency of these movements upon environmental and/or organic variables. That behavior is indeed contingent upon environmental and organic variables is, I suppose, not to be denied;

yet the generalizations were not forthcoming. Why? There's a standard answer: It's because behavior consists of actions, and actions cross-classify movements. The generalization is that the burnt child avoids the fire; but what movement constitutes avoidance depends on where the child is, where the fire is . . . and so, drearily, forth. If you want to know what generalizations subsume a behavioral event, you have to know what *action type* it belongs to; knowing what *motion type* it belongs to usually doesn't buy anything. I take all that to be Gospel.

Yet it is generally assumed that this situation *must* be remediable, at least in principle. After all, the generalizations of a completed physics would presumably subsume every motion of every thing, hence the motions of organisms *inter alia*. So, if we wait long enough, we will after all have counterfactual-supporting generalizations that subsume the motions of organisms *under that description*. Presumably, God has them already.

This is, however, a little misleading. For, the (putative) generalizations of the (putative) completed physics would apply to the motions of organisms qua motions, but not qua organismic. Physics presumably has as little use for the categories of macrobiology as it does for the categories of commonsense psychology; it dissolves the behav*er* as well as the behav*ior*. What's left is atoms in the void. The subsumption of the motions of organisms—and of everything else—by the counterfactual-supporting generalizations of physics does not therefore guarantee that there is any science whose ontology recognizes organisms and their motions. That is: The subsumption of the motions of organisms—and of everything else—by the laws of physics does not guarantee that there are any laws about the motions of organisms qua motions of organisms. So far as anybody knows— barring, perhaps, a little bit of the psychology of classical reflexes— there are no such laws; and there is no metaphysical reason to expect any.[1]

Anyhow, this is all poppycock. Even if psychology were dispensable *in principle*, that would be no argument for dispensing with it. (Perhaps geology is dispensable in principle; every river is a physical object after all. Would that be a reason for supposing that rivers aren't a natural kind? Or that 'meandering rivers erode their outside banks' is untrue?) What's relevant to whether commonsense psychology is worth defending is its dispensability *in fact*. And here the situation is absolutely clear. We have no idea of how to explain ourselves to ourselves except in a vocabulary which is *saturated* with belief/desire psychology. One is tempted to transcendental argument: What Kant said to Hume about physical objects holds, mutatis mutandis, for the propositional attitudes; we can't give them up *because we don't know how to.*[2]

So maybe we had better try to hold onto them. Holding onto the attitudes—vindicating commonsense psychology—means showing how you could have (or, at a minimum, showing *that* you could have) a respectable science whose ontology explicitly acknowledges states that exhibit the sorts of properties that common sense attributes to the attitudes. That is what the rest of this book is about. This undertaking presupposes, however, some consensus about what sorts of properties common sense does attribute to the attitudes. That is what the next bit of this chapter is about.

The Essence of the Attitudes

How do we tell whether a psychology *is* a belief/desire psychology? How, in general, do we know if propositional attitudes are among the entities that the ontology of a theory acknowledges? These sorts of questions raise familiar and perplexing issues of intertheoretic identification. How do you distinguish elimination from reduction and reconstruction? Is the right story that there's no such thing as dephlogisticated matter, or is 'dephlogistinizing' just a word for oxidizing? Even behaviorists had trouble deciding whether they wanted to deny the existence of the mental or to assert its identity with the behavioral. (Sometimes they did both, in successive sentences. Ah, they really knew about insouciance in those days.)

I propose to stipulate. I will view a psychology as being commonsensical about the attitudes—in fact, as endorsing them—just in case it postulates states (entities, events, whatever) satisfying the following conditions:

> (*i*) They are semantically evaluable.
> (*ii*) They have causal powers.
> (*iii*) The implicit generalizations of commonsense belief/desire psychology are largely true of them.

In effect, I'm assuming that (*i*)–(*iii*) are the essential properties of the attitudes. This seems to me intuitively plausible; if it doesn't seem intuitively plausible to you, so be it. Squabbling about intuitions strikes me as vulgar.

A word about each of these conditions.

(i) Semantic Evaluation
Beliefs are the kinds of things that are true or false; desires are the kinds of things that get frustrated or fulfilled; hunches are the kinds

of things that turn out to be right or wrong; so it goes. I will assume that what makes a belief true (/false) is something about its relation to the nonpsychological world (and not—e.g.—something about its relation to other beliefs; unless it happens to be a belief about beliefs). Hence, to say of a belief that it is true (/false) is to evaluate that belief in terms of its relation to the world. I will call such evaluations 'semantic.' Similarly, mutatis mutandis, with desires, hunches, and so forth.

It is, as I remarked in the preface, a puzzle about beliefs, desires, and the like that they are semantically evaluable; almost nothing else is. (Trees aren't; numbers aren't; people aren't. Propositions *are* [assuming that there are such things], but that's hardly surprising; propositions exist to be what beliefs and desires are attitudes *toward*.) We will see, later in this book, that it is primarily the semantic evaluability of beliefs and desires that gets them into philosophical trouble—and that a defense of belief/desire psychology needs to be a defense of.

Sometimes I'll talk of the *content* of a psychological state rather than its semantic evaluability. These two ideas are intimately interconnected. Consider—for a change of plays—Hamlet's belief that his uncle killed his father. That belief has a certain semantic value; in particular, it's a *true* belief. Why true? Well, because it corresponds to a certain fact. Which fact? Well, the fact that Hamlet's uncle killed Hamlet's father. But why is it *that* fact that determines the semantic evaluation of Hamlet's belief? Why not the fact that two is a prime number, or the fact that Demetrius didn't kill Lysander? Well, because the *content* of Hamlet's belief is *that* his uncle killed his father. (If you like, the belief 'expresses the proposition' that Hamlet's uncle killed his father.) *If you know what the content of a belief is, then you know what it is about the world that determines the semantic evaluation of the belief;* that, at a minimum, is how the notions of content and semantic evaluation connect.

I propose to say almost nothing more about content at this stage; its time will come. Suffice just to add that propositional attitudes have their contents essentially: the canonical way of picking out an attitude is to say (a) what sort of attitude it is (a belief, a desire, a hunch, or whatever); and (b) what the content of the attitude is (that Hamlet's uncle killed his father; that 2 is a prime number; that Hermia believes that Demetrius dislikes Lysander; or whatever). In what follows, nothing will count as a propositional-attitude psychology—as a reduction or reconstruction or vindication of commonsense belief/desire explanation—that does not acknowledge states that can be individuated in this sort of way.

(ii) Causal Powers

Commonsense psychological explanation is deeply committed to mental causation of at least three sorts: the causation of behavior by mental states; the causation of mental states by impinging environmental events (by 'proximal stimulation,' as psychologists sometimes say); and—in some ways the most interesting commonsense psychological etiologies—the causation of mental states by one another. As an example of the last sort, common sense acknowledges *chains of thought* as species of complex mental events. A chain of thought is presumably a *causal* chain in which one semantically evaluable mental state gives rise to another; a process that often terminates in the fixation of belief. (That, as you will remember, was the sort of thing Sherlock Holmes was supposed to be very good at.)

Every psychology that is Realist about the mental ipso facto acknowledges its causal powers.[3] Philosophers of 'functionalist' persuasion even hold that the causal powers of a mental state determine its identity (that for a mental state to be, as it might be, the state of believing that Demetrius killed Lysander is just for it to have a characteristic galaxy of potential and actual causal relations). This is a position of some interest to us, since if it is true—and if it is also true that propositional attitudes have their contents essentially—it follows that the causal powers of a mental state somehow determine its content. I do not, however, believe that it is true. More of this later.

What's important for now is this: It is characteristic of commonsense belief/desire psychology—and hence of any explicit theory that I'm prepared to view as vindicating commonsense belief/desire psychology—that it attributes contents and causal powers *to the very same mental things that it takes to be semantically evaluable.* It is Hamlet's belief that Claudius killed his father—the very same belief which is true or false in virtue of the facts about his father's death—that causes him to behave in such a beastly way to Gertrude.[4]

In fact, there's a deeper point to make. It's not just that, in a psychology of propositional attitudes, content and causal powers are attributed to the same things. It's also that causal relations among propositional attitudes somehow typically contrive to respect their relations of content, and belief/desire explanations often turn on this. Hamlet believed that somebody had killed his father because he believed that Claudius had killed his father. His having the second belief explains his having the first. How? Well, presumably via some such causal generalization as 'if someone believes Fa, then ceteris paribus he believes $\exists x(Fx)$.' This generalization specifies a causal relation between two kinds of mental states picked out by reference to (the logical form of) the propositions they express; so we have the usual pattern of a simultaneous attribution of content and causal powers. The present point, however, is that the contents of the mental states that the causal generalization subsumes are themselves semantically related; *Fa entails* $\exists x(Fx)$, so, of course, the semantic value of the latter belief is not independent of the semantic value of the former.

Or, compare the pattern of implicit reasoning attributed to Hermia at the beginning of this chapter. I suggested that she must be relying crucially on some such causal generalization as: 'If x wants that P, and x believes that $-P$ unless Q, and x believes that it is within his power to bring it about that Q, then ceteris paribus x tries to bring it about that Q.' Common sense seems pretty clearly to hold that something like that is true and counterfactual supporting; hence that one has explained x's attempt to bring it about that Q if one shows that x had beliefs and desires of the sort that the generalization specifies. What is absolutely typical is (a) the appeal to causal relations among semantically evaluable mental states as part and parcel of the explanation; and (b) the existence of content relations among the mental states thus appealed to.

Witness the recurrent schematic letters; they function precisely to constrain the content relations among the mental states that the generalization subsumes. Thus, unless, in a given case, what x wants is the same as what x believes that he can't have without Q, and unless what x believes to be required for P is the same as what he tries to bring about, the generalization isn't satisfied and the explanation fails. It is self-evident that the explanatory principles of commonsense psychology achieve generality by quantifying over agents (the 'practical syllogism' purports to apply, ceteris paribus, to all the x's). But it bears emphasis that they also achieve generality by abstracting over *contents* ('If you want P and you believe not-P unless Q . . . you try to bring it about that Q,' whatever the P and Q may be). The latter strategy works only because, very often, the same P's and Q's—the same contents—recur in causally related mental states; viz., only because causal relations very often respect semantic ones.

This parallelism between causal powers and contents engenders what is, surely, one of the most striking facts about the cognitive mind as commonsense belief/desire psychology conceives it: the frequent similarity between trains of thought and *arguments*. Here, for example, is Sherlock Holmes doing his thing at the end of "The Speckled Band":

> I instantly reconsidered my position when . . . it became clear to me that whatever danger threatened an occupant of the room couldn't come either from the window or the door. My attention

> was speedily drawn, as I have already remarked to you, to this
> ventilator, and to the bell-rope which hung down to the bed. The
> discovery that this was a dummy, and that the bed was clamped
> to the floor, instantly gave rise to the suspicion that the rope was
> there as a bridge for something passing through the hole, and
> coming to the bed. The idea of a snake instantly occurred to me,
> and when I coupled it with my knowledge that the Doctor was
> furnished with a supply of the creatures from India I felt that I
> was probably on the right track.

The passage purports to be a bit of reconstructive psychology: a capsule history of the sequence of mental states which brought Holmes
first to suspect, then to believe, that the doctor did it with his pet
snake. What is therefore interesting, for our purposes, is that
Holmes's story isn't *just* reconstructive psychology. It does double
duty, since it also serves to assemble *premises* for a plausible inference
to the *conclusion* that the doctor did it with the snake. Because his
train of thought is like an argument, Holmes expects Watson to be
convinced by the considerations which, when they occurred to
Holmes, caused his own conviction. What connects the causal-history
aspect of Holmes's story with its plausible-inference aspect is the fact
that the thoughts that fix the belief that P provide, often enough,
reasonable *grounds* for believing that P. Were this not the case—were
there not this general harmony between the semantical and the causal
properties of thoughts, so that, as Holmes puts it in another story,
"one true inference invariably suggests others"—there wouldn't,
after all, be much profit in thinking.

All this raises a budget of philosophical issues; just *what sorts* of
content relations are preserved in the generalizations that subsume
typical cases of belief/desire causation? And—in many ways a harder
question—how could the mind be so constructed that such generalizations are true of it? What sort of mechanism could have states that
are both semantically and causally connected, and such that the
causal connections respect the semantic ones? It is the intractability of
such questions that causes many philosophers to despair of commonsense psychology. But, of course, the argument cuts both ways: if the
parallelism between content and causal relations is, as it seems to be,
a deep fact about the cognitive mind, then unless we can save the
notion of content, there is a deep fact about the cognitive mind that
our psychology is going to miss.

(iii) Generalizations Preserved
What I've said so far amounts largely to this: An explicit psychology
that vindicates commonsense belief/desire explanations must permit

the assignment of content to causally efficacious mental states and must recognize behavioral explanations in which covering generalizations refer to (or quantify over) the contents of the mental states that they subsume. I now add that the generalizations that are recognized by the vindicating theory mustn't be *crazy* from the point of view of common sense; the causal powers of the attitudes must be, more or less, what common sense supposes that they are. After all, common-sense psychology won't be vindicated unless it turns out to be at least approximately true.

I don't, however, have a shopping list of commonsense generalizations that must be honored by a theory if it wants to be ontologically committed to bona fide propositional attitudes. A lot of what common sense believes about the attitudes must surely be false (a lot of what common sense believes about *anything* must surely be false). Indeed, one rather hopes that there will prove to be many more—and much odder—things in the mind than common sense had dreamed of; or else what's the fun of doing psychology? The indications are, and have been since Freud, that this hope will be abundantly gratified. For example, contrary to common sense, it looks as though much of what's in the mind is unconscious; and, contrary to common sense, it looks as though much of what's in the mind is unlearned. I retain my countenance, I remain self-possessed.

On the other hand, there is a lot of commonsense psychology that we have—so far at least—no reason to doubt, and that friends of the attitudes would hate to abandon. So, it's hard to imagine a psychology of action that is committed to the attitudes but doesn't acknowledge some such causal relations among beliefs, desires, and behavioral intentions (the 'maxims' of acts) as decision theories explicate. Similarly, it's hard to imagine a psycholinguistics (for English) which attributes beliefs, desires, communicative intentions, and such to speaker/hearers but fails to entail an infinity of theorems recognizably similar to these:

> • 'Demetrius killed Lysander' is the form of words standardly used to communicate the belief that Demetrius killed Lysander.
> • 'The cat is on the mat' is the form of words standardly used to communicate the belief that the cat is on the mat.
> • 'Demetrius killed Lysander or the cat is on the mat' is the form of words standardly used to communicate the belief that Demetrius killed Lysander or the cat is on the mat.

And so on indefinitely. Indeed, it's hard to imagine a psycholinguistics that appeals to the propositional attitudes of speaker/hearers of English to explain their verbal behavior but that doesn't entail that they *know* at least one such theorem for each sentence of their language. So there's an infinite amount of common sense for psychology to vindicate already.

Self-confident essentialism is philosophically fashionable this week. There are people around who have Very Strong Views ('modal intuitions,' these views are called) about whether there could be cats in a world in which all the domestic felines are Martian robots, and whether there could be Homer in a world where nobody wrote the *Odyssey* or the *Iliad*. Ducky for them; their epistemic condition is enviable, but I don't myself aspire to it. I just don't know how much commonsense psychology would have to be true for there to be beliefs and desires. Let's say, some of it at a minimum; lots of it by preference. Since I have no doubt at all but that lots of it *is* true, this is an issue about which I do not stay up nights worrying.

RTM

The main thesis of this book can now be put as follows: *We have no reason to doubt—indeed, we have substantial reason to believe—that it is possible to have a scientific psychology that vindicates commonsense belief/ desire explanation.* But though that is my thesis, I don't propose to argue the case in quite so abstract a form. For there is already in the field a (more or less) empirical theory that is, in my view, reasonably construed as ontologically committed to the attitudes and that— again, in my view—is quite probably approximately true. If I'm right about this theory, it *is* a vindication of the attitudes. Since, moreover, it's the only thing of its kind around (it's the *only* proposal for a scientific belief/desire psychology that's in the field), defending the commonsense assumptions about the attitudes and defending this theory turn out to be much the same enterprise; extensionally, as one might say.

That, in any event, is the strategy that I'll pursue: I'll argue that the sorts of objections philosophers have recently raised against belief/ desire explanation are (to put it mildly) not conclusive against the best vindicating theory currently available. The rest of this chapter is therefore devoted to a sketch of how this theory treats the attitudes and why its treatment of the attitudes seems so promising. Since this story is now pretty well known in both philosophical and psychological circles, I propose to be quick.

What I'm selling is the Representational Theory of Mind (hence RTM; for discussion see, among other sources, Fodor, *PA*; Fodor, *LOT*; Field, *MR*). At the heart of the theory is the postulation of a language of thought: an infinite set of 'mental representations' which function both as the immediate objects of propositional attitudes and as the domains of mental processes. More precisely, RTM is the conjunction of the following two claims:

> *Claim 1* (the nature of propositional attitudes):
>
> For any organism *O*, and any attitude *A* toward the proposition *P*, there is a ('computational'/'functional') relation *R* and a mental representation *MP* such that
>
> *MP* means that *P*, and
> *O* has *A* iff *O* bears *R* to *MP*.

(We'll see presently that the biconditional needs to be watered down a little; but not in a way that much affects the spirit of the proposal.)

It's a thin line between clarity and pomposity. A cruder but more intelligible way of putting claim 1 would be this: To believe that such and such is to have a mental symbol that means that such and such tokened in your head in a certain way; it's to have such a token 'in your belief box,' as I'll sometimes say. Correspondingly, to hope that such and such is to have a token of that same mental symbol tokened in your head, but in a rather different way; it's to have it tokened 'in your hope box.' (The difference between having the token in one box or the other corresponds to the difference between the causal roles of beliefs and desires. Talking about belief boxes and such as a shorthand for representing the attitudes as *functional* states is an idea due to Steve Schiffer. For more on this, see the Appendix.) And so on for every attitude that you can bear toward a proposition; and so on for every proposition toward which you can bear an attitude.

> *Claim 2* (the nature of mental processes):
>
> Mental processes are causal sequences of tokenings of mental representations.

A train of thoughts, for example, is a causal sequence of tokenings of mental representations which express the propositions that are the objects of the thoughts. To a first approximation, to think 'It's going to rain; so I'll go indoors' is to have a tokening of a mental representation that means *I'll go indoors* caused, in a certain way, by a tokening of a mental representation that means *It's going to rain*.

So much for formulating RTM.

There are, I think, a number of reasons for believing that RTM may be more or less true. The best reason is that some version or other of RTM underlies practically all current psychological research on mentation, and our best science is ipso facto our best estimate of what there is and what it's made of. There are those of my colleagues in philosophy who do not find this sort of argument persuasive. I blush for them. (For a lengthy discussion of how RTM shapes current work on cognition, see Fodor, *LOT*, especially chapter 1. For a discussion of the connection between RTM and commonsense Intentional Realism—and some arguments that, given the latter, the former is practically mandatory—see the Appendix.)

But we have a reason for suspecting that RTM may be true even aside from the details of its empirical success. I remarked above that there is a striking parallelism between the causal relations among mental states, on the one hand, and the semantic relations that hold among their propositional objects, on the other; and that very deep properties of the mental—as, for example, that trains of thought are largely truth preserving—turn on this symmetry. RTM suggests a plausible mechanism for this relation, and that is something that no previous account of mentation has been able to do. I propose to spell this out a bit; it helps make clear just *why* RTM has such a central place in the way that psychologists now think about the mind.

The trick is to combine the postulation of mental representations with the 'computer metaphor.' Computers show us how to connect semantical with causal properties for *symbols*. So, if having a propositional attitude involves tokening a symbol, then we can get some leverage on connecting semantical properties with causal ones for *thoughts*. In this respect, I think there really has been something like an intellectual breakthrough. Technical details to one side, this is—in my view—the only aspect of contemporary cognitive science that represents a major advance over the versions of mentalism that were its eighteenth- and nineteenth-century predecessors. Exactly what was wrong with Associationism, for example, was that there proved to be no way to get a *rational* mental life to emerge from the sorts of causal relations among thoughts that the 'laws of association' recognized. (See the concluding pages of Joyce's *Ulysses* for a—presumably inadvertent—parody of the contrary view.)

Here, in barest outline, is how the new story is supposed to go: You connect the causal properties of a symbol with its semantic properties *via its syntax*. The syntax of a symbol is one of its higher-order physical properties. To a metaphorical first approximation, we can think of the syntactic structure of a symbol as an abstract feature of its shape.[5] Because, to all intents and purposes, syntax reduces to shape, and because the shape of a symbol is a potential determinant of its causal role, it is fairly easy to see how there could be environments in which the causal role of a symbol correlates with its syntax. It's easy, that is to say, to imagine symbol tokens interacting causally *in virtue of* their syntactic structures. The syntax of a symbol might determine the causes and effects of its tokenings in much the way that the geometry of a key determines which locks it will open.

But, now, we know from modern logic that certain of the semantic relations among symbols can be, as it were, 'mimicked' by their syntactic relations; that, when seen from a very great distance, is what proof-theory is about. So, within certain famous limits, the semantic relation that holds between two symbols when the proposition expressed by the one is entailed by the proposition expressed by the other can be mimicked by syntactic relations in virtue of which one of the symbols is derivable from the other. We can therefore build machines which have, again within famous limits, the following property:

> The operations of the machine consist entirely of transformations of symbols;
>
> in the course of performing these operations, the machine is sensitive solely to syntactic properties of the symbols;
>
> and the operations that the machine performs on the symbols are entirely confined to altering their shapes.

Yet the machine is so devised that it will transform one symbol into another if and only if the propositions expressed by the symbols that are so transformed stand in certain *semantic* relations—e.g., the relation that the premises bear to the conclusion in a valid argument. Such machines—computers, of course—just *are* environments in which the syntax of a symbol determines its causal role in a way that respects its content. This is, I think, a perfectly terrific idea; not least because it works.

I expect it's clear how this is supposed to connect with RTM and ontological commitment to mental representations. Computers are a solution to the problem of mediating between the causal properties of symbols and their semantic properties. So *if* the mind is a sort of computer, we begin to see how you can have a theory of mental processes that succeeds where—literally—all previous attempts had abjectly failed; a theory which explains how there could be nonarbitrary content relations among causally related thoughts. But, patently, there are going to have to be mental representations if this proposal is going to work. In computer design, causal role is brought into phase with content by exploiting parallelisms between the syntax of a symbol and its semantics. But that idea won't do the theory of *mind* any good unless there are *mental* symbols: mental particulars possessed of both semantical and syntactic properties. There must be mental symbols because, in a nutshell, only symbols have syntax, and our best available theory of mental processes—indeed, the *only* available theory of mental processes that isn't *known* to be false—needs the picture of the mind as a syntax-driven machine.

It is sometimes alleged against commonsense belief/desire psychology, by those who admire it less than I do (see especially Churchland, *EMPA*; Stich, *FFPCS*), that it is a "sterile" theory; one that arguably hasn't progressed much since Homer and hasn't progressed at all since Jane Austen. There is, no doubt, a sense in which this charge is warranted; commonsense psychology may be implicit science, but it isn't, on anybody's story, implicit *research* science. (What novelists and poets do doesn't count as research by the present austere criteria.) If, in short, you want to evaluate progress, you need to look not at the implicit commonsense theory but at the best candidate for its explicit vindication. And here the progress has been enormous. It's not just that we now know a little about memory and perception (qua means to the fixation of belief), and a little about language (qua means to the communication of belief); see any standard psychology text. The real achievement is that we are (maybe) on the verge of solving a great mystery about the mind: *How could its causal processes be semantically coherent?* Or, if you like yours with drums and trumpets: *How is rationality mechanically possible?*[6] Notice that this sort of problem can't even be stated, let alone solved, unless we suppose—just as commonsense belief/desire psychology wants us to—that there are mental states with both semantic contents and causal roles. A good theory is one that leads you to ask questions that have answers. And vice versa, ceteris paribus.

Still, RTM won't do in quite the raw form set forth above. I propose to end this chapter with a little polishing.

According to claim 1, RTM requires both of the following:

> For each tokening of a propositional attitude, there is a tokening of a corresponding relation between an organism and a mental representation;

and

> For each tokening of that relation, there is a corresponding tokening of a propositional attitude.[7]

This is, however, much too strong; the equivalence fails in both directions.

As, indeed, we should expect it to, given our experience in other cases where explicit science co-opts the conceptual apparatus of common sense. For example, as everybody points out, it is simply not true that chemistry identifies each sample of water with a sample of

H_2O; not, at least, if the operative notion of water is the common-sense one according to which what we drink, sail on, and fill our bathtubs with all qualifies. What chemistry does is reconstruct the commonsense categories *in what the theory itself identifies as core cases: chemically pure* water is H_2O. The ecological infrequency of such core cases is, of course, no argument against the claim that chemical science vindicates the commonsense taxonomy: Common sense was right about there being such stuff as water, right about there being water in the Charles River, and right again that it's the water in what we drink that quenches our thirst. It never said that the water in the Charles is chemically pure; 'chemically pure' isn't a phrase in the commonsense vocabulary.

Exactly similarly, RTM vindicates commonsense psychology for what RTM identifies as the core cases; in those cases, what common sense takes to be tokenings of propositional attitudes are indeed tokenings of a relation between an organism and a mental representation. The other cases—where you get either attitude tokenings without the relation or relation tokenings without the attitudes—the theory treats as derivative. This is all, I repeat, *exactly* what you'd expect from scientific precedent. Nevertheless, philosophers have made an awful fuss about it in discussing the vindication of the attitudes (see the controversy over the 'explicit representation'—or otherwise—of grammars recently conducted by, among others, Stabler [*HAGR*] and Demopoulos and Matthews [*HGMR*]). So let's consider the details awhile. Doing so will lead to a sharpening of claim 1, which is all to the good.

Case 1. Attitudes without Mental Representations
Here's a case from Dennett:

> In a recent conversation with the designer of a chess-playing program I heard the following criticism of a rival program: "It thinks it should get its queen out early." This ascribes a propositional attitude to the program in a very useful and predictive way, for as the designer went on to say, one can usually count on chasing that queen around the board. But for all the many levels of explicit representation to be found in that program, nowhere is anything roughly synonymous with "I should get my queen out early" explicitly tokened. The level of analysis to which the designer's remark belongs describes features of the program that are, in an entirely innocent way, emergent properties of the computational processes that have "engineering reality." I see no reason to believe that the relation

between belief-talk and psychological-process talk will be any
more direct (*CCC*, 107; see also Matthews, *TWR*)

Notice that the problem Dennett raises isn't just that some of what
common sense takes to be one's propositional attitudes are *dispositional*. It's not like the worry that I might now be said to believe some
abstruse consequence of number theory—one that I have, commonsensically speaking, never even thought of—because I *would* accept
the proof of the theorem *if* I were shown it. It's true, of course, that
merely dispositional beliefs couldn't correspond to *occurrent* tokenings of relations to mental representations, and claim 1 must therefore be reformulated. But the problem is superficial, since the relevant
revision of claim 1 would be pretty obvious; viz., that for each *occurrent* belief there is a corresponding *occurrent* tokening of a mental
representation; and for each *dispositional* belief there is a corresponding *disposition* to token a mental representation.

This would leave open a question that arises independent of one's
views about RTM: viz., when are attributions of dispositional beliefs
true? I suppose that one's dispositional beliefs could reasonably be
identified with the closure of one's occurrent beliefs under principles
of inference that one explicitly accepts. And, if it's a little vague just
what beliefs belong to such a closure, RTM could live with that. *Qua
dispositional*, attitudes play no causal role in *actual* mental processes;
only occurrent attitudes—for that matter, only occurrent *anythings*—
are actual causes. So RTM can afford to be a little operationalist about
merely dispositional beliefs (see Lycan, *TB*) so long as it takes a hard
line about occurrent ones.

However, to repeat, the problem raised in Dennett's text is not of
this sort. It's not that the program believes 'get your queen out early'
potentially. Dennett's point is that the program actually operates on
this principle; but not in virtue of any tokening of any symbol that
expresses it. And chess isn't, of course, the only sort of case. Behavioral commitment to modus ponens, or to the syntactic rule of 'wh'-
movement, *might* betoken that these are inscribed in brain writing.
But it needn't, since these rules might be—as philosophers sometimes say—complied with but not literally followed.

In Dennett's example, you have an attitude being, as it were, an
emergent out of its own implementation. This way of putting it might
seem to suggest a way of saving claim 1: The machine doesn't explicitly represent 'get your queen out early,' but at least we may suppose
that it *does* represent, explicitly, some more detailed rules of play (the
ones that Dennett says have "engineering reality"). For these rules, at
least, a strong form of claim 1 would thus be satisfied. But that suggestion won't work either. *None* of the principles in accordance with

which a computational system operates need be explicitly represented by a formula tokened in the device; there is no guarantee that the program of a machine will be explicitly represented in the machine whose program it is. (See Cummins, *IMM*; roughly, the point is that for any machine that computes a function by executing an explicit algorithm, there exists another machine—one that's 'hardwired'—that computes the same function but *not* by executing an explicit algorithm.) So what, you might wonder, does the 'computer metaphor' buy for RTM after all?

There is even a point of principle here—one that is sometimes read in (or into) Lewis Carroll's dialogue between Achilles and the Tortoise: Not all the rules of inference that a computational system runs on *can* be represented *just* explicitly in the system; some of them have to be, as one says, 'realized in the hardware.' Otherwise the machine won't run at all. A computer in which the principles of operation are *only* explicitly represented is just like a blackboard on which the principles have been written down. It has Hamlet's problem: When you turn the thing on, nothing happens.

Since this is all clearly correct and arguably important, the question arises how to state RTM so that these cases where programs are hardwired don't count as disconfirmations of claim 1. We'll return to this momentarily; first let's consider:

Case 2. Mental Representations without Attitudes
What RTM borrows from computers is, in the first instance, the recipe for mechanizing rationality: Use a syntactically driven machine to exploit parallelisms between the syntactic and semantic properties of symbols. Some—but not all—versions of RTM borrow more than this; not just a theory of rationality but a theory of intelligence too. According to this story, intelligent behavior typically exploits a 'cognitive architecture' constituted of *hierarchies* of symbol processors. At the top of such a hierarchy might be a quite complex capacity: solving a problem, making a plan, uttering a sentence. At the bottom, however, are only the sorts of unintelligent operations that Turing machines can perform: deleting symbols, storing symbols, copying symbols, and the rest. Filling in the middle levels is tantamount to reducing—analyzing—an intelligent capacity into a complex of dumb ones; hence to a kind of explanation of the former.

Here's a typical example of a kind of representational theory that runs along these lines:

> This is the way we tie our shoes: There is a little man who lives in one's head. The little man keeps a library. When one acts upon the intention to tie one's shoes, the little man fetches down a

volume entitled *Tying One's Shoes*. The volume says such things as: "Take the left free end of the shoelace in the left hand. Cross the left free end of the shoelace over the right free end of the shoelace . . . ," etc. . . . When the little man reads "take the left free end of the shoelace in the left hand," we imagine him ringing up the shop foreman in charge of grasping shoelaces. The shop foreman goes about supervising that activity in a way that is, in essence, a microcosm of tying one's shoe. Indeed, the shop foreman might be imagined to superintend a detail of wage slaves, whose functions include: searching representations of visual inputs for traces of shoelace, dispatching orders to flex and contract fingers on the left hand, etc. (Fodor, *ATK*, 63–65, slightly revised)

At the very top are states which may well correspond to propositional attitudes that common sense is prepared to acknowledge (knowing how to tie one's shoes, thinking about shoe tying). But at the bottom and middle levels there are bound to be lots of symbol-processing operations that correspond to nothing that *people*—as opposed to their nervous systems—ever do. These are the operations of what Dennett has called "sub-personal" computational systems; and though they satisfy the present formulation of claim 1 (in that they involve causally efficacious tokenings of mental representations), yet it's unclear that they correspond to anything that common sense would count as the tokening of an attitude. But then how are we to formulate claim 1 so as to avoid disconfirmation by subpersonal information processes?

Vindication Vindicated

There is a sense in which these sorts of objections to claim 1 strike me as not very serious. As I remarked above, the vindication of belief/desire explanation by RTM does *not* require that every case common sense counts as the tokening of an attitude should correspond to the tokening of a mental representation, or vice versa. All that's required is that such correspondences should obtain in what the vindicating theory itself takes to be the core cases. On the other hand, RTM had better be able to say which cases it does count as core. Chemistry is allowed to hold the Charles River largely irrelevant to the confirmation of 'water is H_2O,' but only because it provides independent grounds for denying that what's in the Charles is a chemically pure sample. Of anything!

So, what are the core cases for RTM? The answer should be clear from claim 2. According to claim 2, mental processes are causal sequences of transformations of mental representations. It follows that tokenings of attitudes *must* correspond to tokenings of mental representations when they—the attitude tokenings—are episodes in mental processes. If the intentional objects of such causally efficacious attitude tokenings are *not* explicitly represented, then RTM is simply false. I repeat for emphasis: If the occurrence of a thought is an episode in a mental process, then RTM is committed to the explicit representation of its content. The motto is therefore No Intentional Causation without Explicit Representation.

Notice that this way of choosing core cases squares us with the alleged counterexamples. RTM says that the contents of a sequence of attitudes that constitutes a mental process must be expressed by explicit tokenings of mental representations. But the rules that determine the course of the transformation of these representations— modus ponens, 'wh'-movement, 'get the queen out early,' or whatever—need not themselves ever be explicit. They can be emergents out of explicitly represented procedures of implementation, or out of hardware structures, or both. Roughly: According to RTM, programs—corresponding to the 'laws of thought'—*may* be explicitly represented; but 'data structures'—corresponding to the contents of thoughts—*have to be.*

Thus, in Dennett's chess case, the rule 'get it out early' may or may not be expressed by a 'mental' (/program language) symbol. That depends on just how the machine works; specifically, on whether *consulting* the rule is a step in the machine's operations. I take it that in the machine that Dennett has in mind, it isn't; *entertaining the thought 'Better get the queen out early' never constitutes an episode in the mental life of that machine.*[8] But then, the intentional content of this thought need *not* be explicitly represented consonant with 'no intentional causation without explicit representation' being true. By contrast, the representations of the board—of actual or possible states of play—over which the machine's computations are defined *must* be explicit, precisely *because* the machine's computations *are* defined over them. These computations constitute the machine's 'mental processes,' so either they are causal sequences of explicit representations, or the representational theory of chess playing is simply false of the machine. To put the matter in a nutshell: Restricting one's attention to the status of rules and programs can make it seem that the computer metaphor is neutral with respect to RTM. But when one thinks about the constitution of mental processes, the connection between the idea that they are computational and the idea that there is a language of thought becomes immediately apparent.[9]

What about the subpersonal examples, where you have mental representation tokenings without attitude tokenings? Commonsense belief/desire explanations are vindicated if scientific psychology is ontologically committed to beliefs and desires. But it's *not* also required that the folk-psychological inventory of propositional attitudes should turn out to exhaust a natural kind. It would be astounding if it did; how could common sense know all that? What's important about RTM—what makes RTM a vindication of intuitive belief/desire psychology—isn't that it picks out a kind that is precisely coextensive with the propositional attitudes. It's that RTM shows how intentional states could have causal powers; precisely the aspect of commonsense intentional realism that seemed most perplexing from a metaphysical point of view.

Molecular physics vindicates the intuitive taxonomy of middle-sized objects into liquids and solids. But the nearest kind to the liquids that molecular physics acknowledges includes some of what common sense would not; glass, for example. So what?

So much for RTM; so much for this chapter, too. There is a strong prima facie case for commonsense belief/desire explanation. Common sense would be vindicated if some good theory of the mind proved to be committed to entities which—like the attitudes—are both semantically evaluable and etiologically involved. RTM looks like being a good theory of the mind that is so committed; so if RTM is true, common sense is vindicated. It goes without saying that RTM needs to make an empirical case; we need good accounts, independently confirmed, of mental processes as causal sequences of transformations of mental representations. Modern cognitive psychology is devoted, practically in its entirety, to devising and confirming such accounts. For present purposes, I shall take all that as read. What the rest of this book is about is doubts about RTM that turn on its *semantic* assumptions. This is home ground for philosophers, and increasingly the natives are restless.

2

Individualism and Supervenience

After the Beardsley exhibit at the V&A, walking along that endless tunnel to South Kensington Station, I thought, why this is 'behavior'—and I had said, perhaps even written: "where does 'behavior' begin and end?"
Barbara Pym

I beg your indulgence. I am about to tell you two stories that you've very probably heard before. Having once told you the stories, I will then spend most of this chapter trying to puzzle out what, if anything, they have to do either with commonsense belief/desire explanation or with RTM. The conclusion will be: not much. That may sound pretty dreary, but I've been to parties that were worse; and there's a sort of excuse in the following consideration: the two stories I'm about to tell you have been at the center of a great lot of recent philosophical discussion. Indeed, contrary to the conclusion that I am driving toward, it is widely held that one or both stories have morals that tend to undermine the notion of content and thereby raise problems for propositional-attitude-based theories of mind.

Since these stories are so well known, I shall tell them in abbreviated form, entirely omitting the bits about the shaggy dog.

The Putnam story. Is there anyone who hasn't heard? There's this place, you see, that's just like here except that they've got XYZ where we've got H_2O. (XYZ is indistinguishable from H_2O by any casual test, though of course one could tell them apart in the chemical laboratory.) Now, in this place where they have XYZ, there's someone who's just like me down to and including his neurological microstructure. Call this guy Twin-Me. The intuition we're invited to share is that, in virtue of the chemical facts and in spite of the neurological ones, the form of words 'water is wet' means something different in his mouth from what it does in mine. And, similarly, the content of the thought that Twin-Me has when he thinks (*in re* XYZ, as one might say) that water is wet is different from the content of the thought that I have when I think that water is wet *in re* H_2O. Indeed, the intuition we're invited to share is that, strictly speaking, Twin-Me can't have the thought that water is wet at all.

The Burge story. The English word 'brisket,' according to the Funk & Wagnalls *Standard Desk Dictionary* and other usually reliable authorities, means "the breast of an animal, esp. of one used as food" (from the Old French 'bruschet,' in case you were wondering). Imagine a guy—call him Oscar—who speaks English all right but who suffers from a ghastly misapprehension: Oscar believes that only certain food animals—only beef, say—have brisket; pork, according to Oscar's mistaken world view, is ipso facto brisketless.

First intuition: Oscar, despite his misapprehension, can perfectly well have brisket-beliefs, brisket-desires, brisket-fears, brisket-doubts, brisket-qualms, and so forth. In general: If the butcher can bear attitude *A* toward the proposition that brisket is *F*, so too can Oscar. Of course, Oscar differs from the butcher—and other speakers of the prestige dialect—in that much of what Oscar believes about brisket is false. The point, however, is that Oscar's false belief that pork isn't brisket is nevertheless a brisket-belief; it *is brisket* that Oscar believes that pork brisket isn't (if you see what I mean). From which it follows that Oscar 'has the concept' BRISKET—whatever exactly that amounts to.

Now imagine an Oscar-Twin; Oscar2 is molecularly identical to Oscar but lives in a language community (and talks a language) which differs from English in the following way. In that language the phonetic form 'brisket' does apply only to breast of beef; so whereas what Oscar believes about brisket is false, what Oscar2 believes about brisket2 is true.

Second intuition: Oscar2 doesn't have brisket-attitudes; it would be wrong for us—us speakers of English, that is—to say of Oscar2 that his wants, beliefs, yearnings, or whatever are ever directed toward a proposition of the form: '. . . brisket . . . .' For Oscar2, unlike his molecularly identical twin Oscar, doesn't have the concept BRISKET; he has the concept BRISKET2 (=brisket of beef, as *we* would say).

So much for the stories. Now for the ground rules: Some philosophers are inclined to claim about the Putnam story that Twin-Me actually *is* just like Me; that it's wrong to think that Twin-Me hasn't got the concept WATER. Analogously, some philosophers are inclined to say that Oscar actually is just like Oscar2; that it's wrong to think that Oscar has the concept BRISKET. (Indeed, if your theory of language is at all 'criteriological,' you quite likely won't be prepared to have the intuitions that Putnam and Burge want you to have.

Criteriological theories of language aren't fashionable at present, but I've noticed that the fashions tend to change.) Anyhow, for purposes of discussion I propose simply to grant the intuitions. If they're real and reliable, they're *worth* discussing; and if they're not, there's no great harm done.

Second, I will assume that the Burge story shows that whatever exactly the moral of the Putnam story is, it isn't specific to terms (/ concepts) that denote 'natural kinds.' In fact, I'll assume that the Burge story shows that if the Putnam story raises *any* problems for the notion of content, then the problems that it raises are completely general and affect all content-bearing mental states.

Third, I will assume that what's at issue in the Putnam and Burge stories is something about how propositional attitudes are individuated; and that the intuitions Putnam and Burge appeal to suggest that the attitudes are in some sense individuated with respect to their *relational* properties. (Thus, my Twin's water2-beliefs are supposed to differ in content from my water-beliefs, and what's supposed to account for the difference is the chemical composition of the stuff *in our respective environments.* Analogously, Oscar's brisket-beliefs are supposed to differ in content from Oscar2's brisket2-beliefs, and what's supposed to account for the difference is what the form of words 'is brisket' applies to *in their respective language communities.*)

Brian Loar, in a recent, important paper (*SCPC*), has argued that these concessions may be too generous. Loar points out that the standard interpretation of the Twin cases takes for granted that if, for example, the predicate 'believes that water is . . .' applies to me but not to my Twin, and the predicate 'believes that water2 is . . .' applies to my Twin but not to me, then it follows that the content of my belief differs in some respect from the content of my Twin's. In effect, according to Loar, Putnam and Burge assume that you can infer identities and differences in beliefs from corresponding identities and differences in the 'that . . .' clauses that are used to ascribe them; and Loar gives grounds for doubting that such inferences are invariably sound. I think Loar may well be right about this, but I propose to ignore it. It's interesting to see what would follow from assuming that people situated the way that the Twins and the Oscars are ipso facto believe different things, whether or not the Burge/Putnam intuitions actually show that they do.

In aid of which, I shall talk as follows: Standards of individuation according to which my beliefs differ in content from my Twin's (and Oscar's differ from Oscar2's) I'll call 'relational.' Conversely, if attitudes are individuated in such fashion that my beliefs and my Twin's are identical in content, then I'll say that the operative standards are 'nonrelational.' It's going to turn out, however, that this terminology is a little coarse and that relational individuation per se isn't really the heart of the matter. So when more precision is wanted, I'll borrow a term from Burge; standards of individuation according to which my Twin and I are in the same mental state are 'individualistic.'

OK, now: What do the Burge and Putnam stories show about the attitudes?

Supervenience

Here's a plausible answer: At a minimum they show that propositional attitudes, as common sense understands them, don't supervene on brain states. To put it roughly: States of type X supervene on states of type Y iff there is no difference among X states without a corresponding difference among Y states. So, in particular, the psychological states of organisms supervene on their brain states iff their brains differ whenever their minds differ. Now, the point about Me and Twin-Me (and about Oscar and Oscar2) is that although we have different propositional attitudes, our brains are identical molecule-for-molecule; so it looks like it just follows that our attitudes don't supervene upon our brain states. But it's arguable that any scientifically useful notion of psychological state ought to respect supervenience; mind/brain supervenience (and/or mind/brain identity) is, after all, the best idea that anyone has had so far about how mental causation is possible. The moral would appear to be that you can't make respectable science out of the attitudes as commonsensically individuated.

I'm actually rather sympathetic to this line of thought; I think there *is* an issue about supervenience and that it does come out that we need, when doing psychology, other identity conditions for mental states than those that common sense prefers. This doesn't bother me much, because (a) redrawing these boundaries doesn't jeopardize the major claim on which the vindication of the attitudes as explanatory constructs depends—viz., that scientific psychological explanation, like commonsense belief/desire explanation, is committed to states to which semantic and causal properties are simultaneously ascribable; and (b) I think it's quite easy to see how the required principles of individuation should be formulated.

All that will take some going into. For starters, however, there's this: It needs to be argued that there *is* any problem about supervenience to be solved. Contrary to first impressions, that doesn't just fall out of the Burge and Putnam stories. Here's why: to get a violation of supervenience, you need not just the relational individuation of mental states; you also need *the nonrelational individuation of brain states.* And the Twin examples imply only the former.

To put the same point minutely differently: My brain states are type-identical to my Twin's only if you assume that such relational properties as, for example, *being a brain that lives in a body that lives in a world where there is XYZ rather than H_2O in the puddles,* do *not* count for the individuation of brain states. But why should we assume that? And, of course, if we *don't* assume it, then it's just not true that my Twin and I (or, mutatis mutandis, Oscars 1 and 2) are in identical brain states; and it's therefore not true that they offer counterexamples to the supervenience of the attitudes.

("Fiddlesticks! For if brain states are individuated relationally, then they will themselves fail to supervene on states at the next level down; on molecular states, as it might be."

"Fiddlesticks back again! You beg the question by assuming that *molecular* states are nonrelationally individuated. Why shouldn't it be relational individuation all the way down to quantum mechanics?")

You will be pleased to hear that I am not endorsing this way out of the supervenience problem. On the contrary, I hope the suggestion that brain states should be relationally individuated strikes you as plain silly. Why, then, did I suggest it?

Well, the standard picture in the recent philosophical literature on cognitive science is the one that I outlined above: The Burge and Putnam stories show that the commonsense way of individuating the attitudes violates supervenience; by contrast, the psychologist individuates the attitudes nonrelationally ('narrowly,' as one sometimes says), thereby preserving supervenience but at the cost of requiring an individualistic (/'nonrelational'/'narrow') notion of content. Philosophers are then free to disagree about whether such a notion of content actually can be constructed. Which they do. Vehemently.

This standard understanding of the difference between the way that common sense construes the attitudes and the way that psychology does is summarized as follows:

Commonsense Taxonomy (Pattern A)

1. Individuates the attitudes relationally; hence, assumes a non-individualistic notion of content.
2. Distinguishes: my beliefs from my Twin's,
          Oscar's beliefs from Oscar2's.
3. Individuates brain states nonrelationally; therefore:
4. Violates supervenience.[1]

Psychological Taxonomy (Pattern B)
1. Individuates the attitudes nonrelationally; hence, assume a narrow notion of content.
2. Identifies: my beliefs with my Twin's,
   Oscar's beliefs with Oscar2's.
3. Individuates brain states nonrelationally; therefore:
4. Preserves supervenience.

One can imagine quite a different reaction to the Twin examples, however. According to this revisionist account, psychology taxonomizes the attitudes precisely the same way that common sense does: Both follow pattern A; both assume principles of individuation that violate supervenience. And so much the worse for supervenience. This, if I understand him right, is the line that Burge himself takes;[2] in any event, it's a line that merits close consideration. If psychology individuates the attitudes relationally, then it is no more in need of a narrow notion of content than common sense is. It would save a lot of nuisance if this were true, since we would not then have the bother of cooking up some narrow notion of content for psychologists to play with. It would also disarm philosophers who argue that cognitive science is in trouble because it needs a notion of narrow content *and can't have one,* the very idea of narrow content being somehow incoherent.

Alas, there is always as much bother as possible; the revisionist reading cannot be sustained. It turns out that the considerations that militate for the nonrelational individuation of mental states (hence, for preserving supervenience at the cost of violating the common-sense taxonomy) are no different from the ones that militate for the nonrelational individuation of brain states, molecular states, and such. This becomes evident as soon as one understands the source of our commitment to nonrelational taxonomy in these latter cases.

All this takes some proving. I propose to proceed as follows: First, we'll consider why we think that brain states and the like should be individuated nonrelationally. This involves developing a sort of metaphysical argument that individuation in science is *always individualistic.* It follows, of course, that the scientific constructs of psychology must be individualistic too, and we'll pause to consider how the contrary opinion could ever have become prevalent. (It's here that the distinction between 'nonrelational' and 'individualistic' individuation is going to have some bite.) We will then be back exactly where we started: Common sense postulates a relational taxonomy for the attitudes; psychology postulates states that have content but are individualistic; so the question arises what notion of content survives this shift in criteria of individuation. It will turn out—contrary to much recent advertisement—that this question is not really very hard to answer. The discussion will therefore close on an uncharacteristic note of optimism: The prospects for a scientifically defensible intentional psychology are, in any event, no worse now than they were before the discovery of XYZ; and brisket is a red herring.

Causal Powers

I have before me this gen-u-ine United States ten cent piece. It has precisely two stable configurations; call them 'heads' and 'tails.' (I ignore dimes that stand on their edges; no theory is perfect.) What, in a time of permanent inflation, will this dime buy for me? Nothing less than control over the state of every physical particle in the universe.

I define 'is an H-particle at t' so that it's satisfied by a particle at t iff my dime is heads-up at t. Correspondingly, I define 'is a T-particle at t' so that it's satisfied by a particle at t iff my dime is tails-up at t. By facing my dime heads-up, I now bring it about that every particle in the universe is an H-particle . . . thus! And then, by reversing my dime, I change every particle in the universe into a T-particle . . . thus! And back again . . . thus! (Notice that by defining H and T predicates over objects at an appropriately higher level, I can obtain corresponding control over the state of every *brain* the universe, changing H–brain states into T–brain states and back again just as the fancy takes me.) With great power comes great responsibility. It must be a comfort for you to know that it is a trained philosopher whose finger is on the button.

What is wrong with this egomaniacal fantasy? Well, in a certain sense, nothing; barring whatever problems there may be about simultaneity, 'is H at t' and 'is T at t' are perfectly well defined predicates and they pick out perfectly well defined (relational) properties of physical particles. Anybody who can get at my dime can, indeed, affect the distribution of these properties throughout the universe. It's a matter of temperament whether one finds it fun to do so.

What *would* be simply mad, however, would be to try to construct a particle physics that acknowledges *being an H-particle* or *being a T-particle* as part of its explanatory apparatus. *Why* would that be mad? Because particle physics, like every other branch of science, is in the business of causal explanation; and whether something is an H-(T-) particle *is irrelevant to its causal powers*. I don't know exactly what that means; but whatever it means, I'm morally cetain that it's true. I propose to wade around in it a bit.

Here are some things it seems to me safe to assume about science:

We want science to give causal explanations of such things (events, whatever) in nature as can be causally explained.[3] Giving such explanations essentially involves projecting and confirming causal generalizations. And causal generalizations subsume the things they apply to in virtue of the causal properties of the things they apply to. Of course.

In short, what you need in order to do science is a taxonomic apparatus that distinguishes between things insofar as they have *different* causal properties, and that groups things together insofar as they have the *same* causal properties. So now we can see why it would be mad to embrace a taxonomy that takes seriously the difference between H-particles and T-particles. All else being equal, H-particles and T-particles have identical causal properties; whether something is an H-$(T$-$)$particle is irrelevant to its causal powers. To put it a little more tensely, if an event e is caused by H-particle p, then that same event e is also caused by p in the nearest nomologically possible world in which p is T rather than H. (If you prefer some other way of construing counterfactuals, you are welcome to substitute it here. I have no axes to grind.) So the properties of being H $(/T)$ are taxonomically irrelevant for purposes of scientific causal explanation.

But similarly, mutatis mutandis, for the properties of being H and T *brain states.* And similarly, mutatis mutandis, for the properties of being H and T *mental states. And similarly, mutatis mutandis, for the property of being a mental state of a person who lives in a world where there is XYZ rather than H_2O in the puddles.* These sorts of differences in the relational properties of psychological (/brain/particle) states are irrelevant to their causal powers; hence, irrelevant to scientific taxonomy.

So, to summarize, if you're interested in causal explanation, it would be mad to distinguish between Oscar's brain states and Oscar2's; their brain states have identical causal powers. That's why we individuate brain states individualistically. And if you are interested in causal explanation, it would be mad to distinguish between Oscar's *mental* states and Oscar2's; their mental states have identical causal powers. But common sense deploys a taxonomy that *does* distinguish between the mental states of Oscar and Oscar2. So the commonsense taxonomy won't do for the purposes of psychology. Q.E.D.[4]

I can, however, imagine somebody not being convinced by this argument. For the argument depends on assuming that the mental states of Twins do in fact have the same causal powers, and I can imagine somebody denying that this is so. Along either of the two following lines:

First line: "Consider the effects of my utterances of the form of words 'Bring water!' Such utterances normally eventuate in somebody bringing me water—viz., in somebody bringing me H_2O. Whereas, by contrast, when my Twin utters 'Bring water!' what he normally gets is water2—viz., XYZ. So the causal powers of my water-utterances do, after all, differ from the causal powers of my Twin's 'water'-utterances. And similarly, mutatis mutandis, for the causal powers of the mental states that such utterances express. And similarly, mutatis mutandis, for the mental states of the Oscars in respect of brisket and brisket2."

Reply: This will not do; identity of causal powers has to be assessed *across* contexts, not *within* contexts.

Consider, if you will, the causal powers of your biceps and of mine. Roughly, our biceps have the *same* causal powers if the following is true: *For any thing x and any context C, if you can lift x in C, then so can I; and if I can lift x in C, then so can you.* What is, however, *not* in general relevant to comparisons between the causal powers of our biceps is this: that there is a thing x and a pair of contexts C and C' such that you can lift x in C and I can not lift x in C'. Thus suppose, for example, that in C (a context in which this chair is not nailed to the floor) you can lift it; and in C' (a context in which this chair *is* nailed to the floor) I cannot lift it. That eventuality would give your biceps nothing to crow about. Your biceps—to repeat the moral—have cause for celebration only if they can lift x's *in contexts in which my biceps can't.*

Well, to return to the causal powers of the water-utterances (/water-thoughts) of Twins: It's true that when I say "water" I get water and when my Twin says "water" he gets XYZ. But that's irrelevant to the question about identity of causal powers, *because these utterances (/thoughts) are being imagined to occur in different contexts* (mine occur in a context in which the local potable is H_2O, his occur in a context in which the local potable is XYZ). What *is* relevant to the question of identity of causal powers is the following pair of counterfactuals: (a) If his utterance (/thought) had occurred in my context, it *would have had* the effects that my utterance (/thought) did have; and (b) if my utterance (/thought) had occurred in his context, it *would have had* the effects that his utterance (/thought) did have. For our utterances (/thoughts) to have the same causal powers, both of those counterfactuals have to be true. But both of those counterfactuals *are* true, since (for example) if I had said "Bring water!" on Twin-Earth, it's XYZ that my interlocutors would have brought; and if he had said "Bring water!" here, his interlocutors would have brought him H_2O.

This line of argument no doubt assumes that I *can* say "Bring water!" on Twin-Earth—that my being on Twin-Earth doesn't ipso facto change my dialect to English2 (and, mutatis mutandis, convert my concept *water* into the concept *water2*). But although I've heard it suggested that mental states construed nonindividualistically are easily bruised and don't 'travel,' the contrary assumption would in fact seem to be secure. The standard intuition about 'visiting' cases is that if, standing on Twin-Earth, I say "That's water" about a puddle of XYZ, then what I say is *false*. Which it wouldn't be if I were speaking English2.

So, OK so far; we have, so far, no reason to suppose that the causal powers of my Twin's mental states are different from the causal powers of mine. On the contrary, since the causal subjunctives about the two states are the same, it must be that they have the *same* causal powers and thus count as the same state by what we're taking to be the relevant typological criteria.

Second line: "Maybe the causal powers of the mental states of Twins are always the same when their effects are *non*intentionally individuated. But consider their effects as intentionally described; consider, in particular, the *behavioral* consequences of the mental states of Oscar and Oscar2. (I assume, here and throughout, that the interesting relations between behaviors and states of mind are typically causal. Philosophers have denied this, but they were wrong to do so.) Oscar's thoughts and desires sometimes eventuate in his *saying* such things as that he prefers brisket to, as it might be, hamburger; Oscar's thoughts sometimes lead to his evincing brisket-eating preferences and brisket-purchasing behavior; and so forth. Whereas Oscar2 never does any of these things. Oscar2 may, of course, say that he likes brisket2; and he may evince brisket2 preferences; and he may, when appropriately stimulated (by, for example, a meat counter), behave brisket2-purchasingly.[5] And, of course, when he says and does these things with brisket2 in mind, he may produce precisely the same bodily *motions* as his counterpart produces when he says and does the corresponding things with brisket in mind. But all that shows is that behaving isn't to be identified with moving one's body; a lesson we ought to have learned long ago."

There's another aspect of this line of reply that's worth noticing: Independent of the present metaphysical issues, anybody who takes the Burge/Putnam intuitions to be decisive for the individuation of the attitudes has a strong motive for denying that Oscar's and Oscar2's behavior (or Mine and My Twin's) are, in general, type-identical. After all, behavior is supposed to be the result of mental causes, and you would generally expect different mental causes to eventuate in correspondingly different behavioral effects. By assumption the Twins' attitudes (and the two Oscars') differ a lot, so if these very different sorts of mental causes nevertheless invariably converge on identical behavioral effects, that would seem to be an accident on a very big scale. The way out is obviously to deny that the behavioral effects *are* identical; to insist that the commonsense way of identifying behaviors, like the commonsense way of identifying the attitudes, goes out into the world for its principles of individuation; that it depends essentially on the relational properties of the behavior. (Burge—who would, of course, accept this conclusion on independent grounds—nevertheless objects that the present sort of argument misunderstands the function of his and Putnam's thought experiments: Since the examples concern the description of circumstances presumed to be counterfactual, the likelihood or otherwise of such circumstances *actually occurring* is not, according to Burge, a relevant consideration. (See *IP*.) But this misses a point of methodology. We do, of course, want to tell the right story about how counterfactual circumstances should be described qua counterfactual. But we *also* want to tell the right story about how such circumstances should be described if they were real. The present intuition is that, were we actually to encounter Twins, what we should want to say of them is *not* that their quite different mental states have somehow managed to converge on the same behaviors; we *can* imagine examples that we'd want to describe that way, but Twins aren't among them. Rather, what we'd want to say about Twins is just that the (putative) differences between their minds are reflected, in the usual way, by corresponding differences between their behaviors. But we *can* say this only if we *are* prepared to describe their behaviors as different. So again it turns out that anyone who counts in a way that distinguishes the minds of Twins should also count in a way that distinguishes their acts.)

In short, Barbara Pym's question "Where does 'behavior' begin and end?" is one that needs to be taken seriously in a discussion of the causal powers of mental states. Claiming, as indeed I have been doing, that my mental states and My Twin's are identical in causal powers begs that question; or so, in any event, the objection might go.

First reply: If this argument shows that my mental state differs from my Twin's, it's hard to see why it doesn't show that our brain states differ too. My Twin is in a brain state that eventuates in his uttering the form of words 'Bring water.' I am in a brain state that eventuates in my uttering the form of words 'Bring water.' If our uttering these forms of words counts as our behaving differently, then it looks as though our brain states differ in their behavioral consequences, hence in their causal powers, hence in the state types of which they are tokens. (Similarly, mutatis mutandis, for our quantum mechanical states.) But I thought we agreed a while back that it would be grotesque to suppose that brain states that live on Twin-Earth are ipso facto typologically distinct from brain states that live around here.

Second reply: Notice that corresponding to the present argument for a taxonomic distinction between my mental state and my Twin's, there is the analogous argument for distinguishing H-particles from T-particles. Here's how it would sound: "Being H rather than T does affect causal powers after all; for H-particles enter into H-particle interactions, and no T-particle does. H-particle interactions may, of course, *look* a lot like T-particle interactions—just as Oscar2's brisket2-eating behaviors look a lot like Oscar's brisket-eating behaviors, and just as my water-requests sound a lot like my Twin's requests for XYZ. Philosophers are not, however, misled by mere appearances; we see where the eye does not."

The least that all this shows is how taxonomic and ontological decisions intertwine: You can save classification by causal powers, come what may, by fiddling the criteria for event identity. To classify by causal powers is to count no property as taxonomically relevant unless it affects causal powers. But x's having property P affects x's causal powers just in case x wouldn't have caused the same events had it not been P. But of course, whether x would have caused the same events had it not been P depends a lot on which events you count as the same and which you count as different. In the present case, whether the difference between being H and being T affects a particle's causal powers depends on whether the very same event that *was* an interaction of H-particles *could have been* an interaction of T particles. (Perhaps it goes without saying that the principle that events are individuated by their causes and effects is perfectly useless here; we can't apply it unless we already know whether an event that *was* caused by an H-particle could have had *the same cause* even if it had been the effect of a T-particle.)

Could it be that this is a dead end? It looked like the notion of taxonomy by causal powers gave us a sort of a priori argument for individualism and thus put some teeth into the idea that a conception of mental state suitable for the psychologist's purposes would have to be interestingly different from the commonsense conception of a propositional attitude. But now it appears that the requirement that states with identical causal powers ought ipso facto to be taxonomically identical can be met *trivially* by anyone prepared to make the appropriate ontological adjustments. Yet surely there has to be something wrong here; because it's false that two events could differ just in that one involves H-particles and the other involves T-particles; and it's false that H-particles and T-particles differ in their causal powers; and—as previously noted—it would be *mad* to suggest saving the supervenience of the propositional attitudes by individuating brain states relationally. Moreover, it is very plausible that all these intuitions hang together. The question is: What on earth do they hang *on*?

I hope I have managed to make this all seem very puzzling; otherwise you won't be impressed when I tell you the answer. But in fact the mystery is hardly bigger than a bread box, and certainly no deeper. Let's go back to the clear case and trace it through.

If H-particle interactions are ipso facto different events from T-particle interactions, then H-particles and T-particles have different causal powers. But if H-particles and T-particles have different causal powers, then the causal powers—not just certain of the relational properties, mind you, but *the causal powers*—of every physical particle in the universe depend on the orientation of my gen-u-ine United States ten cent piece. That includes, of course, physical particles that are a long way away; physical particles on Alpha Centauri, for example. And *that's* what's crazy, because while such relational properties as being H or being T can depend on the orientation of my dime *by stipulation,* how on Earth could the *causal powers* of particles on Alpha Centauri depend on the orientation of my dime? Either there would have to be a causal mechanism to mediate this dependency, or it would have to be mediated by a fundamental law of nature; and there aren't any such mechanisms and there aren't any such laws. *Of course* there aren't.

So, then, to avoid postulating impossible causal mechanisms and/ or impossible natural laws, we will have to say that, all else being equal, H-particle interactions are *not* distinct events from T-particle interactions; hence, that H-particles and T-particles do *not* differ in their causal powers; hence, that the difference between being an H-particle and being a T-particle does *not* count as taxonomic for purposes of causal explanation. Which is, of course, just what intuition tells you that you *ought* to say.

Exactly the same considerations apply, however, to the individuation of mental states.[6] If every instance of brisket-chewing behavior ipso facto counts as an event distinct in kind from any instance of brisket2-chewing behavior, then, since brisket-cravings cause brisket-chewings and brisket2-cravings don't, Oscar's mental state differs in its causal powers from Oscar2's. But then there must be some mechanism that connects the causal powers of Oscar's mental states with the character of the speech community he lives in *and that does so without affecting Oscar's physiology* (remember, Oscar and Oscar2 are molecularly identical). But there is no such mechanism; you *can't* affect the causal powers of a person's mental states without affecting his physiology. That's not a conceptual claim or a metaphysical claim, of course. It's a contingent fact about how God made the world. God made the world such that the mechanisms by which environmental variables affect organic behaviors run via their effects on the organism's nervous system. Or so, at least, all the physiologists I know assure me.

Well then, in order to avoid postulating crazy causal mechanisms, we shall have to assume that brisket chewings are not ipso facto events distinct from chewings of brisket2; hence, that brisket cravings do not ipso facto have different causal powers from brisket2 cravings; hence, that for purposes of causal explanation Oscar's cravings count as mental states of the same kind as Oscar2's.

There is, I think, no doubt that we do count that way when we do psychology, Ned Block has a pretty example that makes this clear. He imagines a psychologist (call her Psyche—the P is silent, as in Psmith) who is studying the etiology of food preferences, and who happens to have both Oscar and Oscar2 in her subject population. Now, on the intuitions that Burge invites us to share, Oscar and Oscar2 have different food preferences; what Oscar prefers to gruel is brisket, but what Oscar2 prefers to gruel is brisket2. Psyche, being a proper psychologist, is of course interested in sources of variance; so the present case puts Psyche in a pickle. If she discounts Oscar and Oscar2, she'll be able to say—as it might be—that there are two determinants of food preference: 27.3 percent of the variance is genetic and the remaining 72.7 percent is the result of early training. If, however, she counts Oscar and Oscar2 in, and if she counts their food preferences the way Burge wants her to, then she has to say that there are *three* sources of variance: genetic endowment, early training, *and linguistic affiliation.* But surely it's *mad* to say that linguistic affiliation is per se a determinant of food preference; how *could* it be?[7]

I think it's perfectly clear how Psyche ought to jump: she ought to say that Oscar and Oscar2 count as having *the same* food preferences and therefore do not constitute counterexamples to her claim that the determinants of food preference are exhausted by genes and early training. And the previous discussion makes clear just *why* she ought to say this: if Oscar and Oscar2 have different food preferences, then there must be some difference in the causal powers of their mental states—psychological taxonomy is taxonomy *by* causal powers. But if there is such a difference, then there must be some mechanism which can connect the causal powers of Oscar's mental states with the character of his linguistic affiliation *without affecting his physiological constitution.* But there is no such mechanism; the causal powers of Oscar's mental states supervene on his physiology, just like the causal powers of your mental states and mine.

So, then, to bring this all together: You can affect the relational properties of things in all sorts of ways—including by stipulation. But for one thing to affect the causal powers of another, there must be a mediating law or mechanism. It's a mystery what this could be in the Twin (or Oscar) cases; not surprisingly, since it's surely plausible that the only mechanisms that *can* mediate environmental effects on the causal powers of mental states are neurological. The way to avoid making this mystery is to count the mental states—and, mutatis mutandis, the behaviors—of Twins (Oscars) as having the same causal powers, hence as taxonomically identical.

So much for the main line of the argument for individualism. Now just a word to bring the reader up to date on the literature.

In a recent paper (*IP*), Burge says that reasoning of the sort I've been pursuing "is confused. The confusion is abetted by careless use of the term 'affect,' conflating causation with individuation. Variations in the environment that do not vary the impacts that causally 'affect' the subject's body may 'affect' the individuation of the . . . intentional processes he or she is undergoing. . . . It does not follow that the environment causally affects the subject in any way that circumvents its having effects on the subject's body" (*IP*, p. 16). But it looks to me like that's precisely what *does* follow, assuming that by "causally affecting" the subject Burge means to include determining the causal powers of the subject's psychological states. You can't both individuate behaviors Burge's way (viz., *non*locally) and hold that the causal powers of mental states are locally supervenient. When individuation is *by* causal powers, questions of individuation and causation don't divide in the way that Burge wants them to.

Consider the case where my Twin and I both spy some water (viz., some H_2O). My seeing the stuff causes me to say (correctly) "That's water!" His seeing the stuff causes him to say (incorrectly) "That's water2!" (His saying this sounds just like my saying "That's water!" of course.) These sayings count as *different behaviors* when you individuate behaviors Burge's way; so the behavioral effects of seeing water are different for the two of us; so the causal powers of the state of seeing water are different depending on which of us is in it. And this difference is uniquely attributable to differences in the contextual background; aside from the contextual background, my Twin and I are identical for present purposes. So if you individuate behavior Burge's way, differences in contextual background effect differences in the causal powers of mental states without having correspondingly different "effects on the subject's body"; specifically, on his neural structure. But is Burge seriously prepared to give up the local supervenience of causal powers? *How could* differences of context affect the causal powers of one's mental states without affecting the states of one's brain?

Burge can say, if he likes, that mind/brain supervenience be damned; though, as I keep pointing out, if mind/brain supervenience goes, the intelligibility of mental causation goes with it. Or he can save mind/brain supervenience by going contextual on *neurological* individuation. (As, indeed, he appears to be tempted to do; see his footnote 18 in *IP*. Here both intuition and scientific practice clearly run against him, however.) But what he can't do is split the difference. If supervenience be damned for individuation, it can't be saved for causation. Burge says that "local causation does not make more plausible local individuation" (p. 16), but he's wrong if, as it would seem, "local causation" implies local supervenience of causal powers. Local causation *requires* local individuation when so construed. You can have contextual individuation if you insist on it. But you can't have it for free. Etiology suffers.

Well, if all this is as patent as I'm making it out to be, how could anyone ever have supposed that the standards of individuation appropriate to the psychologist's purposes are other than individualistic? I cast no aspersions, but I have a dark suspicion; I think people get confused between methodological *individualism* and methodological *solipsism*. A brief excursus on this topic, therefore, will round off this part of the discussion.

Methodological individualism is the doctrine that psychological states are individuated *with respect to their causal powers.* Methodological solipsism is the doctrine that psychological states are individuated *without respect to their semantic evaluation.*[8]

Now, the semantic evaluation of a mental state depends on certain of its relational properties (in effect, on how the state corresponds to the world). So we could say, as a rough way of talking, that solipsistic individuation is *nonrelational.* But if we are going to talk that way, then *it is very important* to distinguish between solipsism and individualism. In particular, though it's a point of definition that solipsistic individuation is nonrelational, there is nothing to stop principles of individuation from being simultaneously relational and individualistic. *Individualism does not prohibit the relational individuation of mental states;* it just says that no property of mental states, relational or otherwise, counts taxonomically unless it affects causal powers.

Indeed, individualism couldn't rule out relational individuation per se if any of what I've been arguing for up till now is true. I've taken it that individualism is a completely general methodological principle in science; one which follows simply from the scientist's goal of causal explanation and which, therefore, all scientific taxonomies must obey. By contrast, it's patent that taxonomic categories in science are *often* relational. Just as you'd expect, relational properties can count taxonomically whenever they affect causal powers. Thus 'being a planet' is a relational property par excellence, but it's one that individualism permits to operate in astronomical taxonomy. For whether you are a planet affects your trajectory, and your trajectory determines what you can bump into; so whether you're a planet affects your causal powers, which is all the individualism asks for. Equivalently, the property of being a planet is taxonomic because there are causal laws that things satisfy in virtue of being planets. By contrast, the property of living in a world in which there is XYZ in the puddles is *not* taxonomic because there are *no* causal laws that things satisfy in virtue of having *that* property. And similarly for the property of living in a speech community in which people use 'brisket' to refer to brisket of beef. The operative consideration is, of course, that where there are no causal laws about a property, having the property—or failing to have it—has no effect on causal powers.[9]

To put the point the other way around, solipsism (construed as prohibiting the relational taxonomy of mental states) is unlike individualism in that it *couldn't conceivably* follow from any *general* considerations about scientific goals or practices. 'Methodological solipsism' is, in fact, an empirical theory about the mind: it's the theory that mental processes are computational, hence syntactic. I think this theory is defensible; in fact, I think it's true. But its defense can't be conducted on a priori or metaphysical grounds, and its truth depends simply on the facts about how the mind works. Methodological solipsism differs from methodological individualism in both these respects.

Well, to come to the point: If you happen to have confused individualism with solipsism (and if you take solipsism to be the doctrine that psychological taxonomy is nonrelational), then you might try arguing against individualism by remarking that the psychologist's taxonomic apparatus is, often enough, nonsolipsistic (viz., that it's often relational). As, indeed, it is. Even computational ('information flow') psychologists are professionally interested in such questions as, 'Why does this organism have the computational capacities that it has?'; 'Why does its brain compute this algorithm rather than some other?'; or even, 'Why is this mental process generally truth preserving?' Such questions often get answered by reference to relational properties of the organism's mental state. See for example Ullman, *IVM*, where you get lovely arguments that run like this: *This perceptual algorithm is generally truth preserving because the organism that computes it lives in a world where most spatial transformations of objects are rigid. If the same algorithm were run in a world in which most spatial transformations were not rigid, it wouldn't be truth preserving, and the ability to compute it would be without survival value. So, presumably, the organism wouldn't have this ability in such a world.* These sorts of explanations square with *individualism,* because the relational facts they advert to affect the causal powers of mental states; indeed, they affect their very existence. But naturally, explanations of this sort—for that matter, *all* teleological explanations—are ipso facto nonsolipsistic. So *if* you have confused solipsistic (viz., nonrelational) taxonomies with individualistic taxonomies (viz., taxonomies by causal powers), then you *might* wrongly suppose that the affection psychologists have for teleological explanation argues that they—like the laity—are prone to individuate mental states nonindividualistically. But it doesn't. And they aren't.

I repeat the main points in a spirit of recapitulation. There are two of them; one is about the methodology of science, and one is about its metaphysics.

Methodological point: Categorization in science is characteristically taxonomy by causal powers. Identity of causal powers is identity of causal consequences across nomologically possible contexts.

Metaphysical point: Causal powers supervene on local microstructure. In the psychological case, they supervene on local neural structure. We abandon this principle at our peril; mind/brain supervenience (/identity) is our only plausible account of how mental states could have the causal powers that they do have. On the other hand, given what causal *powers* are, preserving the principle constrains the way that we individuate causal *consequences.* In the case of the behavioral consequences of the attitudes, it requires us to individuate them in ways that violate the commonsense taxonomy. So be it.

Well, I've gotten us where I promised to: back to where we started. There is a difference between the way psychology individuates behaviors and mental states and the way common sense does. At least there is if you assume that the Burge/Putnam intuitions are reliable.[10] But this fact isn't, in and of itself, really very interesting; scientific taxonomy is forever cross-cutting categories of everyday employment. For that matter, the sciences are forever cross-cutting one another's taxonomies. Chemistry doesn't care about the distinction between streams and lakes; but geology does. Physics doesn't care about the distinction between bankers and butchers; but sociology does. (For that matter, physics doesn't care about the distinction between the Sun and Alpha Centauri either; sublime indifference!)

None of this is surprising; things in Nature overlap in their causal powers to various degrees and in various respects; the sciences play these overlaps, each in its own way.

And, for nonscientific purposes, we are often interested in taxonomies that cross-cut causal powers. Causal explanation is just one human preoccupation among many; individualism is a constitutive principle of science, not of rational taxonomy per se. Or, to put it a little differently—more in the material mode—God could make a genuine electron, or diamond, or tiger, or person, because being an electron or a diamond or a tiger or a person isn't a matter of being the effect of the right kind of causes; rather, it's a matter of being the cause of the right kind of effects. And similarly, I think, for all the other natural kinds. Causal powers are decisively relevant to a taxonomy of natural kinds because such taxonomies are organized in behalf of causal explanation. Not all taxonomies have that end in view, however, so not all taxonomies classify by causal powers. Even God couldn't make a gen-u-ine United States ten cent piece; only the U.S. Treasury Department can do that.

You can't, in short, make skepticism just out of the fact that the commonsense way of taxonomizing the mental differs from the psychologist's way. You might, however, try the idea that disagreement between the commonsense taxonomy and the scientific one matters more in psychology than it does elsewhere *because psychology needs the commonsense notion of mental content*. In particular, you might try the idea that the notion of mental content doesn't survive the transition from the layman's categories to the scientist's. I know of at least one argument that runs that way. Let's have a look at it.

What we have—though only by assumption, to be sure—is a typology for mental states according to which my thoughts and my Twin's (and Oscar's thoughts and Oscar2's) have identical contents. More generally, we have assumed a typology according to which the physiological identity of organisms guarantees the identity of their mental states (and, a fortiori, the identity of the contents of their mental states). All this is entailed by the principle—now taken to be operative—that the mental supervenes upon the physiological (together with the assumption—which I suppose to be untendentious—that mental states have their contents essentially, so that typological identity of the former guarantees typological identity of the latter). All right so far.

But now it appears that even if the physiological identity of organisms ensures the identity of their mental states and the identity of mental states ensures the identity of contents, *the identity of the contents of mental states does not ensure the identity of their extensions:* my thoughts and my Twin's—like Oscar's and Oscar2's—*differ in their truth conditions,* so it's an accident if they happen to have the same truth values. Whereas what makes my water-thoughts true is the facts about H_2O, what makes my Twin's 'water'-thoughts true is the facts about XYZ. Whereas the thought that I have—when it runs through my head that water is wet—is true iff H_2O is wet, the thought that he has—when it runs through his head that 'water' is wet—is true iff XYZ is wet. And it's an accident (that is, it's just contingent) that H_2O is wet iff XYZ is. (Similarly, what I'm thinking about when I think: *water,* is different from what he's thinking about when he thinks: *'water'*; he's thinking about XYZ, but I'm thinking about H_2O. So the denotations of our thoughts differ.) Hence the classical—Putnamian—formulation of the puzzle about Twins: If mental state supervenes upon physiology, then thoughts don't have their truth conditions essentially; two tokens of the *same* thought can have *different* truth conditions, hence different truth values. If thoughts are in the head, then content doesn't determine extension.

That, then, is the 'Twin-Earth Problem.' Except that so far it *isn't* a problem; it's just a handful of intuitions together with a commentary on some immediate implications of accepting them. If that were *all,* the right response would surely be "So what?" What connects the intuitions and their implications with the proposal that we give up on propositional-attitude psychology is a certain *Diagnosis.* And while a lot has been written about the intuitions and their implications, the diagnosis has gone largely unexamined. I propose now to examine it.

Here's the Diagnosis: "Look, on *anybody's* story, the notion of content has got to be at least a little problematic. For one thing, it seems to be a notion proprietary to the information sciences, and *soi-disant* 'emergents' bear the burden of proof. At a minimum, if you're going to have mental contents, you owe us some sort of account of their individuation.

"Now, prior to the Twin-Earth Problem, there *was* some sort of account of their individuation; you could say, to a first approximation, that identity of content depends on identity of extension. No doubt that story leaked a bit: Morning-Star thoughts look to be different in content from the corresponding Evening-Star thoughts, even though their truth conditions are arguably the same. But at least one could hold firmly to this: 'Extension supervenes on content; no difference in extension without some difference in content.' Conversely, it was a *test* for identity of content that the extensions had to come out to be the same. And that was the *best* test we had; it was the one source of evidence about content identity that seemed surely reliable.

Compare the notorious wobbliness of intuitions about synonymy, analyticity, and the like.

"But now we see that *it's not true after all* that difference of extension implies difference of content; so unclear are we now about what content-identity comes to—hence, about what identity of propositional attitudes comes to—that we can't even assume that typologically identical thoughts will always be true and false together. The consequence of the psychologist's insistence on preserving supervenience is that we now have no idea at all what criteria of individuation for propositional attitudes might be like; hence, we have no idea at all what counts as *evidence* for the identity of propositional attitudes.

"Short form: Inferences from difference of extension to difference of content used to bear almost all the weight of propositional-attitude attribution. That was, however, a frail reed, and now it has broken. The Twin-Earth Problem *is* a problem, *because it breaks the connection between extensional identity and content identity.*"

Now, the Twin-Earth intuitions are fascinating, and if you care about semantics you will, no doubt, do well to attend to them. But, as I've taken pains to emphasize, you need the Diagnosis to connect the intuitions about Twins to the issues about the status of belief/desire psychology, and—fortunately for those of us who envision a psychology of propositional attitudes—the Diagnosis rests on a quite trivial mistake: *The Twin-Earth examples don't break the connection between content and extension; they just relativize it to context.*

Suppose that what you used to think, prior to Twin-Earth, is that contents are something like functions from thoughts to truth conditions: given the content of a thought, you know the conditions under which that thought would be true. (Presumably a truth condition would itself then be a function from worlds to truth values: a thought that has the truth condition TC takes the value T in world W iff TC is satisfied in W. Thus, for example, in virtue of its content the thought that it's raining has the truth condition *that it's raining* and is thus true in a world iff it's raining in that world.) I hasten to emphasize that if you don't—or didn't—like that story, it's quite all right for you to choose some other; my point is going to be that if you liked any story of even remotely that kind before Twin-Earth, you're perfectly free to go on liking it now. For even if all the intuitions about Twin-Earth are right, and even if they have all the implications that they are said to have, extensional identity still constrains intentional identity because *contents still determine extensions relative to a context.* If you like, contents are functions from contexts and thoughts onto truth conditions.

What, if anything, does that mean? Well, it's presumably common ground that there's something about the relation between Twin-Earth and Twin-Me in virtue of which his 'water'-thoughts are about XYZ even though my water-thoughts are not. Call this condition that's satisfied by {Twin-Me, Twin-Earth} condition C (because it determines the *Context* of his 'water'-thoughts). Similarly, there must be something about the relation between me and Earth in virtue of which my water-thoughts are about H_2O even though my Twin's 'water'-thoughts are not. Call this condition that is satisfied by {me, Earth} condition C'. I don't want to worry, just now, about the problem of how to articulate conditions C and C'. Some story about constraints on the causal relations between H_2O tokenings and water-thought tokenings (and between XYZ tokenings and 'water'-thought tokenings) would be the obvious proposal; but it doesn't matter much for the purposes now at hand. Because we *do* know this: Short of a miracle, it must be true that if an organism shares the neurophysical constitution of my Twin *and satisfies* C, it follows that its thoughts and my Twin's thoughts share their truth conditions. For example, short of a miracle the following counterfactual must be true: Given the neurological identity between us, in a world where I am in my Twin's context my 'water'-thoughts are about XYZ iff his are. (And, of course, vice versa: In a world in which my Twin is in my context, given the neurological identity between us, it must be that his water-thoughts are about H_2O iff mine are.)

But now we have an extensional identity criterion for mental contents: Two thought contents are identical only if they effect the same mapping of thoughts and contexts onto truth conditions. Specifically, your thought is content-identical to mine only if in every context in which your thought has truth condition *T*, mine has truth condition *T* and vice versa.

It's worth reemphasizing that, by this criterion, my Twin's 'water'-thoughts are intentionally identical to my water-thoughts; they have the same contents even though, since their contexts are de facto different, they differ, de facto, in their truth conditions. In effect, what we have here is an extensional criterion for 'narrow' content. The 'broad content' of a thought, by contrast, is what you can semantically evaluate; it's what you get when you specify a narrow content *and fix a context.*

We can now see why we ought to reject both of the following two suggestions found in Putnam, *MM:* That we consider the extension of a term (/concept/thought) to be an independent component of its "meaning vector"; and that we make do, in our psychology, with stereotypes *instead of* contents. The first proposal is redundant, since, as we've just seen, contents (meanings) determine extensions given a context. The second proposal is unacceptable, because unlike contents, stereotypes *don't* determine extensions. (Since it's untendentious that stereotypes supervene on physiology, the stereotypes for real water and Twin-water must be identical; so if stereotypes did fix extensions, my Twin's 'water'-thoughts would have the same extension as mine.) But, as the Diagnosis rightly says, we need an extension determiner as a component of the meaning vector, because we rely on 'different extension → different content' for the individuation of concepts.

"Stop, stop! I have an objection."

Oh, good! Do proceed.

"Well, since on your view your water-thoughts are content-identical to your Twin's, I suppose we may infer that the English word 'water' has the same intension as its Tw-English homonym (hereinafter spelled 'water2')."

We may.

"But if 'water' and 'water2' have the same intensions, they must apply to the same things. So since 'water2' applies to XYZ, 'water' applies to XYZ too. It follows that XYZ must *be* water (what else could it mean to say that 'water' applies to it?). But, as a matter of fact, XYZ *isn't* water; only H_2O is water. Scientists discover essences."

I don't know whether scientists discover essences. It may be that philosophers make them up. In either event, the present problem doesn't exist. The denotation of 'water' is determined not just by its meaning but by its context. But the context for English "anchors" 'water' to H_2O just as, mutatis mutandis, the context for Tw-English anchors 'water2' to XYZ. (I learned 'anchors' at Stanford; it is a very useful term despite—or maybe because of—not being very well defined. For present purposes, an expression is anchored iff it has a determinate semantic value.) So then, the condition for 'x is water' to be true requires that x be H_2O. Which, by assumption, XYZ isn't. So English 'water' doesn't apply to XYZ (though, of course, Tw-English 'water' does). OK so far.

And yet . . . and yet! One seems to hear a Still Small Voice—could it be the voice of conscience?—crying out as follows: "You say that 'water' and its Tw-English homonym mean the same thing; well then, *what* do they mean?"

How like the voice of conscience to insist upon the formal mode. It might equally have put its problem this way: "What *is* the thought such that when I have it its truth condition is that H_2O is wet and when my Twin has it its truth condition is that XYZ is wet? What is the concept *water* such that it denotes H_2O in this world and XYZ in the next?" I suspect that this—and not Putnam's puzzle about individuation—is 'what *really* bugs people about narrow content. The construct invites a question which—so it appears—we simply don't have a way of answering.

But conscience be hanged; it's not the construct but the question that is ill advised. What the Still Small Voice wants me to do is utter an English sentence which expresses just what my 'water'-thoughts have in common with my Twin's. Unsurprisingly, I can't do it. That's because the content that an English sentence expresses is ipso facto *anchored* content, hence ipso facto *not* narrow.

So, in particular, qua expression of English "water is wet" is anchored to the wetness of water (i.e., of H_2O) just as, qua expression of Tw-English, "water2 is wet" is anchored to the wetness of water2 (i.e., of XYZ). And of course, since it is anchored to water, "water is wet" doesn't—can't—express the narrow content that my water-thoughts share with my Twin's. Indeed, if you mean by content what can be semantically evaluated, then what my water-thoughts share with Twin 'water'-thoughts *isn't* content. Narrow content is radically inexpressible, because it's only content *potentially*; it's what gets to *be* content when—and only when—it gets to be anchored. We can't—to put it in a nutshell—*say* what Twin thoughts have in common. This is because what can be said is ipso facto semantically evaluable; and what Twin-thoughts have in common is ipso facto not.

Here is another way to put what is much the same point: You have to be sort of careful if you propose to co-opt the notion of narrow content for service in a 'Griceian' theory of meaning. According to Griceian theories, the meaning of a sentence is inherited from the content of the propositional attitude(s) that the sentence is conventionally used to express. Well, that's fine so long as you remember that it's *anchored* content (that is, it's the content of anchored attitudes), and hence not narrow content, that sentences inherit. Looked at the other way around, when we use the content of a sentence to specify the content of a mental state (viz., by embedding the sentence to a verb of propositional attitude), the best we can do—in principle, *all* we can do—is avail ourselves of the content of the sentence qua anchored; for it's only qua anchored that sentences *have* content. The corresponding consideration is relatively transparent in the case of demonstratives. Suppose the thought 'I've got a sore toe' runs through your head and also runs through mine; what's the content that these thoughts share? Well, you can't say what it is by using the sentence "I've got a sore toe," since, whenever you use that sentence, the "I" automatically gets anchored to you. You can, however, sneak up on the shared content by *mentioning* that sentence, as I did just above. In such cases, mentioning a sentence is a way of abstracting a form of words from the consequences of its being anchored.

One wants, above all, to avoid a sort of fallacy of subtraction: 'Start with anchored content; take the anchoring conditions away, and you end up with a *new sort of content,* an unanchored content; a *narrow* content, as we say.' (Compare: 'Start with a bachelor; take the unmarriedness away, and you end up with a *new sort of bachelor,* a married bachelor; a *narrow* bachelor, as we say.') Or rather, there's nothing wrong with talking that way, so long as you don't then start to wonder *what the narrow content of—for example—the thought that water is wet could be.* Such questions can't be answered in the nature of things; so, in the nature of things, they shouldn't be asked.[11] People who positively *insist* on asking them generally get what they deserve: phenomenalism, verificationism, 'procedural' semantics, or skepticism, depending on temperament and circumstance.

"But look," the SSV replies, "if narrow content isn't really content, then in what sense do you and your Twin have any water-thoughts in common at all? And if the form of words 'water is wet' doesn't express the narrow content of Twin water-thoughts, how can the form of words 'the thought that water is wet' succeed in picking out a thought that you share with your Twin?"

Answer: What I share with my Twin—what supervenience *guarantees* that we share—is a mental state that is semantically evaluable relative to a context. Referring expressions of English can therefore be used to pick out narrow contents via their *hypothetical* semantic properties. So, for example, the English expression 'the thought that water is wet' can be used to specify the narrow content of a mental state that my Twin and I share (even though, qua anchored to H_2O, it doesn't, of course, *express* that content). In particular, it can be used to pick out the content of my Twin's 'water'-thought via the truth conditions that it *would have had* if my Twin had been plugged into my world. Roughly speaking, this tactic works because the narrow thought that water is wet is the *unique* narrow thought that yields the truth condition H_2O *is wet* when anchored to my context and the truth condition *XYZ is wet* when anchored to his.

You can't, in absolute strictness, express narrow content; but as we've seen, there are ways of sneaking up on it.

SSV: "By that logic, why don't you call the narrow thought you share with your Twin 'the thought that water2 is wet'? After all, that's the 'water-thought' that you would have had if you had been plugged into your Twin's context (and that he *does* have in virtue of the fact that he *has* been plugged into his context). Turn about is fair play."

Answer: (a) 'The thought that water2 is wet' is an expression of Tw-English; I don't speak Tw-English. (b) The home team gets to name the intension; the actual world has privileges that merely counterfactual worlds don't share.

SSV: "What about if you are a brain in a vat? What about then?"

Answer: If you are a brain in a vat, then you have, no doubt, got serious cause for complaint. But it may be some consolation that brains in vats have no special *semantical* difficulties according to the present account. They are, in fact, just special cases of Twins.

On the one hand, a brain in a vat instantiates the same function from contexts to truth conditions that the corresponding brain in a head does; being in a vat does not, therefore, affect the narrow content of one's thoughts. On the other hand, it *may* affect the *broad* content of one's thoughts; it may, for example, affect their truth conditions. That would depend on just which kind of brain-in-a-vat you have in mind; for example, on just what sorts of connections you imagine there are between the brain, the vat, and the world. If you imagine a brain in a vat that's hooked up to *this* world, and hooked up *just* the same way one's own brain is, then—of course— that brain shares one's thought-contents *both* narrow *and* broad. Broad content supervenes on neural state together with connections to context. It had better, after all; a skull is a kind of vat too.

SSV: "But if a brain is a function from contexts to truth conditions, and if a vat can be a context, then when a brain in a vat thinks 'water is wet' the truth condition of its thought will be (not something about H_2O or XYZ but) something about its vat. So it will be thinking something *true*. Which violates the intuiton that the thoughts of brains in vats have to be *false* thoughts."

Answer: You're confused about your intuitions. What they really tell you isn't that the thoughts of brains in vats have to be false; it's that being in a vat wouldn't stop a brain from having the very thoughts that you have now. And that intuition is *true,* so long as you individuate thoughts narrowly. It's tempting to infer that if a brain has your thoughts, and has them under conditions that would make your thoughts false, then the thoughts that the brain is having must be false too. But to argue this way is exactly to equivocate between the narrow way of individuating thoughts and the broad way.

SSV: "Mental states are supposed to cause behavior. How can a function cause anything?"

Answer: Some functions are implemented in brains; and brains cause things. You can think of a narrow mental state as determining an equivalence class of mechanisms, where the criterion for being in the class is *semantic.*

SSV: "I do believe you've gone over to Steve Stich. Have you no conscience? Do you take me for a mere expository convention?"

Answer: There, there; don't fret! What is emerging here is, in a certain sense, a 'no content' account of narrow content; but it is nevertheless also a fully intentionalist account. According to the present story, a narrow content is *essentially* a function from contexts onto truth conditions; different functions from contexts onto truth conditions are ipso facto different narrow contents. It's hard to see what more you could want of an intentional state than that it should have semantic properties that are intrinsic to its individuation. In effect, I'm prepared to give Stich everything except what he wants. (See Stich, *FFPCS.*)

Now, sleep conscience!

What I hope this chapter has shown is this: Given the causal explanation of behavior as the psychologist's end in view, he has motivation for adopting a taxonomy of mental states that respects supervenience. However, the psychologist needs a way to reconcile his respect for supervenience with the idea that the extension of a mental state constrains its content; for he needs to hold onto the argument from *difference* of extension to *difference* of content. When it comes to individuating mental states, that's the best kind of argument he's got, just as Putnam says. It turns out, however, that it's not hard to reconcile respecting supervenience with observing extensional constraints on content, because you can relativize the constraints to context: given a context, contents are different if extensions are. There isn't a shred of evidence to suggest that this principle is untrue—surely the Twin cases provide no such evidence—or that it constrains content attributions any less well than the old, unrelativized account used to do. The point to bear in mind is that if 'difference in extension → difference in intension' substantively constrains the attribution of propositional attitudes, then so too does this same principle when it is relativized to context. *The Moral:* If the worry about propositional attitudes is that Twin-Earth shows that contents don't determine extensions, the right thing to do is to *stop worrying.*

So it looks as though everything is all right. Super; Let, you might suppose, rejoicing be unconstrained. But if you do suppose that, that's only because you've let the Twin problems distract you from the hard problems. The hard problems start in chapter 3.[12]

3
Meaning Holism

I thought chapter 2 was actually sort of interesting. We saw how the standard intuitions about Twin cases pose a threat to the notion of mental content which (on my view) intentional psychology requires; and, toward the end of the chapter, we saw how it might be possible to construct a notion of narrow content that's adequate to meet the threat. The present issues about Meaning Holism are, alas, a lot less clear cut. Meaning Holism is a doctrine that is widely supposed to raise problems for a Realistic view of the attitudes; but it's remarkably hard to say just what the doctrine is, or precisely what the problems are that it raises, or just which arguments are the ones that require us to take the doctrine seriously. So I propose to scout around; to make as clear as I can how issues about Meaning Holism connect with other big issues in the philosophy of language and the philosophy of mind, and to try to convince you—by the time we get to the end—that because these connected issues are unresolved the arguments from Meaning Holism to Irrealism about content are profound, disturbing, unsettling . . . and inconclusive. In this chapter I'll settle for a Scotch verdict.

The Background to the Problem

Pick a proposition that you understand, any proposition that you understand. Let it be: the proposition that *Callas was a better singer than Tebaldi*. Since—by assumption—you understand this proposition, I suppose that you have some idea of what it would be like for *Callas was a better singer than Tebaldi* to be true. And since you have some idea of what it would be like for *Callas was a better singer than Tebaldi* to be true, I suppose there must be many *other* propositions whose truth (/falsity) you take to be relevant to the semantic evaluation of this one. For example, I expect that you would take many of the propositions that *Callas was better than Tebaldi* 'closely' entails to be relevant to its semantic evaluation (so that you would cease to hold that Callas was better than Tebaldi if you were to come to doubt that Callas was better than anyone). Similarly, I expect that you would take many propositions that 'closely' entail *C was better than T* to be relevant to its semantic evaluation (so that you would come to believe that C was better than T if you were to come to believe C was better than everyone).

When an intentional system takes the semantic value of *P* to be relevant to the semantic evaluation of *Q*, I shall say that *P* is an *epistemic liaison of Q* (for that system at that time). Please note the relativization to agents and times. 'Epistemic liaison' is really a *psychological* notion, not an *epistemological* one. That is, what counts isn't the *objective* dependencies between the semantic values of the propositions; it's what the agent *supposes* those dependencies to be.

A lot could be done to clean up 'epistemic liaison,' but I'm not going to bother; it isn't a notion that I propose to build on. (Indeed, the main contention of this chapter is that it is inadvisable to try to build semantics on it.) And even without further elaboration it will serve to do the job at hand, which is to introduce the doctrine of Meaning Holism. Meaning Holism is the idea that the identity— specifically, the intentional content—of a propositional attitude is determined by the *totality* of its epistemic liaisons. We'll see more and more of what this doctrine comes to as we go along; but you can get the intuition by thinking about examples. Suppose that you and I don't agree about Robert J. Lurtsema's reliability in judging sopranos; for you, but not for me, Robert J.'s views are relevant to the semantic evaluation of *Callas was better than Tebaldi*. Then, by definition, the epistemic liaisons of the belief that *C > T* are different for the two of us. But Meaning Holism says that the identity of a belief depends upon the totality of its epistemic liaisons. It therefore follows, if Meaning Holism is true, that *C > T* is a belief that you and I *cannot share*.

Strictly speaking, I suppose that Meaning Holism is compatible with a Realistic reading of intentional ascriptions. For even if, under the conditions just described, you and I can't *both* have the belief that Callas was better than Tebaldi, nothing so far prohibits *one* of us from having it. But that Meaning Holism is, in this minimal sense, compatible with intentional Realism affords small comfort to working intentionalists. For Meaning Holism looks to be entirely destructive of the hope for a propositional attitude psychology.

Presumably an event (e.g., the production of behavior by some organism) would fall within the domain of such a psychology in virtue of instantiating one of its generalizations. And presumably such generalizations would apply to an organism at a time in virtue of the intentional state(s) that the organism is in at the time. The way it ought to go is that the theory says things like: 'From any organism x that believes such and such and desires so and so, you get behaviors of the type . . . blah.' You can, therefore, use the theory to predict that *this* organism x will give behavior of the type . . . blah *if* you can identify this x as believing such and such and desiring so and so. This is just a long form of the truism that one way that intentional psychologies achieve generality is by *quantifying over all the organisms that are in a specified intentional state.*

But now, if—as is surely the case—people quite generally differ in their estimates of epistemic relevance, and if we follow Meaning Holism and individuate intentional states by the *totality* of their epistemic liaisons, it's going to turn out de facto that no two people (for that matter, no two time slices of the *same* person) ever *are* in the same intentional state. (Except, maybe, by accident.) So no two people will ever get subsumed by the same intentional generalizations. So intentional generalizations won't, in fact, succeed in generalizing. So there's no hope for an intentional psychology.

To put it another way: Chapter 2 suggested a notion of narrow content that preserves supervenience. On that notion, neurological identity is a sufficient condition for identity of mental state. But so far we have nothing like a *necessary and* sufficient condition for identity of content; and if Meaning Holism is true, it looks like we aren't going to get one.

Now, Meaning Holism has something of the status of the received doctrine in current philosophy of language. We are thus arrived at a tactical watershed. One option is to live with Meaning Holism and look for ways to mitigate its consequences for intentional psychology; another is to attempt to undermine Meaning Holism. Though most of the discussion in this chapter will pursue the second route, I now propose to spend a paragraph or two considering the first. Perhaps we could cook up a graded notion of 'same intentional state' according to which you and I might both *more or less* believe that Callas is better than Tebaldi. If we could do that, we could presumably also get a graded notion of being subsumed by an intentional generalization, and that would—at least in principle—be enough to buy back the predictive power of intentional psychologies.

That is the kind of yucky solution that they're crazy about in AI. What makes it seem plausible is that it's easy to confuse two quite different senses of 'more or less believing that P.' On the one hand, there's the relatively banal and commonsensical idea that agents can differ in the degree of their epistemic commitment to P (so that while John will go to the wall for P, Jane grants P only her provisional assent). This last is just garden-variety Baysianism. It may be wrong, but it is not yucky and it is perfectly OK with me. But whereas it's common sense that you can grade epistemic commitment, *it is far from common sense that you can grade propositional identity.* There's all the difference in the world between 'one can more-or-less-believe that P' and 'what one believes can be more-or-less-that-P.' And it is emphatically the second claim that is presently on offer. If its epistemic liaisons determine the identity of an attitude's object, and if you and I acknowledge different epistemic liaisons for the belief that $C > T$, then the current proposal must be that $C > T$ is unequally the object of our attitudes: Whereas what *you* believe is *almost* the proposition that Callas was better than Tebaldi, what I believe is that proposition's very self. Yuck! There is, in my view, no sense to be made of the suggestion that something might be almost—but not quite—the proposition that Callas was better than Tebaldi.

A slightly less unaesthetic way of making one's peace with Meaning Holism would be first to admit, but then to 'idealize away from,' variations in estimates of epistemic relevance. In effect, you imagine the generalizations of an intentional psychology to be *strictly* satisfied only in the case of communities of ideally homogeneous believers; so, in practice, the predictive power of the theory increases asymptotically as the domain that it's applied in approaches this ideal. The model here is the appeal, in theory construction even in the respectable sciences, to ideal gases, chemically pure samples, frictionless planes, and other such Platonic constructs.

I used to think this second move would work, at least for the polemical purpose of defanging Meaning Holism. But I don't think so any more. The problem isn't that Meaning Holism forces us to scientific idealization; it's rather that Meaning Holism makes any old idealization seem just about as good as any other. For example, I remarked earlier that even if we can't *both* believe that Callas was better than Tebaldi, it's OK with Meaning Holism that one of us does. Fine, but *which* one? You, who hold that 'Robert J. likes Callas best' is epistemically relevant to '$C > T$'? Or I, who hold that it is not? Or, to put the question more in the terms of the present proposal: Which 'ideally homogeneous' community of intentional systems should we idealize to when we specify the domain of intentional generalizations about people who believe that C is better than T? The ideally homogeneous community in which Robert J.'s views are epistemic liaisons of that belief, or the ideally homogeneous community in which they aren't? Meaning Holism says we *must* choose; since epistemic liaisons are what *individuate* beliefs, each belief has its epistemic liaisons *necessarily.* But though Meaning Holism demands that we choose, it gives us no idea of how we are to do so.

It's important to see how much this objection militates against the possibility of establishing a modus vivendi between Meaning Holism and intentional psychology. If (in despite of the good advice previously tendered) you take what I called the AI approach, you will need a notion of believing P to degree n; two people share the belief that P iff what both believe is that-P to a degree $n > 0$. (This they are both allowed to do even though—since, by assumption, they differ in their epistemic liaisons for P—what at least one of them believes must be that-P to degree $n < 1$.) But surely such a notion could make sense for $n < 1$ only if it makes sense for $n = 1$; if it is possible for a belief to be that-P more or less, it must be possible for a belief to be that-P tout court. But again: Meaning Holism says that whether you believe that P is a question of what epistemic liaisons you take your belief to have. So not even opting for a graded notion of propositional identity will get you off having to decide which epistemic liaisons determine which beliefs.

Similarly if you take the Platonic line. The function of a scientific idealization is (*inter alia*) to tell you how the observed values should vary as experimental conditions move toward the asymptote. But idealization can't serve that function unless the theory says *where the asymptote is*. (E.g., at asymptote the planes are frictionless, the molecules are infinitely inelastic, the chemical samples are pure, . . . etc.) The application of this methodological principle to belief/desire psychology seems clear. Such a theory can idealize to a homogeneous community of believers-that-P only if it can say *what it is like* to believe that P in the ideal case. If, therefore, epistemic liaisons individuate states of P-believing, licit idealization requires intentional theory to say *which* such liaisons the belief that P ideally has. The Platonic reply to Meaning Holism raises this question without suggesting any way of answering it, so it's not much help to Intentional Realists. Even if Platonism is assumed, intentional psychology still requires—and is still without—reasonable principles of individuation for the attitudes. So it is still to that extent in trouble. (The last three paragraphs are indebted to McClamrock, *IC*.)

So much for trying to reconcile a substantive Intentional Realism with a holistic account of the individuation of the attitudes. There remains, of course, the alternative tactic. One might argue that if Meaning Holism is incompatible with intentional psychology, then so much the worse for Meaning Holism. Prima facie, the prospects for such an argument seem pretty good. On the one hand, our commonsense psychological generalizations are surely more likely to be true than any of our philosophical theories about how the attitudes are individuated; the former, unlike the latter, are required to *work* for their living. And, second, Meaning Holism really is a *crazy* doctrine. To defend Individualism, as we did in chapter 2, is perhaps to sail against the prevailing intuitions; but common sense surely suggests that you and I can contrive to agree—or disagree—about the respective merits of Callas and Tebaldi, and that our ability to do so is *metaphysically independent* of our agreeing—or disagreeing—about Robert J.'s reliability as a judge of sopranos. Anti-individualism one may have learned at Mother's knee, but you have to go to Harvard to learn to be a Meaning Holist. This means that the burden of proof is on the Visitors; all the Home Team has to do to win is show why the arguments that have been alleged for Meaning Holism are inconclusive. That is what this chapter will be up to, as previously announced.

There are, so far as I can see, three ways that philosophers have tried to establish Meaning Holism: from epistemology via the assumption of *confirmation* holism, from the philosophy of mind via the assumption of 'psychofunctionalism,' and from the philosophy of language via a 'functional role' theory of meaning. The third route is far the most interesting, but we'll have to look at all three. Before we do, however, it will pay to consider the general structure that all these arguments share. It is very easy to get confused about what a holist can reasonably take for granted and what he is obliged to argue for. I think this sort of confusion abounds in the literature and makes the case for holism seem better than in fact it is. Therefore:

A Methodological Digression. In which the general form of arguments for Meaning Holism is set forth; and the Reader makes the acquaintance of Mrs. T.

After a while all the arguments for Meaning Holism begin to sound rather alike. That is because all the arguments for Meaning Holism *are* rather alike. They're all specializations of a sort of Ur-argument, which goes like this:

The Ur-Argument for Meaning Holism

Step 1. Argue that *at least some* of the epistemic liaisons of a belief determine its intentional content.

Step 2. Run a 'slippery slope' argument to show that there is no principled way of deciding *which* of the epistemic liaisons of a belief determine its intentional content. So either none does or they all do.

Step 3. Conclude that they all do. (1,2: modus tollens.)

Notice that, the way I've set this up, step 2 takes you to Meaning Holism from an *independently established* connection between epistemic liaisons and intentional content. *First* you show that at least some epistemic liaisons are semantically relevant, *then* you use the slippery slope to argue that all of them are. The point is that step 2 does you no good unless you've also—*and independently*—got step 1.

Compare, however, the following:

> I want to demonstrate that . . . intuitive judgments about whether a subject's belief can be characterized in a given way . . . are often very sensitive . . . to other beliefs that the subject(s) are assumed to have. The content we ascribe to a belief depends, more or less holistically, on the subject's entire network of related beliefs.
>
> The cleanest case I have been able to devise to illustrate the holism in content ascription turns on the sad fate of people afflicted with progressive loss of memory. . . . As a young woman, around the turn of the century, Mrs. T had an active interest in politics and was well informed on the topic. She was deeply shocked by the assassination of President . . . McKinley. . . . As Mrs. T advanced into her seventies . . . her memory was fading. . . . Some weeks before her death, something like the following dialogue took place:
>
> S[tich]: Mrs. T, tell me, what happened to McKinley?
> Mrs. T: Oh, McKinley was assassinated.
> S: Where is he now?
> Mrs. T: I don't know.
> S: I mean, is he alive or dead?
> Mrs. T: Who?
> S: McKinley.
> Mrs. T: You know, I just don't remember.
> . . .
> S: But you do remember what happened to McKinley?
> Mrs. T: Oh, yes. He was assassinated.
> . . .
>
> Now the question I want to pose for our intuitive judgment is this: Shortly before her death, Mrs. T had lost all memory about what assassination is. She had even forgotten what death itself is. She could, however, regularly respond to the question, "What happened to McKinley?" by saying, "McKinley was assassinated." Did she, at that time, *believe* that McKinley was assassinated? For just about everyone to whom I have posed this

question, the overwhelmingly clear intuitive answer is no. (Stich, *FFPCS*, 54–56)

I think the received view is that Mrs. T makes a case for the holism of belief content. Clearly, Stich thinks she does. But in fact she doesn't, and it's important from a methodological point of view to understand why this is so.

What's uncontroversial about Mrs. T is only that she forgot many things about death, assassination, and President McKinley *and* that she ceased to believe that McKinley was assassinated. But what needs to be shown to make a case for Meaning Holism is that she ceased to believe that President McKinley was assassinated *because* she forgot many things about death, assassination, and President McKinley; indeed, that her forgetting many things about death, assassination, and McKinley *was constitutive of* her ceasing to believe that he was assassinated. Barring the fallacy *post hoc, ergo propter hoc*, however, the uncontroversial facts about Mrs. T do not show this. Nothing but an independent justification of the claim that epistemic liaisons individuate the attitudes—that is, an independent justification of step 1 of the Ur-Argument—*could* show it. To repeat: Mrs. T makes a case for holism *only given that the semantic relevance of epistemic liaisons has been independently established.* She preaches only to the converted.[1]

If I am pounding the desk about this methodological point—and I am, I am—that is because the strategy of the present discussion depends upon it. What I've called the three 'ways' to Meaning Holism are just three considerations that philosophers have offered to establish the first stop of the Ur-argument. Correspondingly, the burden of this chapter is that none of these considerations is decisive; that we have, in fact, no very good reason to believe that epistemic liaisons *are* determinants of content. Clearly, however, it's no good my going to all that trouble if, as Stich implies, holism follows straight-off from consideration of cases like that of Mrs. T. But it doesn't. All Mrs. T's case shows is that either epistemic liaisons determine content or, if they don't, we need some other story about why, when you lose epistemic liaisons, you (sometimes? often? in extremis?) lost content too.

We'll come to that eventually. For now, let's turn to the 'three ways.' Long is the path, and hard is the good; but at least we don't take wooden nickels.

The First Way: From Confirmation Holism to Meaning Holism
Think of a scientific theory as represented by an infinite, connected graph. The nodes of the graph correspond to the entailments of the

theory, and the paths between the nodes correspond to a variety of semantically significant relations that hold among its theorems: inferential relations, evidential relations, and so forth. When the theory is tested, confirmation percolates from node to node along the connecting paths. When the theory is disturbed—e.g., by adding or abandoning a postulate or a principle of inference—the local geometry of the graph is distorted, and the resulting strains distribute themselves throughout the network, sometimes showing up in unanticipated deformations of the structure of the graph far from the initial locus of the disturbance.

That picture has done a lot of work for philosophers since Quine introduced it in "Two Dogmas of Empiricism." And, here as elsewhere, cognitive psychology may well prove to be the philosophy of science writ small. If holism seems a plausible account of how the scientific community achieves the semantic evaluation of its theories, it also looks not bad as a psychology of how individuals achieve the fixation of their beliefs. Like confirmation, belief fixation appears to be a *conservative* process: the goal of the game is to accomplish the maximum in accommodating data at the minimum cost in overall disturbance to previous cognitive commitments. And, precisely because it is *overall* disturbance that one seeks to minimize, there's no way of telling just where one may have to make the adjustments that new data demand of prior theory; the operative hyperbole is that the minimum unit of belief fixation is *the whole belief system*. It is this holism that we understand least about the higher mental processes. It makes psychologists old before their time, since it's hard even to imagine a mechanism whereby the whole cognitive background can contribute to determining the local tactics of problem solving. And it gives them fits in AI, where it crops up as the notoriously intractable 'frame problem' (see Fodor, *MOM*). A decent compassion can but avert the gaze.

Which is pretty much what I propose to do for present purposes. Confirmation Holism is of interest to us here only because it is often taken to suggest a correspondingly holistic treatment of semantics. It's not, after all, a long step from the doctrine that the belief system is *the minimal unit of confirmation* to the doctrine that the belief system is *the minimal unit of intentional content*. If you're a verificationist, it's no step at all. Verificationism plus holism about the means of confirmation literally *entails* holism about content, since verificationism is the doctrine that the content of a belief *is identical to* the means of its confirmation. I think that many philosophers have crossed this bridge without even noticing.

So you can get from Confirmation Holism to Meaning Holism. But to offer confirmation holism as an *argument* for Meaning Holism would nevertheless be ill advised. For one thing, as we've just seen, it looks like you'd need verificationism as a premise in such an argument, and verificationism is false. Moreover, an inference from Confirmation Holism to Semantic Holism courts circularity. This is because Semantic Holism (or, anyhow, the rejection of semantic *localism*)—is actually *presupposed* by the standard arguments for Confirmation Holism. This is all rather confusing, but it's essential to understanding how holism about meaning connects with holism about confirmation. So we shall have to sort it out.

We can start by disapproving of a piece of historical analysis that Hilary Putnam offers in a recent paper. According to Putnam, "Quine's argument for meaning holism in 'Two Dogmas of Empiricism' is set out against the meaning theories of the positivists. Sentences, he insisted, do not have their own range of confirming experiences. . . . Frege taught us that words have meaning only in the sense of making a systematic contribution to the truth-conditions of whole sentences. Quine argues that . . . individual sentences are meaningful in the sense of making a systematic contribution to the functioning of the whole language . . . (p. 1)" (Putnam, *MH*). Now, part of this is true. Positivists did hold a semantical thesis to which Quine took exception. And Quine did argue, in "Two Dogmas," that sentences taken severally don't have associated ranges of confirming experiences. But "Two Dogmas" doesn't espouse Meaning Holism; a fortiori, it doesn't infer Meaning Holism from a holistic view of confirmation. And to read Quine—*Quine* of all people—as a sort of supercharged Frege . . .oh dear, oh dear! Let us, however, endeavor to remain calm.[2]

The Positivists held—one seems to recall—that there is a certain condition on the meaningfulness of theoretical sentences: For each such sentence in the 'theory language,' there must be at least one sentence in the 'data language' to which it is connected by 'strictly semantic' implications. What exactly 'strictly semantic' implications are supposed to be was, to put it mildly, an issue. But the intended effect was clear enough: it was precisely to *localize* questions of confirmation. So, consider a very strong form of Positivism which requires that for each theory sentence there must be logically necessary conditions expressible by data sentences. Patently if D is a data sentence the truth of which is logically necessary for the truth of theory sentence S, then the disconfirmation of D entails the disconfirmation of S. Which is to say that if D is disconfirmed, then S is disconfirmed *regardless of what is in the rest of the theory*. But Confirmation Holism says that *every* claim that a theory makes is, in principle, relevant to the (dis)confirmation of every other. So this sort of Positivism would be incompatible with Confirmation Holism;[3] as, indeed, the other sorts of Positivism were also supposed to be.

Now, the localist picture of confirmation that Positivists endorsed rests on a semantical thesis which Quine made explicit and unpopular: that 'strictly semantic' implications can be distinguished from 'merely empirical' ones (in effect, that the analytic/synthetic distinction can be made sense of). This semantical thesis, Quine argues, must be false. For if an implication were strictly semantic, then presumably the statement which expresses it would have to be empirically unrevisable (i.e., unrevisable without change of meaning). But the contemplation of actual scientific practice suggests that empirical theories do not contain statements that exhibit a principled immunity from revision. Anything a scientist believes may be rationally revised under pressure from 'systematic' considerations of the unity, coherence, conservatism, simplicity, or plausibility of his whole body of doctrine (such pressures being felt, no doubt, more at the periphery than at the core; centrality is the closest thing to analyticity that science actually offers).

It's important to keep the direction of this argument in mind: Quine rejects the Positivist account of confirmation because it assumes that there are 'local' semantic connections (between 'data sentences' and 'theory sentences'). He rejects local semantic connections because they would imply that there are unrevisable statements. And he rejects the claim that there are unrevisable statements because it is false to scientific practice. In short, Quine's tactic is to infer Confirmation Holism from the refutation of semantic localism, and *not the other way round*. If, however, that is how the argument goes, then a Quinean cannot offer Confirmation Holism as an *argument* for Meaning Holism. That would be to argue backwards.

As, indeed, it is easy enough to find oneself doing. Here is the whole of the first paragraph of the Putnam article that I quote from before:

> Quine's argument for meaning holism in "Two Dogmas of Empiricism" is set out against the meaning theories of the positivists. Sentences, he insisted, do not have their own "range of confirming experiences." Assertibility depends on trade-offs between such desiderata as preserving the observation reports to which we are prompted to assent, preserving past doctrine, and securing or preserving simplicity of theory. The idea that the meanings of individual sentences are mental or Platonic entities must be abandoned. Instead we must recognize that it is a body

of sentences, and ultimately our whole system of evolving doctrine, which faces the "tribunal of experience as a corporate body."

Note carefully the direction of *this* argument. Putnam starts off intending to expound the (purportedly Quinean) defense of a *semantic* thesis ("Quine's argument for meaning holism . . . is set out against the meaning theories of the positivists"). But what he's got at the end of the paragraph isn't a semantic thesis at all; it's an *epistemic* one, a doctrine about *confirmation* ("Our whole system of evolving doctrine . . . faces the 'tribunal of experience as a corporate body' "). Surely something has gone wrong in the course of Putnam's exegesis.

What's gone wrong is that, *pace* Putnam's reading, Quine doesn't offer an "argument for meaning holism in 'Two Dogmas of Empiricism' " or elsewhere. Quine isn't a meaning *holist;* he's a meaning *nihilist.* Quine's disagreement with the Positivists isn't about the size of "the unit of empirical significance"; it's about the coherence of the notion of 'strictly semantic' implication (and of such consort notions as unrevisability and apriority) in terms of which 'empirical significance' was itself supposed to be construed. Putnam's Quine rejects Semantic Localism because he thinks meaning is global. But Quine's Quine rejects Semantic Localism because he thinks meaning is nonsense. But if so, he must, in all conscience, reject Semantic Holism too.

Or so it seems to me. But I'm not a Quine scholar, and I don't actually care much about who wins the historical argument. What I do want to emphasize is the geographical moral: *Confirmation Holism doesn't, after all, imply holism about meaning.* You can perfectly well have holism about confirmation *without* Semantic Holism, since (a) what holism about confirmation needs is the rejection of Semantic Localism (specifically, the rejection of the claim that theory sentences are severally semantically connected to data sentences), and (b) the choice between Semantic Holism and Semantic Localism is not exhaustive; witness the possibility of Quinean nihilism. It is just as well that you can have Confirmation Holism without Semantic Holism, since the former doctrine may quite possibly be true.

Now so far this may seem to be a species of cold comfort. For from the intentional psychologist's point of view, Meaning Nihilism is in no way preferable to Meaning Holism. If the latter undermines the predictive power of intentional generalizations, the former undermines the notion of intentional content, without which there's nothing much left of the notion of a propositional attitude. But as a matter of fact, the choice between Semantic Localism, Semantic Holism, and

Quinean Nihilism isn't exhaustive either, and everything is going to be all right.

Semantic Holism and Semantic Localism both identify the content of a belief with its position in a system of beliefs. Their disagreement is only about how much of the system counts semantically. (Localists claim that you can draw a line around the part that counts; holists deny that this is so.) Nihilism, by contrast, dispenses with the notion of content, thereby exempting itself from this controversy about line drawing, which it takes (if only on inductive grounds) to be not resolvable. Patently, however, there is logical room for a fourth possibility alongside these three: Beliefs have contents, but their contents are not determined by their systemic connections; specifically, the contents of a belief are not determined by its epistemic liaisons.

To which we will return presently.

The Second Way: From Psychofunctionalism to Meaning Holism
A Meaning Holist has to make a case that the content of a belief is determined by its epistemic liaisons; that what determines the propositional object of a belief is its place in a belief system. It is best for him (though not for me) if the case he makes is neither circular nor question begging. We've looked at the possibility of going at this from a theory of confirmation. We now consider the possibility of going at it from an ontological theory, a metaphysical story about the nature of the attitudes. Here, in convenient capsule form, is the metaphysical story about the nature of the attitudes that is currently received.

Once upon a time, if you wanted to be a *physicalist* about the attitudes (i.e., as opposed to being a *dualist*) and if you also wanted to be a *Realist* about the attitudes (i.e., as opposed to being an *eliminativist*), then you were supposed to have only two alternatives to choose from. You could say, 'Intentional states are really logical constructs out of bodily movements' (which made you a Logical Behaviorist), or you could say, 'Intentional states are really neural conditions' (which made you a Central State Identity Theorist). Neither of these options seemed entirely attractive. Behaviorists had trouble providing a robust construal of mental causation (and hence had no logical space for a psychology of mental processes), and central state identity theorists had trouble providing for the nomological possibility of rational machines (and hence had no logical space for a nonbiological—e.g., a computational—theory of intelligence). Considerable ingenuity was expended in trying to devise palatable versions of one or other of these accounts; without, however, much success. The more physicalists assured one another that everything was metaphysically OK in the philosophy of mind, the more the conviction spread that it wasn't.

Enter Psychofunctionalism: According to functionalists, physicalism is true of particulars but not of universals; everything spatiotemporal is de facto a physical particular (so, for example, chains of thought are, de facto, causal sequences of neural events), but lots of properties aren't physical properties. Among the plausible candidates for nonphysical properties are: being a chair; being a nose; being a river; being a number greater than 3; being a friend of mine; being a token of the type *itch;* being a token of the type 'itch'; being the thought that *P.* (The physical properties include, presumably, being a charged particle, having determinate mass, and so forth. Roughly, they're the properties that get mentioned in physical laws.)

If being the thought that *P* isn't a physical property, what sort of property is it? (Equivalently: What has to be true of a physical event in order that it count as a having of the thought that *P*?) Psychofunctionalist answer: "Psychological event types are relationally defined; specifically, they are defined by the actual and potential causal relations that their tokens enter into: causal relations to inputs, outputs, and one another. Since I am very busy just now, please do not ask me what 'inputs' and 'outputs' are."

Psychofunctionalism was (indeed, still is) alleged to have certain advantages as compared to the traditional materialist alternatives. Since psychological particulars are physical, they can enter into whatever causal relations physics acknowledges; which makes Psychofunctionalism better than Behaviorism. Since psychological properties are relational, they can be exhibited by non-neural particulars; which makes Psychofunctionalism better than the Central State Identity theory. It is observed, from time to time, that being better than Behaviorism and the Central State Identity theory may not be the same as being *true.* Some philosophers are never satisfied.

Why am I telling you all this old news? Well, there is a temptation to argue as follows: "Psychofunctionalism says that psychological kinds are relationally defined; more specifically, it says that what makes something a belief state is certain of its actual and potential causal relations to such other mental particulars as beliefs, perceptions, desires, memories, actions, intentions, and so on. (Just the very sorts of causal relations, notice, that Mrs. T's mental state *lost* when it ceased to be the belief that McKinley was assassinated.) But if anything remotely like this is true, then its epistemic liaisons will surely be among the mental particulars relations to which individuate the belief that *P.* And now look back at step 1 of the Ur-Argument; it requires exactly what we've just seen that Psychofunctionalism supplies: an argument that its epistemic liaisons are among the relations that a belief state has essentially. So there is a route from Psychofunctionalism to Meaning Holism, Q.E.D."

I think that, just as many philosophers have crossed the bridge from Confirmation Holism to Meaning Holism without hardly noticing, so too many philosophers have slipped into Meaning Holism from Psychofunctionalism in a state near to unconsciousness. And in fact, the form of the inference is all right: if Psychofunctionalism says that mental states are individuated by their relations, then Psychofunctionalism implies that believing P is individuated by *its* relations; hence, presumably, by its relations to its epistemic liaisons.

The trouble is with the premise of the argument. Specifically, our best grounds for Psychofunctionalism don't justify a version of that doctrine nearly as strong as what the inference to Meaning Holism requires.

I suppose we like Psychofunctionalism (those of us who do) because it provides us with a reasonable account of the difference between systems to which belief/desire ascriptions are appropriate and systems to which they are not. "It's a question of internal organization," Psychofunctionalism says. "People and machines have the right sort of internal organization to satisfy belief/desire explanations; rocks and such, by contrast, don't." This does look better than either the Central State Identity theory (which has to say that rocks don't have beliefs and desires because they're made of rock) or Logical Behaviorism (which has to say that rocks don't have beliefs and desires because they don't move around enough).

If, however, *that's* what you want Psychofunctionalism for, then all you need is the claim that *being a belief* is a matter of having the right connections to inputs, outputs, and other mental states. What you *don't* need—and what the philosophical motivations for Psychofunctionalism therefore do not underwrite—is the much stronger claim that being the belief *that P*, being a belief that has a certain *content*, is a matter of having the right connections to inputs, outputs, and other mental states.

So, suppose that a belief state is by definition one that causally interacts with desires and actions in the way that your favorite decision theory specifies; and that causally interacts with memories and percepts in the way that your favorite inductive logic specifies; and so forth. Then that would suffice to explain why rocks don't believe things (none of their internal states enter into the right causal relations); why people do believe things (some of our internal states do enter into the right causal relations); why computers might believe things (some of their internal states might enter into the right causal relations); and so forth. In short, a functionalist definition of 'believe' would do the sorts of work that Psychofunctionalism is supposed to do in the philosophy of mind, even if we don't have a functionalist account of *belief content;* a functional account of believing *that P.*

The philosophical arguments for Psychofunctionalism do not, therefore, constitute arguments for a functionalist theory of intentional content. This is just the not very sophisticated observation that Psychofunctionalism might perfectly well be so formulated as to give a necessary but not a sufficient condition for psychological type identity. Moreover, a division of the question that yields a functionalist answer to 'what is believing?' but a nonfunctionalist answer to 'what is believing that P?' might actually be rather natural; or so, at least, the following considerations suggest.

Psychofunctionalism type-individuates mental states by reference to the psychological generalizations that subsume them. On a functionalist analysis, a pair of mental states will be type-distinct just in case there are psychological generalizations that subsume one but not the other. *Functional analysis provides no basis for a more refined taxonomy,* however well motivated further distinctions might seem from other points of view (which is, of course, why Psychofunctionalists have a problem about inverted spectra). Well, my point is that—as I remarked in chapter 1—psychological theories typically achieve generality by *quantifying over* the objects of the attitudes. In consequence, many of the most powerful psychological generalizations don't care about content per se; what they care about is only relations of *identity and difference* of content.

Suppose that the 'practical syllogism' is more or less true (as, after all, it surely is). What it says is that if you want that *P* and you believe that not-*P* unless *Q,* then all else being equal, you try to bring it about that *Q for any P and Q whatever.* So formulated, the generalization purports to apply to *all* beliefs and wants, *regardless* of their contents. So the taxonomy of mental states that it implies distinguishes believing from wanting, but not believing that such and such from believing that so and so. If, as I rather suspect, the best candidates for taxonomically relevant psychological generalizations are like this, then Psychofunctionalism *can't* reconstruct individuation by content; the psychological generalizations that it relies upon for its criteria of individuation are, de facto, insufficiently fine grained.[4]

Or, again: It's an embarrassment for attempts to construct content from functional role that quite different—indeed, quite opposed—sorts of mental states can nevertheless *share* their contents. John hopes that it will snow on Tuesday (because on Tuesday he proposes to ski); Jane dreads that it will snow on Tuesday (because on Tuesday she proposes to pot petunias). John's hope that it will snow interacts with his belief that it will to cause elation; Jane's dread that it will snow interacts with her belief that it will to cause despair; so it's hard to see that the causal roles of the hope and the dread have much in common. *But how, then, can it be their causal roles that determine their content?* This is, of course, just the argument from functionalism to holism read as a *reductio ad absurdum.* For a Realist, the interesting thing about intentional content is its ability to survive variations in functional role. And this relative independence of content from functional role provides a prima facie reason for doubting that the former notion reduces to the latter.

So, to put it at a minimum: It looks as though our best arguments for Psychofunctionalism do not entail that the sorts of (relational) properties that make a thing a belief are also the sorts of properties that make a thing the belief that *P.* And we've seen that there are straws in the wind that suggest that espousing a Psychofunctionalist account of belief content might be positively ill advised. But it's only Psychofunctionalism about *content* that offers a route to Meaning Holism; functionalism about *believing* (as opposed to believing-that-*P*) isn't a *semantical* doctrine at all.

It appears that we are still in want of a compelling defense of step 1 of the Ur-Argument.

The Third Way: From Functional-Role Semantics to Meaning Holism
We are interested in arguments that the functional role of a belief (most notably, its causal connections to its epistemic liaisons) is among the determinants of its content. We care about such arguments because they appear to be the crucial step on the route to Meaning Holism. And we are interested in Meaning Holism because it's the best reason philosophers have so far proposed for irrealism about the attitudes.

The arguments we've looked at so far are noticeably indirect. They seek to establish the semantical relevance of causal roles from considerations that arise elsewhere in philosophy: either in epistemology or in metaphysics. You therefore need a lot of apparatus to run these arguments, which may be why they don't create much conviction. Forthright is best: The really interesting case for the semantic relevance of causal roles turns on considerations *internal* to the theory of content. "Quite aside from whatever epistemic, metaphysical—or, indeed, psychological—axes you may have it in mind to grind, you can't get *semantics* to work unless you appeal to functional role in the determination of meaning. Any science which proposes to exploit the notion of content must learn to live with this fact." So the argument goes. And I think one has to take it seriously.

There are, however, tactical problems in trying to do so. The claim is that a theory of meaning won't work unless it takes functional role to be a determinant of content. Clearly, the best way to meet this argument would be to set out a theory of meaning that does work but does *not* take functional role to be a determinant of content. I suffer from an embarrassment: I have no workable theory of meaning in hand. This is, however, an embarrassment that my antagonists share; *nobody* has a workable theory of meaning in hand, functional-role theorists notably included. Arguments in this area are thus, perforce, nonconstructive.

I suffer from a further embarrassment. I think that it's probably right that some aspects of functional role have semantic force. What I hold (to put it very roughly) is that functional role is a marginal—a not very important—determinant of meaning. And, in particular, that since the contribution of functional role to the determination of meaning is marginal and not very important, you can get from functional role everything that semantics demands without opening the floodgates to Meaning Holism. To put it another way: Semantic considerations make the first step of the Ur-Argument true, strictly speaking; but when you see how they do it, you see that they do it in a way that makes the second step false.

What, then, prompts the appeal to functional role in theories of content? I think one does best to view the situation in its dialectical context: a certain, relatively unsophisticated view of meaning appears to fail; a certain diagnosis of the failure comes to be widely accepted, viz., that the unsophisticated theory went wrong because it ignored the contribution of functional role to the determination of content. So you get functional-role semantics by a process of reaction.

The relatively unsophisticated view that is supposed to have failed is what I'll call the 'denotational' theory of meaning. The denotational theory says something like this: For a mental entity to have content is just for it to have a denotation. (The denotation of a thought is whatever it is about the world that makes—or would make—the thought true. The denotation of a concept is whatever it is about the world that the concept does—or would—apply to.) You specify the content of a mental entity by saying what it denotes. So, for example, the concept RED has content because there is a color that it applies to (viz., the color red). And you say what the content of the concept RED is in just the way that I just did, viz., by saying that it's the concept *of the color red*.[5]

It is widely held (or at least it was till recently; how the fashions in philosophy do change!) that this sort of unsophisticated theory of meaning is false *root and branch*. Whereas I'm inclined to believe that it is *very nearly* true; that it is false in ways that matter *only for semantics*, not for psychology or the philosophy of mind. I can't, alas, prove this; but I hope to provide enough argument to make it seem, in any event, a possibility worth taking seriously.

To recapitulate: Once you buy wide-open functional-role semantics, you have step 1 of the Ur-Argument, hence Meaning Holism, hence skepticism about the attitudes. For functional roles—unlike, notice, denotations—aren't, even in principle, things that mental states can have *severally;* the functional roles of mental states are *made* of their interrelations. But who says you have to buy wide-open functional-role semantics? Looked at the other way, if there is nothing against mental content except Meaning Holism, and if Meaning Holism is plausible only if functional-role semantics is assumed, then all that the enthusiast for mental content need do to shift the burden of argument is to show that alternatives to wide-open functional-role semantics are *not out of the question.* As I remarked above, shifting the burden of argument *is* all that's required since the prima facie case for intentional explanation is *terrific.*

So here is how I propose to carry on. First, I'll run through a kind of case that is classically supposed to make trouble for denotational theories of meaning. Then I'll sketch the treatment that such cases might receive in a functional-role semantics. This will illustrate in microcosm how functional-role semantics is supposed to work and how problems with denotational theories can motivate the adoption of functional ones. So much for exposition. I shall then argue that there are serious problems for the functionalist program in semantics; so serious, indeed, that it's not clear that there *is*—even programmatically—a coherent functionalist alternative to the denotational view. Finally, then, I'll come back to the denotational story, survey some more of the standard objections, and end on a note of, of all things, hope! The problems for denotational semantics are perhaps less intractable than they are often supposed to be. It may be possible—at least, we don't know that it's *not* possible—to get a denotational theory to work without making the wholesale concessions to inferential role—hence to holism—that functional-role semanticists contemplate. In which case functional-role theory emerges as one of those cures philosophers from time to time devise for which there is no adequate disease.

Here's a classical problem for denotational semantics: *denotational theories slice meanings* (hence concepts; hence mental states) *too thick.* If you identify contents with denotations, you fail to distinguish between contents that are in fact distinct.

Oedipus's state of mind was this: he wanted to marry Jocasta but he did not want to marry his mother. Or, formal mode, 'wanted to marry Jocasta' was true of Oedipus and 'wanted to marry Oedipus's mother' was false of him. The story has it, however, that Jocasta and Oedipus's mother were the same person; hence, that 'Jocasta' and 'Oedipus's mother' have the same denotation; hence, that they have the same *meaning*, assuming that denotation and meaning are the same thing. If, however, 'Jocasta' and 'Oedipus's mother' are synonymous, then 'wanted to marry J' and 'wanted to marry Oedipus's mother' are synonymous too. But then it can't be that one of them is true of O while the other is false of him. This, however, contradicts the original assumption, so something has gone wrong—presumably with the way that denotational theories individuate meanings.

Moreover, what has gone wrong is particularly bad from the point of view of psychological theory. It is precisely the psychologist, professional of commonsensical, who *needs* the present distinction between O's mental states; how, without it, can he say why it was that O's behavior was conflicted? Suppose the psychological theory is this:

> Unconsciously, O was seething to marry his mother. In fact, O wanted to marry J precisely *because* he knew—still unconsciously, of course—that 'is Mother' was true of her. "Ist eine wienerische Maskerad."

The point is: We want our theory of mental content to allow us to formulate such psychological stories as may seem plausible for the explanation of behavior. And *all* the plausible stories about Oedipus—not just Freud's story, but also Sophocles' story—turn on which identity statements Oedipus knew to be true about Jocasta. Telling the stories therefore requires distinguishing between believing that $a = b$ and believing that $a = c$, even in the case where 'b' and 'c' both denote a. It is, to put the moral briefly, beliefs and desires *sliced thin* that organisms act out of.

But what could a semantic distinction between codenotational mental states amount to? Here is where functional-role theories of meaning begin to seem plausible. The fundamental idea is that although O's thought that it would be nice to marry J and his thought that it would be nice to marry Mother have the same truth conditions, what keeps them semantically separate is the fact that they have different roles to play in O's mental economy. Most notably, they differ in their epistemic liaisons. (So, for example, 'incest is improper' is, for O, an epistemic liaison of one thought but not of the other; he takes it to make false the thought that it would be nice to marry Mother, but he takes it to be neutral in respect of the thought that it would be nice to marry J.) If, therefore, we individuate O's thoughts by reference to their epistemic liaisons—as, indeed, functional-role semantics invites us to do—we see how it is possible that O should come to be in the condition in which we in fact find him.

That's the burden of the proposed solution, but we can't, without begging the question, put it in quite that way. For from the point of view of a denotational theory, the suggestion that the thought that . . . Jocasta . . . and the thought that . . . Mother . . . might have different epistemic liaisons for O is simply incoherent. Remember that since these thoughts have the same truth conditions, they are, from the point of view of a denotational theory of content, *the same thought*. What we therefore need, if we are to characterize the functional-role theory un–question-beggingly, is some way of characterizing thoughts that is *neutral* about their denotations; in effect, something that does for thoughts what recourse to syntactic structural description does for sentences.

There's no problem about saying that the English *sentence* 'O marries J' differs from the English sentence 'O marries O's mother'; this is because the device of quotation picks out sentences in virtue of their *syntax*, leaving open issues of semantical identity and difference. Correspondingly, what we'd like to be able to do in the present case is *quote thoughts*, leaving open the question of their semantic values. In particular, we'd like to be able to quote the thought that it would be nice to marry J and the thought that it would be nice to marry Mother, leaving open the question whether they're to count as the same when thoughts are individuated by their contents. Functional-role theory could then step in to close this open question by applying the principle that thoughts are the same iff they have the same functional roles (e.g., iff they have the same epistemic liaisons). This would leave us with the thought that . . . J . . . being *not* identical to the thought that . . . Mother . . . , which, as we have seen, is just where we wanted to get.

Hence the traditional connection between functional-role theories of mental content and the Representational Theory of Mind (see, for example, Block, *ASP*): the former needs the latter (though not, I propose to argue later, the other way round). RTM says that token thoughts are (or involve) relations to token symbols in a 'language of thought.' Roughly, RTM claims that to think that P is to be in a certain relation to a symbol that means that P (see chapter 1 and the Appendix). It is, however, in the nature of symbols that they have *both* syntactic and semantic properties. So, if you assume RTM, you can set out the functional-role story about Oedipus's case as follows (I assume, for purposes of exposition, that O's language of thought was English. This assumption is, no doubt, implausible.):

> Among the well-formed formulas of O's language of thought there are the expressions 'I shall marry J' and 'I shall marry Mother.' These expressions are distinct not only syntactically but also semantically, since, by assumption, they differ in their functional roles. And since they are semantically distinct, the thoughts whose propositional objects they express differ in content. O's conflicted condition consisted in this: though O's marrying J and O's marrying Mother are, de facto, the same state of affairs, nevertheless he wanted the thought that O marries J to be true and he wanted the thought that O marries Mother to be false. O therefore *could not*, in principle, get what he wanted. No wonder the poor man was upset.

It looks as though, given a functional-role theory of meaning, together with the mechanisms for individuating thoughts that RTM provides, we can say everything that needs to be said.

I'm prepared to admit that this seems pretty good; certainly quite a number of semanticists have found it attractive. But I suspect that the reason it looks good is just that nothing much has happened, the hard problem for a functional-role theory of meaning having thus far been dodged. The hard problem is this: Functional-role semantics says that content is constituted by function. Very well, then, just *how* is content constituted by function? How does the fact that a symbol or a thought has the content that it does manage to be—how does it manage to "reduce to"—the fact that it has the function that it does?[6]

What makes the hard problem so *very* hard is this: the vocabulary that is required for the individuation of contents is, by assumption, *not* available for the individuation of functional roles. In particular, if the theory is to be other than question begging, functional roles must be picked out *nonsemantically and nonintentionally*. So, in particular, when you specify the functional roles of the internal sentences '. . .J . . .' and '. . . Mother . . . ,' you may *not* refer to such of their relations to other mental sentences as, for example, entailment or logical compatibility; for these are the sorts of relations that a theory of content is committed to *explaining*, and what is to be explained is ipso facto not to be assumed. Similarly, you may not refer to the epistemic liaisons of a belief—not, at least, under that description—when you undertake to specify its functional role. For B is an epistemic liaison of B1 for *x* iff *x takes B to be relevant to the semantic evaluation of B1;* and, of course, *taking to be* is an intentional relation.

By contrast, you *may* refer to *causal* relations among mental representations when specifying their functional roles, since, presumably, causal relations are themselves neither semantic nor intentional. You are thus allowed to say, for example, that whereas tokenings of O's mental symbol 'I am about to marry Mother' cause—or would cause—tokenings of his mental symbol 'How frightful!', tokenings of O's mental symbol 'I am about to marry Jocasta' cause—or would cause—tokenings of his mental symbol 'How nice!' *That's* the sort of stuff from which functional roles may legitimately be constructed in aid of a functional-role theory of meaning.

In practice, then, functional-role theory comes down to the idea that causal interrelations among thoughts are determinants of their content. And the hard problem is: How do identities and differences among patterns of causal connection give rise to identities and differences of meaning? It is a worry about functional-role semantics—it is indeed a *serious* worry about functional-role semantics—that there are no good answers to this question. I want to look at this at some length, because I would like to convince you that even if denotational theories are as defective as they're advertised to be, still going functional is quite probably not going to make things any better. Then we'll return to the denotational story with an eye to whether we mightn't, after all, learn to live with it. The implied conclusion will be that it's no good offering functional-role semantics in support of Meaning Holism because functional-role semantics (a) doesn't work and (b) isn't needed. This is, to be sure, rather a long route to take to deal with Meaning Holism. But I suppose we're in no hurry, and the ground to be traveled is inherently very interesting. We are now right at the point where the theory of meaning comes together with the theory of mind.

Let us start with Psychofunctionalism, according to which the attitudes are type-individuated by reference to their (actual and potential) causal roles; specifically, according to their causal relations to inputs, outputs, and one another. Psychofunctionalism implies a model of the mind as a network of causal relations, where each node corresponds to a nomologically possible mental state and each path corresponds to a nomologically possible causal relation among the nodes that it connects. In this notation the functional role of a mental state is just its location in this causal network, and the holism problem is to find a notion of type identity for nodes that does not require the type identity of the entire networks they belong to. (Viewing things this way adds nothing to what Psychofunctionalism claims about the individuation of the attitudes, and it's useful for the semantical purposes at hand. For further discussion see the Appendix.)

Right, then; here's the 'hard question' slightly reformulated: "How does locating a mental state in a causal network determine its intentional content?"

Well, notice that, just as there is a network that is generated by the *causal* interrelations among *mental states,* so too there is a network that is generated by the *semantic* interrelations among *propositions.* (Never mind what propositions are; it doesn't matter for the purposes at hand. Let's just suppose that they constitute an infinite class of abstract objects over which appropriate semantic relations can be defined.) Thus, for example, it is presumably a property of the proposition that Aunty is shorter than Uncle Wilifred that it entails the proposition that Uncle Wilifred is taller than Aunty. And it is surely a property of the proposition that $P \& Q$ that it entails the proposition that P and the proposition that Q. It seems safe to assume that such semantic relations are among the properties that propositions have *essentially;* that, for example, a proposition which failed to entail that P would thereby fail to be the proposition that $P \& Q$. Perhaps there are also *evidential* relations that propositions have essentially; perhaps, for example, it is constitutive of the proposition that many of the G's are F that it is, ceteris paribus, evidence for the proposition that all of the G's are F. If this be so, then so be it. Anyhow, there's a network of propositions generated by their semantic relations, however, precisely, "semantic' may be understood.

The basic idea for a functionalist solution to the hard problem is that, given the two networks just described, we can establish partial isomorphisms between them; and that, under such an isomorphism, *the causal role of an attitude mirrors the semantic role of the proposition that is its object.*

So, for example, there is the proposition that John left and Mary wept; and it is partially constitutive of this proposition that it has the following semantic relations: it entails the proposition that John left; it entails the proposition that Mary wept; it is entailed by the pair of propositions {John left, Mary wept}; it entails the proposition that somebody did something; it entails the proposition that John did something; it entails the proposition that either it's raining or John left and Mary wept . . . and so forth. Likewise, however, there may be, among the potential episodes in an organism's mental life, instantiations of states which we may wish to construe as: (S1) having the belief that John left and Mary wept; (S2) having the belief that John left; (S3) having the belief that somebody did something; (S4) having the belief that Mary wept; (S5) having the belief that either it's raining or John left and Mary wept . . . and so forth. The crucial point is that it constrains the assignment of these propositional contents to these mental states that the latter exhibit a pattern of *causal* relations appropriate to the *semantic* relations among the former. In particular, it must be true (if only under idealization) that being in S1 tends to cause the organism to be in S2 and S3; that being in S1 tends to cause the organism to be in S4; that being (simultaneously) in states {S2,S3} tends—very strongly, one supposes—to cause the organism to be in state S1; that being in state S1 tends to cause the organism to be in state S5 (as does being in state S6, viz., the state of believing that it's raining). And so forth.

This answers the "hard question": 'How does functional (viz., *causal*) role engender content?' For a mental state to *have* content is for there to be a proposition that is its object. And the proposal is that we can make nonarbitrary assignments of propositions as the objects of propositional attitudes *because* there is this isomorphism between, on the one hand, the network generated by the constitutive semantic relations among the propositions and, on the other hand, the network generated by the constitutive causal relations among the mental states. The assignment is nonarbitrary precisely in that it is constrained to preserve the isomorphism. And because the isomorphism is perfectly objective (which is not, of course, to say that it is perfectly unique), knowing which proposition gets assigned to a mental state—what the object of an attitude is—is knowing something useful. For, within the limits of the operative idealizations, *you can deduce the causal role of a mental state from the semantic relations of its propositional object.* To know that John thinks that Mary wept is to know that it is highly probable that he thinks that someone wept. To know that Sam thinks that it is raining is to know that it is highly probable that he thinks that either it is raining or John left and Mary wept. To know that Sam thinks that it's raining and that he thinks that if it is raining it is well to carry an umbrella is to be far along the way to predicting a piece of Sam's behavior. (The sort of view I've been sketching is currently very popular in philosophy; perhaps the most lucid proponent is Brian Loar. See Loar, *MAM*, for the full treatment.)

One further expository comment about this story before we look to see what's wrong with it: the commitment to *propositions* is, in a sense, dispensable. *Any* collection of objects which exhibit the appropriate semantic relations would do for the purposes at hand. For example, you could use the sentences, assuming that there are enough sentences to express the objects of all the attitudes. (The objections to doing so is extrinsic to the present concerns: viz., that you can't explicate the semantics of the attitudes by reference to the semantical relations among sentences if, like me, you believe that the meaning of a sentence derives from its use in expressing an attitude.)

Alternatively, you might consider the commitment to propositions to be just *de jure* and hope for 'naturalistic' (nonintentional, nonsemantic) translations of formulas in which references to propositions occur. (Indeed, it's arguable that you'd better hope for some such naturalization in *any* case, since it's not clear what the point would be of an explanation of the intentionality of the attitudes which presupposes objects that are intentional intrinsically. Why not just say that the attitudes are?) However, let's put this sort of worry to one side; we'll have it in abundance in chapter 4. For now, I'm prepared to spot you the propositions, since what I regard as the most serious problems about semantic functionalism arise in other quarters.

To see what they are, let's assume, in the spirit of the present proposal, that the propositional content of a mental state is a function of its causal role. And let's ask the following question: What, according to this assumption, is the relation between the propositional content of a mental state and its denotation?

Well, at first blush there would appear to be two options. You could say that content determines denotation, or you could say that content and denotation are, as it were, independent components of meaning. At second blush, however, the Twin cases (see chapter 2) would seem to mandate the latter option. For consider: If functional role determines content, then (assuming that the functional role of my mental states supervenes on my neurology) it follows that my Twin's WATER-concept has the same content as mine. So if the two concepts have the same content, then they have the same denotation, assuming that content determines denotation. But as a matter of fact, they *don't* have the same denotation, according to the standard intuitions. So denotation is not determined by content, contrary to option one.

This is, in fact, pretty generally the way that semantic functionalists have read the moral of the Twin stories. The popular version of semantic functionalism is therefore something called 'two-factor' theory: the isomorphism between the network of causally interconnected mental states and the network of implicationally interconnected propositions engenders propositional content; and something *different* engenders denotation. Like what, for example? Well, like, maybe, the *causal connections between concepts (thoughts, etc.) and things in the world.*

So: Oedipus's JOCASTA-concept differs from his MOTHER-concept in virtue of the difference in their functional roles. But the concepts are *identical in denotation* because (unbeknownst to Oedipus, of course) the etiology of their tokenings traces back *to the same woman.* Conversely, my Twin and I have, content-wise, the *same* WA-

TER-concept (because WATER2-thoughts occupy the same position in his network of mental states that WATER-thoughts occupy in mine); but the concepts *differ* in their denotations because, whereas the etiology of his WATER2-thoughts connects them to XYZ, the etiology of my WATER-thoughts connects them to H_2O. In effect, a mental state has sense and denotation, the former in virtue of its domestic relations and the latter in virtue of its foreign affairs.

As previously remarked, this two-factor story is currently the standard version of semantic functionalism. It is now very popular among philosophers who count themselves as more or less Intentional Realists; see, for example, Block, Loar, McGinn. Nevertheless, I'm pretty sure it won't do. Consider the following:

Semantic functionalism is explicit that one of the two factors it postulates opens a route from mental states to the world via the causal connections that each such state has to its denotation. Causal chains connect WATER-thoughts to samples of H_2O, WATER2-thoughts to samples of XYZ, and so forth. On consideration, however, it seems that the theory must imply a *second* such route as well. For according to the theory, functional roles associate mental states with propositional objects, and, of course, *propositions have satisfaction conditions*. Indeed, propositions have satisfaction conditions *essentially*; it is, to put it mildly, no accident that the proposition that Granny takes snuff is the very proposition that is true (or false) in virtue of Granny's taking snuff (or failing to take it). The situation isn't materially altered if you think of functional roles as associating mental states with *sentences* as objects (rather than propositions). Sentences too have associated satisfaction conditions since they're used to make statements, and statements have truth values. Thus the form of words 'Granny takes snuff' is the conventional vehicle of the very statement whose truth depends on whether the contextually relevant Granny is a snuffnut. And that, too, is no accident.

So: Two-factor theories imply semantically salient mind-world relations via the causal connections between thoughts and their denotations; and two-factor theories *also* imply semantically salient mind-world relations via the internal connections between propositions and their satisfaction conditions. And now the problem arises: *What keeps these two kinds of implications mutually coherent?*

The problem is most obvious in the Twin cases. My Twin's WATER2-thoughts are causally connected with XYZ; so his thought WATER2 IS WET is true in virtue of the wetness of XYZ. But also the propositional content of my Twin's thought WATER2 IS WET is identical to the propositional content of my thought WATER IS WET. For (1) by assumption, propositional content is determined by functional role; and (2) by assumption, my thoughts and my Twin's thoughts have the *same* causal roles. Well, but surely my thought WATER IS WET expresses the proposition *water is wet* if it expresses any proposition at all. And now we've got trouble. Because, notice, the proposition *water is wet* has, intrinsically, a certain satisfaction condition; viz., it's true iff water is wet. But being true iff water is wet is not the same as being true iff XYZ is wet, what with water not being XYZ. So it looks as though there is a flat-out contradiction: the theory says of my Twin both that it is and that it isn't the case that his WATER2-thoughts are true in virtue of the facts about water.

But you don't really need the Twin cases to make trouble for the two-factor version of functional-role semantics. It's quite enough that there's nothing in the theory to prevent a situation where a thought inherits, for example, the truth condition *dogs are animals* from its causal connections and the truth condition *grass is purple* from its functional role. What on Earth would the content of such a thought be? What sentence would one use to express it? And, worst of all, would it be true or would it be false?

I think that this is no joke. Functional-role theory works by associating functional roles with semantical objects; viz., with objects which—like propositions—are assumed to have semantical properties essentially. However, at least as far as anybody knows, you can't be a thing that has semantical properties essentially without also being a *thing that has satisfaction conditions*. In short, it looks unavoidable that two-factor theories are going to assign satisfaction conditions to a mental state not only via its causal connections to the world but also via the propositional interpretation of its functional role. And, as previously noted, *the theory has no mechanism at all for keeping these two assignments consistent*. The one obvious way to keep them consistent would be to let content determine denotation; and that's what the Twin cases won't allow.

I don't take it that this is a knockdown argument (though I think it comes within inches). You might, after all, try to find a domain of semantical objects to map the functional roles onto, such that (a) these objects differ in ways that will allow the difference between O's thinking J-thoughts and O's thinking MOTHER-thoughts to consist in O's thoughts having different images under the mapping; but also such that (b) the postulated semantic objects *don't have satisfaction conditions*; i.e., that they are semantical in some way that can be explicated without appeal to notions like truth. I doubt that much would come of such an undertaking, though of course I wish you luck.[7]

It is worth adding that purely denotational theories of meaning don't have this sort of problem. Denotational theories recognize only *one* semantic factor—viz., denotation—and you don't have to worry much about how to coordinate the factors of a one-factor theory.

For analogous reasons, the account of 'narrow content' proposed in chapter 2 also doesn't have a coordination problem. In particular, that notion of narrow content is quite compatible with a one-factor—e.g., a purely denotational—theory of meaning. You can have narrow content without functional-role semantics because *narrow contents aren't semantically evaluable;* only wide contents have conditions of satisfaction. *If there were* a proposition that was simultaneously the intentional object of my belief that water is wet and my Twin's belief that water2 is wet, then, of course, the question would arise what the satisfaction condition of that proposition could be. But, by assumption, there isn't; so, in consequence, it doesn't. This is what you bought when you paid the price of making narrow contents 'inexpressible.' It was well worth the price, in my view.

To summarize: One-factor functional-role semantics is out because of the Twin cases; and two-factor functional-role semantics is out because of the problem of coordinating the factors. Looked at one way, this is all rather encouraging: we've seen that taking functional-role semantics for granted is a—maybe *the*—preferred route to justifying the first step in the Ur-Argument, hence to Meaning Holism. So it's just as well for Intentional Realists if, as now appears, that route isn't going anywhere. On the other hand, this victory is distinctly Pyrrhic if functional-role theory is the last hope for semantics. An Intentional Realist wants there to be a defensible theory of content; it's just that he wants it not to be a theory that implies Meaning Holism. What to do, what to do?

The following seems to me to be, at very worst, a tenable polemical stance: We don't really *know* that a denotational theory won't work; it may be that the standard objections can be met without going over to a functional-role semantics. And, unlike functional-role semantics, denotational semantics is not inherently holistic. Whereas their causal relations to one another are, by definition, not things that mental states can have severally, the denotational relations of a mental state may depend just on its causal connections to things in the world (as, indeed, one of the two-factor theorist's two factors assumes). And—in principle at least—there seems to be no reason why mental states shouldn't enter into such causal connections *one by one.* Suppose, for example, that whether the denotation-making causal relations hold between the (mental) symbol 'horse' and horses is nomologically independent of whether the denotation-making causal relations hold between the (mental) symbol *cow* and cows. Then a creature could have the concept HORSE *whether or not* it has the concept COW; and holism is, to that extent, undone.

So the situation in respect of the burden of argument is this: Unless the intentional irrealist has a knockdown argument against equating meaning with denotation, he lacks a knockdown semantic argument for holism. But, as I keep pointing out, the utility of content psychology is such that the lack of a knockdown argument against it is tantamount to a decisive argument for it. So let's look at what's supposed to be wrong with denotational semantics, and at the prospects for fixing it.

The issues in this area are quite well known; there are volumes about them. Indeed, it's an appreciable irony that while philosophers of language generally assume that denotational semantics can't be saved and that a functional-role theory must therefore be endorsed, formal semanticists routinely take it for granted that denotational theories are the only serious options and that the problem is to construct one that works. It's the difference, I suppose, between talking about semantics and actually doing some. Anyhow, the general tactic for saving denotational semantics in face of its embarrassments—in face of the thinness-of-slice problem, for example—is to assume a richer ontology than the minimalist apparatus of actual individuals and sets. So, if the concept JOCASTA needs to be distinguished from the coextensive concept OEDIPUS'S MOTHER, that's all right because the two concepts are connected with (denote or express) *different properties;* viz., with the property of *being Jocasta* in the first case and with the property of *being Oedipus's mother* in the second. In this example (though, notoriously, not in all the examples; see below) the nonidentity of the properties shows up in differences in the truth of corresponding modals: Jocasta couldn't but have been Jocasta; but she might have had no children.

As I say, the technical problems are well known; I don't propose to try to solve them here. But I'll mention one or two just by way of suggesting the feel of the thing.

Names

Maybe some thinness-of-slice problems can be solved by proliferating properties, but it's implausible that all of them can. Consider the belief that Tully was wet and the belief that Cicero was. Though Cicero and Tully were the same person, it looks possible that someone could have the one belief and not have the other. And prima facie it's implausible that being Cicero and being Tully could be *different properties,* so here's a case where the tactic of saving denotational semantics at the cost of a rich ontology maybe won't work.

The obvious suggestion is that 'Cicero' means something like *the person called 'Cicero'* and 'Tully' means something like *the person called 'Tully';* or, to put this more in the present terms, the obvious suggestion is that 'is Tully' and 'is Cicero' do express different properties after all; viz., they express different *linguistic* properties. But, as Kripke has insisted, this obvious suggestion has problems. Though it explains how 'Cicero is Tully' could be informative, it implies that 'Cicero was called "Cicero" ' is a necessary truth. Which, in fact, it isn't; there are, as one says, 'possible worlds' in which Cicero was called 'Psmith.' So now what?

This is a hard problem. But it bears emphasis that it's a hard problem for everybody, not just for denotational semanticists. Even if you propose to pull the meanings of 'Cicero' and 'Tully' apart by reference to the distinctness of their functional roles—and quite aside from the holism issues about which bits of their functional roles count for their meanings and which bits don't—you're still left with a question that nobody can answer: What *do* 'Cicero' and 'Tully' mean if, on the one hand, they mean different things and, on the other, they don't mean something linguistic? This doesn't look to be noticeably easier than the question 'Which properties *do* "Cicero" and "Tully" denote if they don't denote the same property?' So—in this case, at least—it doesn't look as though appeal to functional role is actually buying much.

The course of wisdom would be to reiterate the moral—viz., that names are a hard problem for everybody—and then to shut up and leave it alone. Still, how about this: 'Cicero' and 'Tully' are synonymous but differ in presupposition. (Slightly like 'and' and 'but'; rather more like 'he' and 'she.' The idea is that proper names are, as it were, *dedicated* demonstrative pronouns: whereas 'he/she' are indexicals that one has to share with many other denotees, one's name is an indexical that one gets to keep for one's own.) Then 'Cicero was wet' says, in effect, that *he was wet* and presupposes that he was called 'Cicero.' 'Tully was wet' says that *he was wet* too, but it presupposes that he was called 'Tully.' 'Cicero is Tully' is informative because, although it doesn't *say* that the guy who was called 'Cicero' was called 'Tully,' it "carries the information" that he was. (For more on this notion of carrying information, see Dretske, *KFI,* and Barwise and Perry, *SA.*)

This picture would comport with a denotational view of meaning, since—on some theories at least—presupposition is itself to be explicated by appeal to the notion of a truth-value gap. If 'Cicero was wet' and 'Tully was wet' differ in presupposition, then they ipso facto differ in truth conditions: the former is not-true unless the relevant Roman has the (linguistic) property of being called 'Cicero,' whereas the latter is not-true unless that same Roman has the (different) linguistic property of being called 'Tully.' On the other hand, 'Cicero was called "Cicero" ' isn't a necessary truth; we can coherently describe a world in which Cicero is called 'Psmith.' That's because what is presupposed by our use of 'Cicero' to refer to Cicero in some non-actual world is only that Cicero is called 'Cicero' *here,* in our world.

Finally, the psychology works out all right, since, on this sort of account of names, entertaining the thought that Cicero was wet is after all a different state of mind from entertaining the thought that Tully was. The two thoughts presuppose different things.

If this sort of denotational account of names won't work, perhaps some other sort will.

Fatness of Slice

It's plausible that the property of being water is the property of being H_2O. So, how do you keep the thought that water is wet distinct from the thought that H_2O is wet if you hold that identity of denotation makes identity of content?

I think the way to fix the fatness-of-slice problem is to let in a moderate, restricted, and well-behaved amount of functional-role semantics. The point about the formulas 'water' and 'H_2O' is that though they—presumably—express the same property, the second is a complex, built out of formulas which themselves denote hydrogen and oxygen. And I do want to let into meaning those implications that accrue to an expression in virtue of its *compositional* semantics; i.e., in virtue of its relation to such other expressions as occur as its grammatical constituents. In effect, this is to say that the difference between the *concept* WATER and the concept H_2O is that you can have the former but not the latter even if you lack the concepts HYDROGEN and OXYGEN. Which does, indeed, seem to be true.

The point to emphasize is that letting in this much functional role does not, in and of itself, open the floodgates. I've emphasized throughout how much you need step 1 of the Ur-Argument to make a case for Meaning Holism. But you need step 2 too, and the present appeal to functional role as a component of meaning *doesn't concede it.* True enough, having the concept H_2O requires more than just having a concept that expresses the property of being water; it also requires that you have some beliefs about hydrogen and oxygen (viz., that water has them as constituents). But it doesn't begin to follow that *all* of your beliefs constrain the individuation of each of your concepts. (For example, believing that Cicero was wet is irrelevant to having the concept H_2O because neither the concept CICERO nor the concept WET is a constituent of the concept H_2O.) And Meaning Holism is false if *any* of your mental states is irrelevant to the individuation of any of your others.[8]

The same line of thought bears on another of denotational semantics' standard embarrassments: the problem of *equivalent* properties. We satisfied ourselves that *being Jocasta* and *being Oedipus's mother* are not the same property by reflecting that Jocasta could have been childless, in which case she would have had the one property but not the other. But this tactic doesn't always work: thoughts about closed trilaterals are prima facie distinct from thoughts about closed triangulars; but every closed triangular is *necessarily* a closed trilateral and vice versa, so there are no modals conveniently true of the one and false of the other.

I'm actually a bit inclined to reject this sort of objection out of hand. After all, it's not an argument that a denotational semantics can't distinguish thoughts about triangulars from thoughts about trilaterals. It's just an argument that drawing the distinction requires making an assumption that is not *independently* motivated; viz., that *being triangular* and *being trilateral* are different properties. But, one might reasonably wonder, so what? Why aren't *internal* motivations enough? Why isn't it enough that if we assume that the properties are different, we get corresponding distinctions among mental states just where our psychology requires us to draw them?

But never mind; even if the properties *are* the same, the concepts don't have to be; you can't have the concept TRIANGLE without having the concept ANGLE, because the second is a structural ingredient of the first. See above.

So it goes. There are lots—batches; a plethora—of unsolved technical problems about saving denotational semantics. But that's no argument for Meaning Holism unless there's reason to believe that these unsolved problems are unsolvable. Which, as things now stand, we need not suppose.

And, actually, I don't think that it's the technical problems that put people off. There are deeper—or, anyhow, vaguer and more 'philosophical'—objections to the project; ones that have motivated a whole tradition of 'use' theories of meaning, functional-role semantics being—explicitly; see Block, *ASP*—just the most recent of these. It's a little hard to get one's hands on these objections, but I propose to give it a try.

'Philosophical' Objections

1. A purely denotational semantics breaks the connection between content and consequence. If the content of your belief is independent of its functional role, then believing that P is compatible with believing practically anything else; even −P.

The trouble with reductio ad absurdum arguments, however, is that it matters *very much* that their conclusions should be false. I'm inclined to think it's roughly *true* that believing that *P* is compatible with believing practically anything else; even −*P*.

I say I think it's *roughly* true because though there are, on my view, approximately no functional-role constraints on the *content* of a mental state, there *are* functional-role constraints on its *character*. On my view *believing* is functionally defined although believing that *P* isn't; and it may be that it's part of the analysis of believing that if two of the intentional states of an organism at a time have *P* and −*P* as their respective propositional objects, then it can't be that both are states of belief. I don't think that this claim is actually very plausible; but for what it's worth, it's compatible with a purely denotational view of content. (Of course, it's one thing to believe that *P* and believe that not-*P*; it's quite another thing to believe that *P* and not-*P*. Maybe the second really *doesn't* count as believing.) Barring that, however, I accept—in fact, welcome—what amounts to the conclusion that people can believe things that are *arbitrarily* mad.

For example: Consider what (some of) the ancient Greeks believed about the stars. They believed that stars are little holes in the sky which the heavenly fires show through. Now, as it turns out, this view of the stars is badly mistaken; so badly, that practically every inference that the Greeks drew from their beliefs about the stars is false. After all, people who think that stars are holes in the sky don't even think that stars are *things;* things are the sorts of things whose identity is independent of their spatial position. Holes aren't.

So if you're a functional-role theorist, it is hard to say how these Greeks could have had (de dicto) beliefs about stars at all. For surely *we* have de dicto beliefs about stars; and ex hypothesi beliefs are individuated by their functional roles; and de facto the functional roles of our star beliefs and Greek star beliefs have practically nothing in common. The line of thought is familiar and leads to a sort of Kuhnian relativism; viz., to the view that the Greeks didn't have thoughts that were de dicto about stars after all; indeed, that we can't say/know/even imagine what the de dicto content of Greek star-thoughts was.

I think that really *is* a reductio ad absurdum; a reductio ad absurdum of the idea that what beliefs a guy has is a matter of what consequences he's prepared to draw. For of course, we know perfectly well what the Greeks thought about stars. In fact, I just *told* you what they thought about stars; they thought that stars are little holes in the sky which the heavenly fires show through. Any theory of content which says that I can't tell you what I just did tell you has got to be false. (You'll remember that Putnam says that Quine says that whereas Frege held that the unit of meaning must be at least as big as a sentence, in fact it has to be at least as big as a theory. Well, Quine doesn't say that, because, as we've seen, Quine is a Meaning Nihilist, not a Meaning Holist. But if he *did* say it, then the right reply would surely have been: So much the worse for Quine's theory of meaning.)

"But look, if you radically detach content from functional role, then why does one have to draw *any* consequences from one's thoughts? On your view, entertaining (as it might be) the thought that three is a prime number could constitute an *entire mental life?*" This too is satisfactory as a reductio ad absurdum argument only on the assumption that its conclusion is false. But its conclusion doesn't strike me as *self-evidently* false. (I envy philosophers who have clear intuitions about propositions this abstruse, but I do not seek to emulate them. And I do not trust them worth a damn.) What would therefore seem to be required is non–question-begging grounds for this assumption; specifically, grounds that do not presuppose functional-role semantics. I don't know what they might be. Do you?[9]

2. A purely denotational semantics breaks the connection between content and behavior.

In a key passage in "Intentional Systems" (*IS*, 11), Dennett writes as follows: ". . . one gets nowhere with the assumption that an entity x has beliefs p,q,r . . . unless one also supposes that x believes what follows from p,q,r . . . ; otherwise there is no way of ruling out the prediction that x will, in the face of its beliefs p,q,r . . . do something utterly stupid, and, if we cannot rule out *that* prediction, we will have acquired no predictive power at all."

I should emphasize that Dennett *isn't*, at this point, arguing for a functional-role theory of content; but you can see how his observation might easily be parlayed into such an argument. Viz., that what you pay for a semantic theory that denies that there is an internal connection between content and functional role is a philosophy of mind that denies that there is an internal connection between believing such and such and behaving in such and such a way.

But here again the right strategy is simply to outSmart the opposition. (The Philosopher's Lexicon, as everybody knows, defines 'out-

Smarting' as embracing the conclusion of one's opponent's reductio ad absurdum arguments.) There is indeed no *internal* connection between believing a certain thing and behaving in a certain way. It does not follow, however, that since there is no such connection we cannot derive behavioral predictions from belief attributions.

Behavioral predictions follow from belief attributions via *ancillary hypotheses* about (e.g.) other such states of the organism as interact with the belief (and, of course, about the laws that govern the interactions). This observation is simply the application to psychology of standard Duhemian considerations about empirical prediction at large. To get predictions ('observation statements,' as one used to call them) from claims specified in theoretical vocabulary, you *always* need ancillary hypotheses. (If, for example, what you're predicting is an experimental outcome, then you need, inter alia, a specification of the theory of the experimental apparatus.) The question that's relevant for our present considerations, however, is whether the 'ancillary hypotheses' required to connect mental content ascriptions to behavioral outcomes *should be viewed as among the determinants of the contents.* Whether, for example, given that you need to assume beliefs that Q and R to get behavioral consequences from ascriptions of beliefs that P, it follows that believing that Q and R is a (conceptually or logically or metaphysically or even empirically) necessary condition for believing that P.

Now, once upon a time there were such things as *Operationalists,* and Operationalists were precisely people who held that the ancillary hypotheses required to get predictions from theory statements are somehow constitutive of the meaning of the theory statements. To which Anti-Operationalists replied that ancillary hypotheses can't be determinants of content because—in point of scientific practice— questions about how to test a theory are frequently viewed as wide open even among scientists who agree about what the theory *is.* Operationalism systematically underestimated the importance of *experimental ingenuity* in science. Whereas figuring out how to test a theory ought, on Operationalist principles, to be a matter of mere semantic analysis, it in fact often requires the most creative exercise of scientific imagination. This is immediately comprehensible on the view that the content of a theory is largely independent of the means of its confirmation; but not, apparently, on any other view.

I think these Anti-Operationalist considerations are decisive. And I see no reason why they shouldn't hold in the case where the "theory" is a belief ascription and the "observables" are behaviors. But if they do hold, then it's perfectly possible to agree that you need lots of 'ancillary hypotheses' about the functional role of an intentional state if you're going to get behavioral predictions from ascriptions of that state; and yet to deny that the functional role of an intentional state is a determinant of its content. That's just the application of Anti-Operationalist good sense to the context of belief/desire explanation.

So much for the current objection.

3. *Purely denotational semantics doesn't solve the problem about individuating contents; it only begs them.*

Here's how this objection is supposed to go. The semantic argument for skepticism about the attitudes proceeds from the observation that

    (a) functional roles individuate intentional contents

and

    (b) there is no nonarbitrary way to individuate functional roles

to the conclusion that

    (c) there is no nonarbitrary way to individuate contents.

I've proposed to avoid this argument by denying (a); on my view, concepts are individuated by reference to the properties they express, thoughts by the states of affairs they correspond to, and so forth.

But of course that reply presupposes principles of individuation for properties, states of affairs, and the like; if not that we have such principles, at least that we could have. Suppose, however, that the right such principles are that properties are identical iff synonymous concepts express them, and states of affairs are identical iff synonymous thoughts correspond to them. Clearly this won't do; it can't be both that ontological individuation presupposes individuation of intentional contents *and* that the individuation of intentional contents presupposes principles of individuation for the ontology.

People who don't like the sort of semantics I've been gesturing toward often assume that this circle is unbreakable, so that all that happens in denotational theories of content is that the individuation problem gets moved around without getting solved. And they may be right to assume this. It is, however, relevant to assessing the polemical situation that they may *not* be right. The idea that property identities—for example—are generated by semantic equivalences is not a revealed truth but an ontologist's theory. By and large, it's been a Positivist ontologist's theory; it belongs in the same camp as the idea that modal (e.g., logical and mathematical) facts are generated by analyticities. Prima facie, it doesn't look as though either theory has much to recommend it. It counts against linguistic accounts of modality that one can know one's language exhaustively and have no idea whether there could be an even number that is not the sum of two primes; and it counts against linguistic accounts of property identity that one can know one's language exhaustively and have no idea that being water is being H_2O. I agree that neither of these considerations counts decisively; but it does seem to me that they shift the burden of proof. It may be, in short, that there is an ontological argument for skepticism about the attitudes; but to make such an argument, you are actually going to have to *do* the ontology. (For evidence that it's possible for a perfectly reasonable person to hold the sort of view of the relation between ontology and semantics that I've been commending, see Jubien, *OPPT*).

I propose to round off this discussion by returning to Mrs. T. It illuminates the denotational picture of meaning to see what her case looks like when viewed in that theoretical context.

You'll remember that what we had was (a) some facts, (b) an intuition, and (c) an analysis. To wit:

(a) The facts: Mrs. T didn't know who McKinley was, or what death is, or whether assassination is fatal. But—to put it as neutrally as I'm able—she took the form of words 'McKinley was assassinated' to express something true.

(b) The intuition: Mrs. T. didn't believe (a fortiori, didn't remember) that McKinley was assassinated.

(c) The analysis: The mental states to which content ascriptions correspond are holistic, not just epistemically but *metaphysically;* knowing who McKinley was, knowing that assassination is fatal, and so forth, are somehow *constitutive* of believing that McKinley was assassinated. An immediate implication is that you can't, after all, have a mental life that consists just of the thought that McKinley was assassinated (or that three is prime; see above). Entertaining the thought that McKinley was assassinated is *internally* connected with being in other intentional states.

Now, as I remarked before, (c) doesn't follow from (a) and (b); what *does* follow is that *either* belief content is holistic *or* we require some alternative story about why people who fail to have the right views about what assassination is . . . etc. *also* fail to have mental states whose intentional content is that McKinley was assassinated. And we are now in a position to provide an alternative story. Namely: One can't have the belief that McKinley was assassinated, *or* the belief that assassination is fatal, *or* the belief that if McKinley was assassinated then he is dead . . . etc., unless one has (inter alia) the concept ASSASSINATION; for the concept ASSASSINATION is a *constituent* of all of these beliefs. So if Mrs. T ceased, in extremis, to have the concept ASSASSINATION, then of course she ceased to have any of the beliefs of which it is a constituent. But—according to the present view—to have the concept ASSASSINATION is to have a concept which expresses a certain property, viz., the property of assassination. So it would explain the connection between (a) and (b) if there were reason to believe that Mrs. T had no concept that expressed the property of assassination. Well, *is* there reason to believe that? Of course there is. Indeed, it's hard to imagine *any* account—holistic or otherwise—of what it is for a concept to express a property that failed to imply that Mrs. T lacked a concept of assassination.

Here, for example, is an unholistic story about what it is for concept C to express property P: C expresses P iff there is a certain kind of causal connection between (actual and counterfactual) tokenings of P and (actual and counterfactual) tokenings of C. (Never mind about the details; we'll come back to them in chapter 4.) The present point is that however you flesh this story out, it's plausible that in Mrs. T's case all the relevant causal connections were broken. In no useful way were her tokenings of ASSASSINATION (or, a fortiori, her tokenings of 'assassination') causally connected with assassinations. Remember, Mrs. T was prepared to apply 'assassinated' to people whom she didn't even think were dead. What better evidence could we have that, for Mrs. T, ASSASSINATION and assassinations had come unstuck?

"Ah! But 'at what point' did they come unstuck?"

The answer depends on two unknowns: (a) in virtue of *what* connections between (actual and counterfactual) tokenings of ASSASSINATION and (actual and counterfactual) instances of assassination does that concept express that property; and (b) when, in the case of Mrs. T, did these semantically relevant connections cease to obtain? It would indeed be bad news for Intentional Realism if there were principled reasons to hold that such questions have no answers. But so far we haven't had a shred of argument that that is so.

I repeat: What Mrs. T's case tells us is something we already knew; you can't believe that McKinley was assassinated unless you have a concept of assassination. But it's neutral on whether the conditions for having a concept of assassination—or, indeed, any other concept—are themselves holistic.[10]

Exactly similarly for a puzzle that Putnam proposes in "Computational Psychology and Interpretation Theory"; Putnam's case is just like Stich's case, except that it's run on *acquiring* concepts rather than losing them.

> Imagine that there is a country somewhere on Earth called Ruritania. In this country . . . there are small differences between

the dialects which are spoken in the north and in the south. One of these differences is that the word 'grug' means silver in the northern dialect and aluminum in the southern dialect. Imagine two children, Oscar and Elmer . . . alike in genetic constitution and environment as you please, except that Oscar grows up in the south of Ruritania and Elmer grows up in the north of Ruritania. Imagine that in the north . . . pots and pans are normally made of silver, whereas in the south [they] are normally made of aluminum. So [both] children grow up knowing that pots and pans are normally made of 'grug' . . . . But if the word 'grug' and the mental representations that stand behind the word . . . have the same content at this stage, *when do they come to differ in content?* By the time Oscar and Elmer have become adults, have learned foreign languages and so on, they certainly will not have the same conception of grug . . . [but] . . . this change is *continuous.* (*CPIT*, 144–146)

No problem. When Elmer and Oscar start out—when, intuitively speaking, they have the same beliefs about 'grug'—theirs is just a Twin case: *different wide contents* because of the difference in contexts, but *the same narrow contents* because there's the same mapping from contexts onto truth conditions realized in each of their heads (see chapter 2). As they get older, however, things change. Whereas at first tokenings of 'grug' would have been elicited from *either* child by *either* aluminum or silver, at the end only silver controls 'grug' for Elmer and only aluminum controls 'grug' for Oscar. So at the end, Oscar and Elmer are different functions from contexts to extensions, and the narrow contents of their concepts differ accordingly.

Just when the change in narrow content happens depends on just when Oscar and Elmer cease to be the same function from contexts onto extensions. And *that* depends, in turn, on just which factuals and counterfactuals have to be true for there to be the semantically relevant sort of connection between the instancing of a property in a context and the tokening of a concept in that context. Once again, it would be bad news for Intentional Realism if it turned out that that sort of question hasn't got an answer. But Putnam provides no reason to suppose that it doesn't, or even that its application in the Oscar/ Elmer case is of any special theoretical interest.

By the way, parity of analysis requires us to say, vis a vis the Twin cases, that learning that water is H_2O changes one's narrow concept of water. Why? Well, consider somebody who learns that water is H_2O and thus comes to distinguish between water and XYZ (much as the adult Oscar and Elmer have come to distinguish between northern and southern grug). This person has *no* concept which denotes water in my context and water2 in my Twin's, for the narrow WATER concept that he applied to H_2O he ipso facto withholds from XYZ, and vice versa. So he's not the same function from contexts to truth conditions that my Twin and I are. So learning what water really is has changed his narrow concept of water. Mutatis mutandis: Learning what *anything* really is changes one's narrow concept of that thing. I take this to settle an old philosophical disagreement.

On which, however, nothing much would seem to turn. For example, changing the narrow content of the concept WATER doesn't, in and of itself, "change the topic" of water-conversations. (Old-timers will remember the idea that the central state identity theory "changes the topic" of conversations about minds.) The topic of water-conversations always was, and always will be, H_2O. It's not *narrow* content that fixes topics, it's *broad* content that does.[11]

Well, we've looked at three main ways that philosophers have tried to argue for Meaning Holism, and none of them seems to be all that convincing. *Surely* none of them seems as convincing as routine belief/desire explanations often are. If we have to give up either the belief/desire explanations or the arguments for holism, rationality would therefore seem to indicate the latter course.

Scotch verdict?

4

Meaning and the World Order

I suppose that sooner or later the physicists will complete the catalogue they've been compiling of the ultimate and irreducible properties of things. When they do, the likes of *spin, charm,* and *charge* will perhaps appear upon their list. But *aboutness* surely won't; intentionality simply doesn't go that deep. It's hard to see, in face of this consideration, how one can be a Realist about intentionality without also being, to some extent or other, a Reductionist. If the semantic and the intentional are real properties of things, it must be in virtue of their identity with (or maybe of their supervenience on?) properties that are themselves *neither* intentional *nor* semantic. If aboutness is real, it must be really something else.

And, indeed, the deepest motivation for intentional irrealism derives not from such relatively technical worries about individualism and holism as we've been considering, but rather from a certain ontological intuition: that there is no place for intentional categories in a physicalistic view of the world; that the intentional can't be *naturalized.* It is time that we should face this issue. What is it, then, for a physical system to have intentional states?[1]

Let's, to begin with, try to get clear on just *where* the naturalization problem arises in the sort of account of propositional attitudes that I've been pushing. I've assumed that what most needs to be explained about the attitudes is that they have conditions of semantic evaluation; such facts as that beliefs have truth conditions, for example. Now, according to my story, you generate conditions for the semantic evaluation of an attitude by *fixing a context* for the tokenings of certain symbols; symbols which jointly constitute a system of mental representations. (The reader will recall that RTM is operative, and that RTM identifies token attitudes with relations between organisms and the token mental representations that they entertain.) So, then, what is it to fix a context for a system of mental representations?

Well, whatever else you have to do, you must at least specify an interpretation for items in the primitive nonlogical vocabulary of the language to which the symbols belong.[2] For example, you fix a context for tokenings of the (Mentalese) expression 'this is water' by specifying—inter alia—that in the context in question the symbol 'water' expresses the property H_2O, or the property XYZ, or whatever. Granting an interpretation of the primitive nonlogical vocabulary, the business of generating conditions of evaluation for derived formulas can proceed by means which, though certainly not unproblematic, are at least familiar; viz., by the construction of a truth definition. In short: Given RTM, the intentionality of the attitudes reduces to the content of mental representations. Given a truth definition, the content of mental representations is determined by the interpretation of their primitive nonlogical vocabulary. So it's the interpretation of the primitive nonlogical vocabulary of Mentalese that's at the bottom of the pile according to the present view. Correspondingly, we would have largely solved the naturalization problem for a propositional-attitude psychology if we were able to say, in nonintentional and nonsemantic idiom, what it is for a primitive symbol of Mentalese to have a certain interpretation in a certain context.

Alas, I don't know how to carry out this program. But I see no principled reason why it can't be carried out; I even imagine that we might make a little progress within the foreseeable future. In particular, I think it's plausible that the interpretation of (primitive, nonlogical; from now on I'll omit these qualifiers) Mentalese symbols is determined by certain of their causal relations. For example, what makes it the case that (the Mentalese symbol) 'water' expresses the property H_2O is that tokens of that symbol stand in certain causal relations to water samples. Presumably if tokens of 'water' have a different interpretation on Twin-Earth (or, equivalently, if Twin-Earth counts as a *different context* for tokens of 'water'; or, equivalently, if tokens of 'water' are type-distinct from tokens of 'water2'; or, equivalently, if Mentalese2 counts as a different language from Mentalese), that is all because it's XYZ that bears to 'water2' tokens the sort of causal relations that H_2O bears to tokens of 'water.'

So the causal story goes. I think it points a promising route to the naturalization of such semantics as RTM requires. At a minimum, I think that some of the standard objections to that sort of story can be met; that's what I propose to argue in the following.

Here, then, are the ground rules. I want a *naturalized* theory of meaning; a theory that articulates, in nonsemantic and nonintentional terms, sufficient conditions for one bit of the world to *be about* (to express, represent, or be true of) another bit. I don't care—not just now at least—whether this theory holds for *all* symbols or for all things that represent. Maybe the occurrence of smoke expresses the proximity of fire; maybe the number of tree rings expresses the age of the tree; maybe the English predicate 'is red' expresses the property of being red; maybe the thermostat represents the temperature of the ambient air (see note 1). It's OK with me if any or all of this is so; but I'm not particularly anxious that the theory that naturalizes the semantic properties of mental representations should work for smoke, tree rings, or English words. On the contrary, I'm prepared that it should turn out that smoke and tree rings represent only relative to our interests in predicting fires and ascertaining the ages of trees, that thermostats represent only relative to our interest in keeping the room warm, and that English words represent only relative to our intention to use them to communicate our thoughts. I'm prepared, that is, that only mental states (hence, according to RTM, only mental representations) should turn out to have semantic properties *in the first instance*; hence, that a naturalized semantics should apply, strictu dictu, to mental representations only.

But it had better apply to them.

The Crude Causal Theory

Let's start with the most rudimentary sort of example: the case where a predicative expression ('horse,' as it might be) is said of, or thought of, an object of predication (a horse, as it might be). Let the Crude Causal Theory of Content be the following: In such cases the symbol tokenings denote their causes, and the symbol types express the property whose instantiations reliably cause their tokenings. So, in the paradigm case, my utterance of 'horse' says *of* a horse that it *is* one.

'Reliable causation' requires that the causal dependence of the tokening of the symbol upon the instancing of the corresponding property be counterfactual supporting: either instances of the property actually do cause tokenings of the symbol, or instances of the property *would* cause tokenings of the symbol *were they to occur,* or both. I suppose that it is necessary and sufficient for such reliable causation that there be a nomological—lawful—relation between certain (higher-order) properties of events; in the present case, between the property of being an instance of the property *horse* and the property of being a tokening of the symbol 'horse.' The intuition that underlies the Crude Causal Theory is that the semantic interpretations of mental symbols are determined by, and only by, such nomological relations.

You can see straight off why the Crude Causal Theory has a much better chance of working for mental representations than it does for (e.g.) English words. CCT wants the tokening of a symbol to depend upon the instantiation of the property it expresses. But whether an English word gets tokened (e.g., uttered) depends not just on what it means but also upon the motivations, linguistic competences, and communicative intentions of English speakers. Giving voice to an utterance, unlike entertaining a thought, is typically a voluntary act.

So, for example, suppose Smith notices that Mary's hair is on fire—and hence, perforce, thinks: *Mary's hair is on fire,* thereby tokening the Mentalese expression whose truth condition is that Mary's hair is on fire. Whether he then chooses to *say* 'Mary's hair is on fire,' thereby tokening the English expression whose truth condition is that Mary's hair is on fire, depends on whether he thinks that Mary (or some other suitably situated auditor) would be interested to know that Mary's hair is on fire. Paul Grice has made us all aware how complex these sorts of pragmatic determinants of speech acts can become.

In short, the causal dependence of tokenings of mental representations upon semantically relevant situations in the world is typically more reliable than the causal dependence of tokenings of English expressions upon semantically relevant situations in the world. That's because the chains that connect tokenings of mental representations to their semantically relevant causes are typically *shorter than* (indeed, are typically links in) the chains that connect tokenings of English sentences to their semantically relevant causes. This is the principal reason why it is mental representations, and not the formulas of any natural language, that are the natural candidates for being the primitive bearers of semantic properties. If, however, mental representations are the bearers of semantic properties in the first instance, then it is the semantic properties of mental representations that are, in the first instance, apt for naturalization. CCT and RTM are made for one another.

Which is not, of course, to say that the Crude Causal Theory will work for mental representations; only that it's unlikely to work for anything else. CCT has—I admit it—lots of problems. I want to argue, however that some of what look to be its worst problems have natural and appealing solutions. This makes me hopeful that maybe, someday, some refinement of the Crude Causal Theory might actually be made to work. Maybe.

The Crude Causal Theory says, in effect, that a symbol expresses a property if it's nomologically necessary that *all* and *only* instances of the property cause tokenings of the symbol. There are problems with the 'all' part (since not all horses actually do cause 'horse' tokenings) and there are problems with the 'only' part (cows sometimes cause 'horse' tokenings; e.g., when they are mistaken for horses). The main business of this chapter will be the consideration of these problems; in reverse order.

So here is what I am going to do. I shall start by assuming—contrary to fact, of course—that *all* horses cause 'horses,' and I'll show you why a causal theory doesn't need to require that *only* horses do consonant with 'horse' meaning HORSE. Having thus fixed the 'only' clause, I'll then go back and fix the 'all' clause. We will then have a Slightly Less Crude Causal Theory; one that requires neither that all horses cause 'horses' nor that only horses do, but that nevertheless claims that it's in virtue of the causal connections between horses and 'horses' that 'horse' means what it does. This Slightly Less Crude Causal Theory I shall then commend to your kind consideration.

Error in the Crude Causal Theory
An embarrassment: It seems that, according to CCT, there can be no such thing as *misrepresentation*. Suppose, for example, that tokenings of the symbol 'A' are nomologically dependent upon instantiations of the property *A*; viz., upon A's. Then, according to the theory, the tokens of the symbol denote A's (since tokens denote their causes) and they represent them *as* A's (since symbols express the property whose instantiations cause them to be tokened). But symbol tokenings that represent A's as A's are ipso facto veridical. So it seems that the condition for an 'A'-token meaning *A* is identical to the condition for such a token being true. How, then, do you get *un*veridical 'A' tokens into the causal picture?

This may not look awfully worrying so far, since it invites the following obvious reply: "*Sometimes* 'A' tokens are caused by A's (and thus represent their causes as A's, and are thus veridical); but other times 'A' tokens are caused by B's where, as we may suppose, whatever is B is *not* A. Well, since 'A' tokens express the property of being A, 'A' tokens that are caused by B's represent B's as A's and are ipso facto not veridical. 'A' tokens that are caused by B's are ipso facto *mis*representations of their causes. *That's* how misrepresentation gets into the causal picture."

But though that answer sounds all right, CCT can't make it stick. Since there are B-caused tokenings of 'A,' it follows that the causal dependence of 'A's upon A's is imperfect; A's are sufficient for the causation of 'A's, *but so too are B's*. If, however, symbols express the properties whose instantiations reliably cause them, it looks as though what 'A' must express is not the property of *being A* (or the property of *being B*) but rather the *disjunctive property of being (A v B)*.

But if 'A' expresses the property *(A v B)*, then B-caused 'A' tokenings
are veridical after all. They're not misrepresentations since, of course,
B's *are A v B*. But if B-caused 'A' tokenings are true of their causes,
then we don't yet have a theory of misrepresentation.

That's what I'll call the 'disjunction problem.' We can put it that a
viable causal theory of content has to acknowledge *two* kinds of cases
where there are disjoint causally sufficient conditions for the tokenings of a symbol: the case where the content of the symbol is disjunctive ('A' expresses the property of *being (A v B)*) and the case where
the content of the symbol is *not* disjunctive and some of the tokenings
are false ('A' expresses the property of *being A,* and B-caused 'A'
tokenings misrepresent). The present problem with the Crude Causal
Theory is that it's unable to distinguish between these cases; it always
assigns disjunctive content to symbols whose causally sufficient conditions are themselves disjoint.

The disjunction problem is extremely robust; so far as I know, it
arises in one or another guise for every causal theory of content that
has thus far been proposed. Accordingly, there are various ideas for
circumventing it in the literature in which such theories are espoused.
None of these proposals has been very satisfactory, however; and the
rumor has gotten around that the problem that causal theories have
with misrepresentation is perhaps intrinsic and ineliminable (see, for
example, Matthews, *TWR*). I'm about to try and scotch that rumor.
First, however, let's look at the remedies currently on offer.

Dretske's Solution
Fred Dretske's important book *Knowledge and the Flow of Information*
was largely responsible for the present widespread enthusiasm for
causal theories of content, so his treatment of misrepresentation bears
careful consideration.[3] For Dretske, the cardinal semantic relation is
the one that holds between two events when one of them (the tokening of a symbol, as it might be) *transmits information about* the other.
Here is how he proposes to construe misrepresentation in that theoretical context:

> In the learning situation special care is taken to see that incoming
> signals have an intensity, a strength, sufficient unto delivering
> the required piece of information *to* the learning subject. . . . Such
> precautions are taken in the learning situation . . . in order to
> ensure that an internal structure is developed with . . . the
> information that s is F. . . . But once we have meaning, once the
> subject has articulated a structure that is selectively sensitive to
> information about the F-ness of things, instances of this

structure, tokens of this type, can be triggered by signals that *lack* the appropriate piece of information. . . . We [thus] have a case of misrepresentation—a token of a structure with a false content. We have, in a word, meaning without truth. (*KFI*, 194–195; emphases Dretske's)

All you need to know to understand this well enough for present purposes is that Dretske's notion of information is fundamentally that of counterfactual-supporting correlation: events of type 'A' carry information about events of type A to the extent that the latter sort of events are reliably causally responsible for events of the former sort. (There is, in fact, rather more than this to Dretske's official account of information; but none of the rest is essential to his treatment of the problem of false content.)

So information reduces to a certain sort of correlation. And the problem is this: Correlations can be better or worse—more or less reliable—but there is no sense to the notion of a *mis*correlation, so there appears to be nothing for Dretske to make a theory of misinformation out of. His solution is to enforce a strict distinction between what happens in the learning period and what happens thereafter. The correlation that the learning period establishes determines what 'A' events represent, and it's the teacher's function to ensure that this correlation reliably connects 'A' tokens to A's. It may be, however, that *after* the learning period 'A' tokens are brought about by something *other than* A's (by B's, for example); if so, then these are, as I'll sometimes say, 'wild' tokenings, and their content is false.

I think this move is ingenious but hopeless. Just for starters, the distinction between what happens in the learning period and what happens thereafter surely isn't principled; there is no time after which one's use of a symbol stops being merely shaped and starts to be, as it were, in earnest. (Perhaps idealization will bear some of the burden here, but it's hard to believe that it could yield a notion of *learning period* sufficiently rigorous to underwrite the distinction between truth and falsity; which is, after all, exactly what's at issue.) Moreover, if Dretske insists upon the learning-period gambit, he thereby limits the applicability of his notion of misrepresentation to *learned* symbols. This is bad for me because it leaves no way for innate information to be false; and it's bad for Dretske because it implies a dichotomy between *natural* representation (smoke and fire; rings in the tree and the age of the tree) and the intentionality of mental states. Dretske is explicit that he wants a naturalized semantics to apply in the same way to all such cases.

But the real problem about Dretske's gambit is internal. Consider a trainee who comes to produce 'A' tokens in A circumstances during the learning period. And suppose that the teacher does his job and ensures that *only* A's elicit 'A' tokenings in the course of training. Well, time passes, a whistle blows (or whatever), and the learning period comes to an end. At some time later still, the erstwhile trainee encounters an instance of B and produces an 'A' in causal consequence thereof. The idea is, of course, that this B-elicited tokening of 'A' is ipso facto wild and, since it happened after the training ended, it has the (false) content *that A.*

But this won't work; it ignores counterfactuals that are clearly relevant to determining *which* symbol-to-world correlation the training has brought about. Imagine, in particular, what *would have* happened if an instance of B *had* occurred during the training period. Presumably what would have happened is this: it would have caused a tokening of 'A.' After all, B's are supposed to be sufficient to cause 'A' tokenings *after* training; that's the very supposition upon which Dretske's treatment of wild 'A' tokenings rests. So we can also assume—indeed, we can stipulate—that if a B had occurred *during* training, it too would have brought about an 'A.' But that means, of course, that if you take account of the relevant counterfactuals, then the correlation that training established is (not between instances of A and tokenings of 'A' but) between instances of *A v B* and tokenings of 'A.' [Equivalently, what the training established was (not a nomological dependence of 'A's on A's but) a nomological dependence of A's on *(A v B)s.*] So we have the old problem back again. If 'A's are correlated with (A v B)s, then the content of a tokening of 'A' is *that A v B.* So a B-caused 'A' tokening isn't false. So we're still in want of a way out of the disjunction problem.

The Teleological Solution
A suggestion that crops up in several recent papers about causation and content (see Stampe, *TCTLR;* and also a manuscript of mine, ·Fodor, *P)* goes like this:

We suppose that there's a causal path from A's to 'A's and a causal path from B's to 'A's, and our problem is to find some difference between B-caused 'A's and A-caused 'A's in virtue of which the former but not the latter misrepresent. Well, perhaps the two paths differ in their *counterfactual* properties. In particular, though A's and B's both cause 'A's as a matter of fact, perhaps we can assume that only A's *would* cause 'A's in—as one says—"optimal circumstances." We could then hold that *a symbol expresses its 'optimal' property;* viz., the property that would causally control its tokening in optimal circumstances. Correspondingly, when the tokening of a symbol is causally controlled by properties other than its optimal property, the tokens that eventuate are ipso facto wild.

Now, I'm supposing that this story about "optimal circumstances" is proposed as part of a naturalized semantics for mental representations. In which case it is, of course, essential that it be possible to say what the optimal circumstances for tokening a mental representation are *in terms that are not themselves either semantical or intentional.* (It wouldn't do, for example, to identify the optimal circumstances for tokening a symbol as those in which the tokens are *true;* that would be to assume precisely the sort of semantical notions that the theory is supposed to naturalize.) Well, the suggestion—to put it in a nutshell—is that appeals to *optimality* should be buttressed by appeals to *teleology:* optimal circumstances are the ones in which the mechanisms that mediate symbol tokenings are functioning "as they are supposed to." In the case of mental representations, these would be paradigmatically circumstances where *the mechanisms of belief fixation* are functioning as they are supposed to.

The reference to 'mechanisms of belief fixation' perhaps makes this look circular, but it's not. At least not so far. Remember that we're assuming a functional theory of *believing* (though not, of course, a functional theory of *believing that P;* see chapter 3). On this assumption, having a belief is just being in a state with a certain causal role, so—in principle at least—we can pick out the belief states of an organism without resort to semantical or intentional vocabulary. But then it follows that we can pick out the organism's mechanisms of belief *fixation* without recourse to semantical or intentional vocabulary: the mechanisms of belief fixation are, of course, the ones whose operations eventuate in the organism's having beliefs.

So, then: The teleology of the cognitive mechanisms determines the optimal conditions for belief fixation, and the optimal conditions for belief fixation determine the content of beliefs. So the story goes.

I'm not sure that this teleology/optimality account is false, but I do find it thoroughly unsatisfying. The story has it that only A's cause 'A's in optimal circumstances; hence, that when the mechanisms of belief fixation are operating properly the beliefs they fix are true. But how do we know—or rather, why should we believe—that the mechanisms of belief fixation *are* designed always to deliver truths? Suppose some of these mechanisms are designed to *repress* truths; truths, for example, the acknowledgment of which would be unbearable.[4] Clearly we can't define "optimal circumstances" in terms of the teleology of *those* mechanisms; not if we're to define truth *conditions* as the ones that are satisfied when a symbol is caused in optimal circumstances. But there's no obvious way to weed mechanisms of repression out of the definition of optimality unless we can independently identify them *as* mechanisms of repression; viz., as mechanisms tending to the fixation of beliefs that are false.

To put this objection in slightly other words: The teleology story perhaps strikes one as plausible in that it understands one normative notion—truth—in terms of another normative notion—optimality. But this appearance of fit is spurious; there is no guarantee that the kind of optimality that teleology reconstructs has much to do with the kind of optimality that the explication of 'truth' requires. When mechanisms of repression are working "optimally"—when they're working "as they're supposed to"—what they deliver are likely to be *falsehoods.*

Or again: There's no obvious reason why conditions that are optimal for the tokening of one sort of mental symbol need be optimal for the tokening of other sorts. Perhaps the optimal conditions for fixing beliefs about very large objects (you do best from the middle distance) are different from the optimal conditions for fixing beliefs about very small ones (you do best from quite close up); perhaps the conditions that are optimal for fixing beliefs about sounds (you do best with your eyes closed) are different form the optimal conditions for fixing beliefs about sights (you do best with your eyes open). But this raises the possibility that if we're to say which conditions are optimal for the fixation of a belief, we'll have to know what the content of the belief is—what it's a belief *about.* Our explication of content would then require a notion of optimality whose explication in turn requires a notion of content, and the resulting pile would clearly be unstable.

As I say, I'm uncertain whether these sorts of objections to the optimality/teleology story can be met; but I propose to delay having to meet them as long as I can. In particular, I think maybe we can get a theory of error without relying on notions of optimality or teleology; and if we can, we should. All else being equal, the less Pop-Darwinism the better, surely.

How to Solve the Disjunction Problem

We need a way to break the symmetry between A-caused 'A' tokenings (which are, by hypothesis, true) and B-caused 'A' tokenings (which are, by hypothesis, false). In particular, we need a difference between A-caused 'A' tokenings and B-caused 'A' tokenings that can be expressed in terms of nonintentional and nonsemantic properties of causal relations; for nonintentional and nonsemantic properties of causal relations are all that the Crude Causal Theory of Content has to play with. My suggestion is that the teleological story was on the

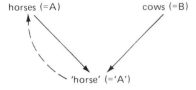

Figure 1

right track in appealing to the *counterfactual* properties of the causal relations between A's and 'A's, on the one hand, and B's and 'A's, on the other. Only the teleological story got hold of the wrong counterfactual properties.

It's an old observation—as old as Plato, I suppose—that falsehoods are *ontologically dependent* on truths in a way that truths are not ontologically dependent on falsehoods. The mechanisms that deliver falsehoods are somehow *parasitic on* the ones that deliver truths. In consequence, you can only have false beliefs about what you can have true beliefs about (whereas you can have true beliefs about anything that you can have beliefs about at all). So the intuition goes, and I think that there is something to it. What's more, I think that it points the way out of the disjunction problem.

Consider the following situation: I see a cow which, stupidly, I misidentify. I take it, say, to be a horse. So taking it causes me to effect the tokening of a symbol; viz., I say 'horse.' Here we have all the ingredients of the disjunction problem (set up, as it happens, for a token of English rather than a token of Mentalese; but none of the following turns on that). So, on the one hand, we want it to be that my utterance of 'horse' means *horse* in virtue of the causal relation between (some) 'horse' tokenings and horses; and, on the other hand, we *don't* want it to be that my utterance of 'horse' means *cow* in virtue of the causal relation between (some) 'horse' tokenings and cows. But if the causal relations are the same, and if causation makes representation, how can the semantic connections not be the same too? What we want is the situation in figure 1 (where the dashed line stands for the representation relation and the other lines stand for causal relations); but how are we to get what we want?

Answer: As previously remarked, the causal relations aren't identical in their counterfactual properties. In particular, misidentifying a cow as a horse wouldn't have led me to say 'horse' *except that there was independently a semantic relation between 'horse' tokenings and horses*. But for the fact that the word 'horse' expresses the property of *being a horse* (i.e., but for the fact that one calls *horses* 'horses', it would not have been *that* word that taking a cow to be a horse would have caused me to utter. Whereas, by contrast, since 'horse' does mean *horse*, the fact that horses cause me to say 'horse' does not depend upon there being a semantic—or, indeed, any—connection between 'horse' tokenings and cows.

From a semantic point of view, mistakes have to be *accidents:* if cows aren't in the extension of 'horse,' then cows being called horses can't be *required* for 'horse' to mean what it does. By contrast, however, if 'horse' didn't mean what it does, being mistaken for a horse wouldn't ever get a cow called 'horse.' Put the two together and we have it that the possibility of saying 'that's a horse' falsely presupposes the existence of a *semantic setup* for saying it truly, but not vice versa.[5] Put it in terms of CCT, and we have it that the fact that cows cause one to say 'horse' depends on the fact that horses do; but the fact that horses cause one to say 'horse' does *not* depend on the fact that dows do.

So, the causal connection between cows and 'horse' tokenings is, as I shall say, *asymmetrically dependent* upon the causal connection between horses and 'horse' tokenings. So now we have a necessary condition for a B-caused 'A' token to be wild: B-caused 'A' tokenings are wild only if they are asymmetrically dependent upon non-B–caused 'A' tokenings.[6]

What we've got so far is, in effect, a theory that understands wildness in terms of an empirical dependence among causal relations. Since all the notions employed are naturalistic, as per prior specifications, we could stop here. Alternatively, we can press the analysis further by reconstructing the notion of an empirical dependence in the familiar way, viz., by reference to subjunctives: If B-caused 'A' tokenings are wild—if they falsely represent B's as A's—then there *would be* a causal route from A's to 'A' even if there *were no* causal route from B's to 'A's; but there would be no causal route from B's to 'A's if there were no causal route from A's to 'A's.

Suppose that a counterfactual is true in a world iff its consequent is true in 'nearby' possible worlds in which its antecedent is true. (One possible world is 'near' another if, by and large, the laws that hold in the first also hold in the second. See Lewis, C.) So 'if I were smart I would be rich' is true here because I'm rich in the nearby possible worlds in which I'm smart. Then we can spell out the proposed condition on wild tokens as follows. In a world where B-caused 'A' tokens are wild (and express the property A), the nomic relations among properties have to be such that

1. A's cause 'A's.
2. 'A' tokens are *not* caused by B's in nearby worlds in which A's *don't* cause 'A's.
3. A's cause 'A's in nearby worlds in which B's don't cause 'A's.

Caveat: These conditions are supposed to apply with—as it were—synchronic force. For imagine a case where someone learns 'horse' entirely from noninstances. For example, from ostensions of cows, all of which happen to look a lot like horses. No doubt, once 'horse' has been mastered, wild (cow-caused) 'horse' tokens would depend upon tame (horse-caused) 'horse' tokenings, exactly as required. But the dependence isn't, in this case, asymmetric, since the speaker's current disposition to apply 'horse' to horses is a historical consequence of his previous disposition to apply it to cows. *Had he not previously applied 'horse' to cows, he would not now apply 'horse' to horses.*[7] So it looks like we've got error *without* asymmetric dependence, contrary to the condition previously endorsed. But this is OK, since, as just remarked, the sort of asymmetrical dependence that's necessary for wildness is *synchronic;* and in the case imagined, my present disposition to apply 'horse' to horses does *not* depend on any corresponding *current* disposition to apply it to cows. We get the asymmetric dependence back when we respect the tenses, to put it in a nutshell.

As things stand thus far, I'm assuming only that the asymmetric dependence of B-caused 'A' tokenings on A-caused 'A' tokenings is *necessary* for B-caused 'A' tokens to be wild. I emphasize this point because, on the one hand, it's more obvious that asymmetric dependence is necessary for wildness than that it's sufficient; and, on the other, mere necessity will do for the purpose at hand.[8]

The purpose at hand, remember, is solving the disjunction problem; and *you don't get the asymmetric dependence of B-caused 'A' tokenings on A-caused 'A' tokenings in the case where 'A' means A v B.* Suppose the form of words 'blue or green' means *blue or green;* then the fact that you use 'blue or green' (rather than 'blue') of a blue thing depends on the fact that you use it of green things; and the fact that you use 'blue or green' (rather than 'green') of a green thing depends on the fact that you use it of blue things. In short, in the case of disjunctive predicates, what you get is *symmetrical* dependence. Asymmetric dependence thus does what it's supposed to do if it's necessary for wildness; viz., it distinguishes wildness from disjunction.

I'm inclined, however, to think that asymmetric dependence is both necessary *and* sufficient for wildness. I don't think there could be, as it were, *adventitious* asymmetric dependence: worlds in which

'A' means $B v C$, but it *just happens* that there's a law that C's don't cause 'A's unless B's do (and no law that B's don't cause 'A's unless C's do).

At a minimum, to suppose that there could be adventitious asymmetric dependence begs the question against causal theories of content. A causal theorist has to rule out this possibility *whatever* he says about error. For consider: according to the causal theory, a symbol expresses a property only if the instantiation of the property is nomologically sufficient for the tokening of the symbol. In particular, if 'A' expresses the property $B v C$, then the instantiation of $B v C$ has to be nomologically sufficient for the tokening of 'A.' But C's *do* instantiate the property $B v C$. So it can't be that 'A' means $B v C$ in a world where C's don't cause 'A's. A causal theorist can acknowledge only one kind of world in which X's don't cause 'X's; viz., the kind of world in which 'X' doesn't mean X.[9]

Time to sum up:
We began with the Very Crude idea that 'A' means A iff all and only A's cause 'A's. Neither the all part nor the only part being defensible as stated, we decided to start by whittling away at the latter. This clause can now be replaced as follows: 'A' means A iff all A's cause 'A's and 'A' tokenings that are caused by non-A's are wild.

Wildness then gets defined by reference to asymmetric dependence: B-caused 'A' tokenings are wild only if B-caused 'A' tokenings are *asymmetrically* dependent on the causation of 'A' tokenings by non-B's.

Correspondingly, B-caused 'A' tokenings express the (disjunctive) property $A v B$ only if B-caused 'A' tokenings are *symmetrically* dependent on A-caused 'A' tokenings.

And just to round things off: Ambiguity—viz., the case where 'A' means A *and* 'A' means B—requires symmetrical *independence*; A's cause 'A's in nearby worlds where B's don't, and B's cause 'A's in nearby worlds where 'A's don't.

A brief aside before we turn to other business. The treatment of error I've proposed is, in a certain sense, purely formal. It invokes a dependence among relations, and it is *compatible* with assuming that the relations among which this dependence holds are causal (that's why it's a help to CCT). But strictly speaking, it doesn't *require* that assumption. On the contrary, it looks like *any* theory of error will have to provide for the asymmetric dependence of false tokenings upon true ones. To that extent, the story I've been telling may be of use to you even if you don't care for causal theories of content and even if you're out of sympathy with the naturalization program. (I'm indebted for this point to Peter Slezak.)

So far, so good; but at best this far is only part way. The Crude Causal Theory (Pocket Version) says that 'A's express the property A iff *all* A's and *only* A's reliably cause 'A's. And, as I remarked earlier on, there are troubles with both clauses: it's not true that only horses cause 'horse' tokenings (sometimes cows do); and it's not true that all horses cause 'horse' tokenings (many horses live and die quite undenoted). Well, it may be that the problems about the 'only' clause are merely technical and that fancy footwork along the lines just reviewed will save it: instead of saying 'only A's cause 'A's' we can say 'only A's are such that 'A's depend upon them asymmetrically.' But the problems about the 'all' clause are, in my view, very deep. It's here that the plausibility of a serious causal theory of content will be tested. And here I can offer no more than a sketch.

Toward a Slightly Less Crude Causal Theory of Content

The idea was that my Mentalese symbol 'horse' expresses the property of being a horse only if *all* instantiations of the property cause the symbol to be tokened in my belief box. But that's preposterous on the face of it. What about Ancient Athenian horses? What about horses on Alpha Centauri? What about fortieth-century horses? What about horses in Peking (where, unlike many horses, I have never been)? I am prepared to assume that 'A's do express A if all A's cause 'A's; for if that's not true, then the causal covariance approach to content is palying in entirely the wrong ball park. But even if it *is* true, it's not much comfort, since not all A's do cause 'A's, as previously noted. What we need is a *plausible* sufficient condition for 'A' expressing A; a condition such that it's plausible that, in at least some cases, 'A's express A *because that condition is satisfied*.

One is, perhaps, inclined to put one's faith in counterfactuals; Pekingese (Antique Greek; Alpha Centaurian; Post-Modern . . . etc.) horses *would cause (/would have caused)* corresponding 'Horse' tokenings if . . . . And here's the rub, because we don't know which counterfactuals to appeal to. The viability of the Causal Theory depends on its being able to specify (in naturalistic vocabulary, hence in nonsemantic and nonintentional vocabulary) circumstances such that (a) in those circumstances, 'horse's covary with horses; i.e., instantiations of *horse* would cause 'horse' to be tokened in my belief box (i.e., would cause me to believe *Here's a horse!*) were the circumstances to obtain; and (b) 'horse' expresses the property *horse* (in my ideolect of Mentalese) in virtue of the truth of (a). Just which circumstances are those, pray?

This is, as I say, a very hard problem. And there's worse; horses aren't the half of it. Suppose that there *are* circumstances under which horse instantiations are, as it were, guaranteed to stuff tokens of the (Mentalese) expression 'horse' down one's throat (more precisely, to stuff them into one's belief box). What about expressions like 'proton' or 'is a segment of curved space-time'? If the Causal Theory is going to work at all, it's got to work for the so-called 'theoretical vocabulary' too. But if protons qua protons affect the content of one's belief box, they must do so via a complicated chain of intermediate causes, and some of the links of this chain must be inferences that one draws from the physical theories that one believes. And of course, neither 'inference' and 'belief'—which are intentional notions—nor 'theory'—which is a semantical notion—are at the disposal of a naturalistic treatment of meaning.

Still, it's an ill wind and all that. If reflection on the semantics of soi-disant theoretical terms makes the prospects for a causal theory of content look glum, reflection on the semantics of soi-disant observation terms makes them look appreciably better.[10] To wit:

The 'Psychophysical' Basis
There *are* circumstances in which beliefs about observables do seem to force themselves upon one in something like the way that the Crude Causal Theory requires. For example: Paint the wall red, turn the lights up, point your face toward the wall, and open your eyes. The thought 'red there' will occur to you; just try it and see if it doesn't. To put it another way (to put it in a way that assumes RTM): If (enough of the) wall is (bright enough) red, and if you're close (enough) to the wall, and if your eyes are pointed toward the wall and your visual system is functioning, then the Mentalese equivalent of 'red there' will get stuffed into your belief box *willy-nilly*.

It goes without saying that not *every* instantiation of *red* affects the contents of your belief box. Think of all the reds in China. But what we've got is just as good for the purposes at hand: there are circumstances such that red instantiations control 'red' tokenings whenever those circumstances obtain; and it's plausible that 'red' expresses the property *red* in virtue of the fact that red instantiations cause 'red' tokenings in those circumstances; *and the circumstances are nonsemantically, nonteleologically, and nonintentionally specifiable*.

In fact, they're *psychophysically* specifiable. Psychophysics is precisely in the business of telling us how much of the wall has to be painted red (more strictly speaking, what angle the retinal image of the red part of the wall has to subtend), and how red it has to be painted, and how close to the wall one has to be, and how bright the lights have to be, and so forth . . . such that if it's that much red, and that bright, and you're that close . . . then you'll think 'red' if your eyes are pointed toward the wall and your visual system is intact. To a close first approximation (caveats to follow), psychophysics is the science that tells us how the content of an organism's belief box varies with the values of certain physical parameters in its local environment. And it does so in nonintentional, nonsemantical vocabulary: in the vocabulary of wavelengths, candlepowers, retinal irradiations, and the like.

Of course, not all the organism's concepts are under the sort of local causal control that psychophysics talks about; for example, the theoretical concept PROTON patently isn't; and we'll see later why middle-sized-object concepts like HORSE aren't either. (Equivalently, not all properties are such that their instances exert the relevant sort of local control on the contents of the belief box; for example, the property of *being a proton* doesn't, and neither does the property of *being a horse*). Still, psychophysics does what it does, and ingratitude is a vice. For the concepts and properties that it applies to, psychophysics is just what the causal theory ordered. The Crude Causal Theory, together with psychophysics, provides a plausible sufficient condition for certain symbols to express certain properties: viz., that tokenings of those symbols are connected to instantiations of the properties they express *by psychophysical law.*

This isn't everything, but it isn't nothing either. You can imagine a whole mental life constituted by beliefs about observables—equivalently, given RTM, a system of mental representations whose nonlogical vocabulary consists exhaustively of observation terms. Perhaps, indeed, the mental life of some animals is rather like this. For such a mind, the Crude Causal Theory, as psychophysically emended, would approximate a complete solution to the naturalization problem. This ought to bother you if your view is that there are principled—metaphysical—reasons why there can't be plausible, naturalistic, sufficient conditions for intentionality.

A couple of caveats: It doesn't, to begin with, matter to this line of thought that the observation/theory distinction isn't epistemologically or ontologically principled; for, in fact, I'm not wanting to do any epistemological or ontological work with it. All that matters is that there are concepts (Mentalese terms) whose tokenings are determined by psychophysical law; and that these concepts are plausibly viewed as expressing the properties upon which their tokening is thus lawfully contingent; and that the psychophysical conditions for the tokenings of these concepts can be expressed in nonintentional and nonsemantical vocabulary.

It also doesn't matter that the tokenings in question be, strictly speaking, 'in the belief box'; i.e., it's not required that we view psychophysics as enunciating sufficient conditions for the fixation of *belief*. It will do, for our purposes, if psychophysics enunciates sufficient conditions for the fixation of *appearances*.

The point is that belief fixation is a *conservative* process. You may stare at what looks to be a paradigm case of red wall, and something you know—some part of the cognitive background—may nevertheless convince you that the wall isn't red after all (where 'after all' means quite literally 'appearances to the contrary notwithstanding'). Belief fixation is about what happens *on balance*. Psychophysics can't do anything about this; it can't guarantee that you'll *believe* 'red there,' only that 'red there' will occur to you.[11] But a guaranteed correlation between instances of red and tokenings of 'red there' in the occurs-to-me box will do perfectly nicely for the purposes of semantic naturalization; all semantics wants is *some* sort of nomologically sufficient conditions for instances of *red* to cause psychologically active tokenings of 'red.' On this view, the theory of belief fixation strictly so called belongs not to semanticists but to cognitive psychologists, among whose goals it is to say what determines which of the things that occur to you you actually come to believe (how information flows from the occurs-to-me box to the belief box, if you like that way of putting it).

Well, where do you go from here? The psychophysical cases are close to ideal from the point of view of a causal theory; they're the ones for which it appears most clearly possible to enumerate the conditions in which (reliable, causal) correlation makes content. So a rational research strategy would be to try to work outward from these cases—somehow to extend an analogous treatment to apparently less tractable examples such as HORSE or PROTON. There's a variety of proposals around that are plausibly viewed as variants of this strategy; the idea that the semantics of observation terms is somehow at the core of the theory of meaning is, after all, pretty traditional among philosophers.

Reduction

For example, it would be extremely convenient if one could talk oneself into a reductionist account of the relation between observation terms and the rest of the nonlogical vocabulary of Mentalese: perhaps something to the effect that any Mentalese formula that can express an intentional content at all is equivalent to some Mentalese formula all of whose nonlogical vocabulary is observational. It would be convenient to believe this because if it were true, the naturalization problem would be largely solved. Psychophysics would be all the theory of mind/world interaction that the semantics of Mentalese requires.

This sort of solution has, of course, a long and respectable history in the tradition of classical Empiricism. In effect, you reduce all concepts to sensory concepts, which are in turn assumed to be connected to their instances by some such 'natural' (viz., putatively nonintentional and nonsemantic) relation as resemblance or causation. This is an appealing idea, one which effectively expresses the intuition that the semantics of observation terms is unproblematic in ways that the semantics of the theoretical vocabulary is not.

But of course it won't do. PROTON and HORSE aren't the concepts of a set of actual or possible experiences. (Nor, mutatis mutandis, are the concepts WATER and WATER2; if they were, they'd be the *same* concept.)[12] Or, to put the same point in terms that are congenial to the causal theory: We need a story about how PROTON connects causally with instantiations of the property of *being a proton*. And our trouble is that *being a proton* is not a property in the domain of psychophysical law.

Psychophysics gives us a naturalization of a certain set of concepts; the reductionist strategy was to show that all other concepts are logical constructions out of these. But there's another alternative to consider. Perhaps we've underestimated the number of concepts that can be treated as psychophysical. Perhaps that treatment can be extended, if not to PROTON, then at least to an indefinite variety of concepts that subtend 'middle-sized' objects. Here is how it might go:

Psychophysical Imperialism
Psychophysics purports to specify what one might call an 'optimal' point of view with respect to red things; viz., a viewpoint with the peculiar property that any intact observer who occupies it *must*— nomologically must; must in point of psychophysical law—have 'red there' occur to him. Well then, why can't a suitably extended psychophysics do as much for HORSE? Of course there are instantiations of *horse* (horses in Peking and so forth) that don't affect the contents of one's belief box; arguably, however, that's only because one doesn't occupy a psychophysically optimal viewpoint with respect to those instantiations. For, plant a horse right there in the foreground, turn the lights up, point the observer hors rards, *rub his nose in horse*, to put the proposal as crudely as possible . . . and surely the thought 'horse there' will indeed occur to him. The suggestion is

that horses *must* cause 'horse' tokenings whenever there is an observer on the spot; and that we can rely on psychophysics to tell us exactly what being on the spot consists in. So, all that's required for a guaranteed correlation between horses and 'horses' is what they call in Europe *being there!* (God's omniscience, according to this view, is largely implicit in His omnipresence. Notes toward a truly *naturalized* theology.)

It's not, then, just for RED, but also for HORSE and CLOCK-TOWER and many, many other such concepts, that psychophysics provides just what a naturalized semantics needs: circumstances in which instances of a property are guaranteed to cause tokens of the symbol that expresses it. This is a proposal rather in the spirit of an eighteenth-century commonplace about how to draw the distinction between perception and thought: Whereas thought is somehow voluntary—so that one can, in Reflection, conjure up the Idea of a horse at will—percepts simply intrude themselves. You *can't but* entertain the Idea HORSE when you're presented with a horse close up. But then, perhaps the fact that horses force 'horses' upon one in psychophysically optimal circumstances is *all there is* to 'horse' expressing *horse*. Just as the fact that red things force 'red' upon one in psychophysically optimal circumstances is arguably all there is to 'red' expressing *red.*

I think that this is all rather pleasing. It is, for example, the grain of sense in the Gibsonian idea that there are 'ecologically' sufficient conditions for perceptual achievements. (See also Fodor, *P,* where something of this sort is argued for, though not in quite the present terms.) But it doesn't work; HORSE won't do as a psychophysical concept. Here's why:

Psychophysics can guarantee circumstances in which you'll see a horse and, presumably, have the appropriate horsy experiences. It can't, however, guarantee the *intentional content* of the mental state that you're in in those circumstances. That's because it can't guarantee that when you see the horse you'll see it *as* a horse. Roughly, seeing a horse as a horse requires applying the concept HORSE to what you see. And of course, intact observers qua intact observers *don't have to have* the concept HORSE. So then, it's perfectly nomologically possible to be in a psychophysically optimal relation to a horse and yet not have the thought *here's a horse* occur to one.

You can now see why Darwinian/teleological apparatus does no good for the purposes at hand. Suppose you *could* get a teleological notion of optimal conditions as—e.g.—the ones that obtain when the cognitive mechanisms are behaving as the forces of selection intended them to. Even so, you still couldn't infer from (a) the presence of a horse and (b) the optimality of the conditions that (c) 'horse' will get tokened. For: there is no Darwinian guarantee that a properly functioning intentional system ipso facto has the concept HORSE (to say nothing of the concept PROTON). And what you don't have, you can't token.

It is, by the way, easy to miss all this if you think of perceiving as just the entertaining of a mental image; that is, as imaging rather than judging. For that sort of treatment leaves the question of the intentional content of the percept wide open. The present point, put in those terms, is that psychophysics can guarantee circumstances in which you'll have a horse image, but not circumstances in which you'll take what you're having to be an image of a horse. Compare Hume, who I'm inclined to think got this wrong for once.

Let's go back to RED. There are, of course, cases where one sees red things but fails to see them *as* red: you're too far away to make out colors; the illumination is bad . . . and so forth. But what makes RED special—what makes it a 'psychophysical concept' within the meaning of the act—is that the difference between merely seeing something red and succeeding in seeing it *as* red vanishes when the observer's point of view is psychophysically optimal. You can't—or so I claim—see something red under psychophysically optimal viewing conditions and *not* see it as red. That is, perhaps, the hard core of truth that underlies the traditional doctrine of the 'theory neutrality' of observation: qua intact observers, we do have some concepts that we token willy-nilly under circumstances about which psychophysicists can tell us the whole story. Perceptual applications of such concepts are, in that sense, independent of—not mediated by—the perceiver's background of cognitive commitments. But most of our concepts—even ones like HORSE; certainly ones like PROTON—just aren't like that. There are no *psychophysically* specifiable circumstances in which it is nomologically necessary that one sees horses as such.

The box score seems to be as follows: Psychophysics naturalizes the semantics of a certain—relatively quite small—set of mental representations; viz., those for which the distinction between seeing and seeing as vanishes in psychophysically optimal circumstances. These representations have the peculiarity that sufficient conditions for their tokenings can be specified in entirely 'external' terms; when one's psychophysical situation is optimal, the world, as it were, reaches in and stuffs them into one's belief box. But it isn't true that these concepts provide a reduction base for the rest of Mentalese; and it isn't true that this psychophysical model can be extended, in any obvious way, to concepts like HORSE whose tokenings—even in psychophysically optimal circumstances—are characteristically inferentially mediated. (To say nothing of PROTON, for whose tokenings the notion of psychophysically optimal circumstances is thus far undefined, since, of course, protons are very small and you can't see them even with the lights turned up.) So what now?

A Demure Foundationalism
Here's what we want: we want circumstances such that (1) they are naturalistically specifiable; (2) horses (/protons) reliably cause 'horses' (/'protons') in those circumstances; (3) it's plausible that 'horse' (/ 'proton') expresses *horse (/proton)* because it's the case that (2). We really do need to know at least roughly what such circumstances might be like, on pain of having the metaphysical worry that— excepting psychophysical concepts—*we have no idea at all* what a naturalized semantics would be like for the nonlogical vocabulary of Mentalese.

Here is how I propose to proceed: first I'll tell you a sketch of a story about (2) and (3), but I'll tell the story in a question-begging vocabulary; viz., in a vocabulary that flouts (1). Then I'll say a little about how it might be possible to tell the same story sketch, only naturalistically. Then I'll ask you to try very, very hard to believe that some day the naturalistic version of this story sketch might actually be filled in, thereby solving the naturalization problem.

The story is, I admit, sort of old-fashioned, since, roughly, it connects having concepts with having experiences and knowing meanings with knowing what would count as evidence. Whenever I tell this story to Granny, she grins and rocks and says "I told you so."

The Question-Begging Version
Horse isn't a psychophysical property (see above); but instantiations of *horse* are, very often, causally responsible for instantiations of what *are* psychophysical properties. It is, for example, because Dobbin is a horse that Dobbin has that horsy look.[13] And it's entirely plausible that having that horsy look reduces to having some or other (maybe quite disjunctive) bundle of psychophysical properties (though, of course, *being a horse* doesn't).

Proton is a little different, because there isn't a look (taste, smell, etc.) that being a proton is typically causally responsible for a thing's having. Protons are, as previously remarked, too small to see. But I think the principle is very much the same. It turns out that it's possible to construct environments in which instantiations of *proton* do have characteristic psychophysical consequences. These are called 'experimental' environments; they involve the deployment of 'instruments of observation'; and they are, more often than not, very expensive to build. The reason they're so expensive is that because protons are very small, the observable effects of instantiating *proton* at a particular position in spacetime tend to be fairly negligible compared to the causal contributions of other sources of variance. It therefore requires great delicacy to ensure that a given psychophysical effect really is specific to the instantiation of *proton*. But, as I say, it turns out to be possible to do so—to an acceptable level of reliability—assuming you're prepared to pay for it.

We're trying to imagine a kind of connection between horses (or protons) in the world and 'horse's (or 'proton's) in the belief box such that it's plausibly because that connection obtains that 'horse' means *horse* (and 'proton' means *proton*). The Crude Causal Theory says that this connection ought to be a species of causally reliable covariation. Aside from that, all we know so far is that the covariation can't be mediated by brute psychophysical law because neither HORSE nor PROTON is a psychophysical concept.

On the other hand, there's no reason why instantiations of psychophysical properties shouldn't be *links in a causal chain* that reliably connects horses and protons with 'horse's and 'proton's respectively. This is a hopeful suggestion, because, as we've seen, there are (presumably naturalistically specifiable) circumstances in which instantiations of psychophysical properties are reliably caused by—indeed, are specific to—instantiations of nonpsychophysical properties such as *horse* and *proton;* and, as we've also seen, there are (naturalistically specifiable) circumstances in which instantiations of psychophysical properties reliably causally control what's in the belief box.

So far, everything is OK: physics—incuding the physics of the experimental environment—guarantees a reliable causal covariation between instantiations of *proton* and the psychophysical properties of the photographic plate, or the cloud chamber, or the voltmeter, or whatever apparatus you're using to detect protons (if physics didn't guarantee this correlation, what you're using wouldn't count as a proton detector). And psychophysics guarantees a reliable causal covariation between the observable properties of the apparatus and the tokening of concepts in the belief box (if psychophysics didn't guarantee this correlation, these properties of the apparatus wouldn't count as observable). And 'reliably causally covaries with' is, I suppose, fairly transitive; transitive enough for the purposes at hand.

Remember that what we wanted for semantics was naturalistically specifiable conditions under which instantiations of *proton* are guaranteed to affect what's in the belief box, our problem being that, patently, not all instances of *proton* succeed in doing so. Well, we can now have what we wanted: for semantical purposes, we require only that instances of *proton* affect the belief box if[14] (a) they take place in an 'experimental environment,' i.e., *they are causally responsible for the instantiation of psychophysical properties;* and (b) the experimental environment is viewed by an observer who is in an optimal psychophysical position with respect to that environment. (So instances of *proton* that leave traces on photographic plates that are never examined are ipso facto *not* required to affect the contents of any belief boxes.) Notice that so far we haven't even cheated. Because physics connects protons with the look of the photographic plate and psychophysics connects the look of the photographic plate with what's in the belief box, we can specify the conditions under which instances of *proton* are required to affect tokens in the belief box nonsemantically and nonintentionally.

This is *much* better than the Crude Causal Theory, since we no longer require that *all* instantiations of *proton* (mutatis mutandis, *horse*) need to affect the belief box in order that 'proton' should express *proton* (mutatis mutandis, in order that 'horse' should express *horse*). In fact, in the case of *proton* (though not, perhaps, in the case of *horse*) the number of instances that have been causally responsible for semantically relevant tokenings of representations in belief boxes is infinitesimally small; vastly, astronomically, unimaginably more protons go undetected than not. On the present view, this is quite compatible with there being mental representations that mean *proton*. Fine so far.

But still no good over all. We've got something into the belief box for which instantiations of *proton* are causally responsible; but it's the wrong thing. It's not a token of the concept PROTON; rather, it's a token of some (probably complex) *psychophysical* concept, some concept whose tokening is lawfully connected with the look of the photographic plate. This is clear from the way that the counterfactuals go. Suppose what happens in the experimental environment is that instances of *proton* turn photographic plates red. Then what we're guaranteed gets into the belief box of an observer whose situation with respect to the plate is psychophysically optimal is a symbol whose tokens are reliably correlated with instantiations of *red whether or not* the instantiations of *red* are causally dependent on instances of *proton*. I.e., it's the same symbol that gets tokened in the belief boxes of observers whose situations are psychophysically optimal with respect to ripe tomatoes.

Something needs to be done about this. Here is where the cheating starts.

It's clear enough what story one *wants* to tell: Some people—

physicists, for example—*know about* the causal relation between, on the one hand, instantiations of *proton* and, on the other, the redness of photographic plates that are exposed in appropriate experimental environments. Such people are thus in a position to draw the relevant inferences from the look of the plate to the presence of the particle. So, for these people, there is the required correlation between 'proton' in the belief box and protons in the world, mediated—as we've seen—by 'automatic' tokenings of psychophysical concepts, but also by theoretical inferences that draw upon the cognitive background for their premises. Alas, this sort of correlation does a naturalized semantics no good at all, because to specify the conditions in which the required connections between protons and 'protons' will obtain you have to talk about states like *knowing physical theories* and processes like *drawing inferences from what one knows*. Utterly anathema, it goes without saying.

Well, but perhaps not *utterly* anathema, on second thought. What we need is some process that will put a token of 'proton' into the belief box whenever a proton in the world is causally responsible (via physical and psychophysical law) for a token of 'red' being in the belief box. Now, what in fact normally performs this function is a theoretically based inference: the observer holds a theory that implies that red plates signal protons, and he applies what he knows to infer the presence of the proton from the color of the plate. When the theory is true, the inferences it mediates will indeed succeed in correlating instantiations of *proton* in the experimental environment with tokenings of 'proton' in the belief box. True theories—when internalized—correlate the state of the head with the state of the world; that's exactly what's so nice about them.

But though protons typically exert causal control over 'protons' via the activation of intentional mechanisms, a naturalistic semantics doesn't need to specify all that. All it needs is that the causal control should actually obtain, *however* it is mediated. The claim, to put it roughly but relatively intuitively, is that it's sufficient for 'proton' to express *proton* if there's a reliable correlation between protons and 'protons,' effected by a mechanism whose response is specific to psychophysical traces for which protons are *in fact* causally responsible. And *that* claim *can* be made in nonintentional, nonsemantic vocabulary. It just was.

No doubt mechanisms that track nonobservables in the required way typically satisfy intentional characterizations (they're typically inferential) and semantic characterizations (they work because the inferences that they draw are sound). But that's OK because on the one hand, the semantic/intentional properties of such mechanisms are, as it were, only *contingently* conditions for their success in tracking protons; and, on the other, what's required for 'proton' to express *proton* is only that the tracking actually be successful. For purposes of semantic naturalization, *it's the existence of a reliable mind/world correlation that counts, not the mechanisms by which that correlation is effected.*

So what's proposed is a sort of foundationalism. The semantics of observation concepts is indeed special: First, in that—given an intact observer—the nomologically sufficient and semantically relevant conditions for their tokenings are specifiable 'purely externally'; viz., purely psychophysically. And second, in that all the other semantically relevant symbol/world linkages run via the tokening of observation concepts. 'Horse' means *horse* if 'horse' tokenings are reliably caused by tokenings of psychophysical concepts that are in turn caused by instantiations of psychophysical properties for which instantiations of *horse* are in fact causally responsible.[15] The causal chain runs from horses in the world to horsy looks in the world to psychophysical concepts in the belief box to 'horse' in the belief box. 'Horse' means *horse* because that chain is reliable.

All right, Granny, have it your way: in effect, the satisfaction of this condition for having a HORSE concept requires that you be able to have certain experiences; and that you be prepared to take your having of those experiences to be evidence for the presence of horses; and, indeed, that you can sometimes be *right* in taking your having of those experiences to be evidence of horses. Only do stop rocking; you make me nervous.

A number of points, all in a jumble and mostly in a concessive and ecumenical tone of voice:

First: There's a detectable family resemblance between the present doctrine and Quine's analysis—in *Word and Object*—of what it is to know a scientific theory like, for example, chemistry. Knowing chemistry, Quine says, is a matter of the associative "interanimation of sentences." It's a matter of having the right psychological connections between, on the one hand, sentences like "This is wet/tasteless/ colorless" and sentences like "This is water"; and, on the other hand, between sentences like "This is water" and sentences like "This is H_2O." "Thus someone mixes the contents of two test tubes, observes a green tint, and says 'There was copper in it.' Here the sentence is elicited by a nonverbal stimulus, but the stimulus depends for its efficacy upon an earlier network of associations of words with words; viz., one's learning of chemical theory. . . . The intervening theory is composed of sentences associated with one another in multifarious ways not easily reconstructed even in conjecture" (*WO*, 11).

Now that is, of course, *not* what it is to know chemistry; at a minimum, knowing chemistry is a matter of judging that certain propositions are true, and there is—as Kant decisively remarked—no way of reducing judging (as it might be, judging that if P then Q) to associating (as it might be, associating 'Q' with 'P').

Nevertheless, there may be a use for Quine's picture; it may be that Quine gives you everything you need to characterize the role of internalized theories in fixing the content of mental representations. Viz., all the internalized theory need do is 'transfer activation' from observation sentences to theoretical sentences on the appropriate occasions; and all *that* requires is that the sentences involved form the right sort of associative network. So, to that extent, Quine's right: the part of the story about how internalized theories operate that's essential to their functioning in supporting semantically relevant concept/world correlations can be told in the (nonintentional, nonsemantic) vocabulary of Associationism.[16]

In similar spirit: There is, in my view, almost nothing to be said for the idea that theories are 'mere calculating devices' when it is proposed as a piece of philosophy of science. But it may be that that's precisely the story that you want to tell about how theories (more generally, bits of the cognitive background) function in fixing the semantics of mental representations.

The picture is that there's, as it were, a computer between the sensorium and the belief box, and that the tokening of certain psychophysical concepts eventuates in the computer's running through certain calculations that in turn lead to tokenings of 'proton' (or of 'horse,' or whatever) on the appropriate occasions. De facto, these would normally be calculations that appeal, for premises, to internalized beliefs; and they would actually succeed in correlating 'proton's with protons only when these beliefs are true. But you don't need to mention any of that to say what it is about the computer's calculations that's relevant to fixing the semantics of 'proton'; all *that* requires is that the computer output 'proton' when its inputs are tokenings of psychophysical concepts for which protons are in fact causally responsible.

To put it in a nutshell: The *epistemological* properties of theories are, of course, sensitive to their intentional and semantic properties; what we want of our beliefs is that their *contents* should be *true*. But maybe only the *computational* properties of our theories matter to their role in fixing the meanings of mental representations; *for those purposes* our theories are just the formalism we use to calculate what to put in the belief box when.

Second: The condition I'm imagining is supposed to be *sufficient* but not *necessary* for 'proton' meaning *proton*. For all I care, there may be other sorts of routes that would connect concepts to their instances in a semantically relevant way; for example, ones that *don't* depend on the existence of psychophysical laws. I emphasize this point because I don't trust Granny; give her an a priori connection between content and (what she calls) 'the possibility of experience' and she's likely to try for antimetaphysical arguments in the familiar, Positivist vein (worse still, for philosophical constraints on the conceptual apparatus of science). Chaque à son rocker; I am *not* doing 'critical philosophy.' Rather, I'm arguing with a guy who says that there are a priori, metaphysical reasons for supposing that semantics can't be naturalized. A plausible, naturalistic, *sufficient* condition for 'A's' meaning A is all I need to win the argument with him.

Third: Although the present condition for 'proton' meaning *proton* is a lot more plausible than the Crude requirement that all protons cause 'protons,' it's still too strong to be *entirely* plausible; for example, it requires the tokening of 'proton' in *all* environments in which psychophysical consequences for which protons are causally responsible are detected. But, of course, there may be correlations between protons and psychophysical traces that nobody knows about, correlations that our (current) physics doesn't specify; and such correlations are ipso facto unlikely to function as links in chains from protons to 'protons.' For instance: for all I know, I am right now registering psychophysical traces that are specific to protons. That my belief box is nevertheless innocent of a tokening of PROTON would not imply that I lack that concept. All that would follow is that my internalized physics is incomplete. Oh boy, is it ever!

But I don't propose to linger over this sort of worry. It seems to me that we're now playing in the right ball park and the rest is arguably just fine tuning. Perhaps what we want to say is sufficient for 'proton' meaning *proton* is that there be *at least one* kind of environment in which there are psychophysical traces of protons which, when detected, cause the tokening of 'proton' in the belief box. Or perhaps, slightly more interesting, the right thing to say is that there should be *a fair number* of such kinds of environments, thereby allowing the concept HAVING THE CONCEPT PROTON to exhibit the sort of vagueness of boundary characteristic of most of the notions that the special sciences employ (cf. RIVER, TORNADO, FEUDAL SOCIETY, FEMALE, and the like).

Fourth: Precisely because the present proposal requires only that there be the right kind of correlation between protons and 'protons,' we're allowing the fixation of meaning by radically false theories. On this view, somebody who believes really crazy things—that protons are alive, as it might be—could still have the concept PROTON. He would do so if his crazy theory happens to have the property of reliably connecting 'protons' with protons via their psychophysical traces. For reasons given in chapter 3, I regard this as a virtue; people *can* have radically false theories and really crazy views, consonant with our understanding perfectly well, thank you, which false views they have and what radically crazy things it is that they believe. Berkeley thought that chairs are *mental*, for Heaven's sake! Which are we to say he lacked, the concept MENTAL or the concept CHAIR?

A consequence of the present view is that although theories mediate symbol/world connections, still Meaning Holism is not thereby implied. That's because the *content* of a theory does *not* determine the meanings of the terms whose connections to the world the theory mediates. What determines their meanings is *which things in the world the theory connects them to*. The unit of meaning is not the theory; it's the world/symbol correlation *however mediated*.

Let me tell you—by way of making the spirit of the proposal clear—a story about what was wrong with Verificationism. Verificationism was the idea that the meaning of an expression could be identified with whatever route connects the use of the expression to its denotation. So, for example, there's something that connects our use of the word 'star' to stars; a causal chain that starts with light leaving stars, passing—maybe—through telescopes, falling on our retinas, and eventuating in utterances of 'star' (mutatis mutandis, with tokenings of 'star' in the belief box). The Verificationist idea was that it's *that sort of thing* that constitutes the meaning of 'star.'

Now, there is something right about this—namely, that tokenings of the verification procedures for 'star' must have stars on one end and 'stars' on the other; it's true a priori that when they work, verification procedures connect terms with their denotations. If they didn't, they wouldn't *be* verification procedures.

But there is something wrong with it too. Namely, that verification procedures connect terms with their denotations *in too many ways*. Think of the routes along which stars can get connected to tokenings of 'star': via just looking; via looking at reflections in a puddle; via inference from astronomical theory; via inference from astrological theory; via inference from what somebody happened to say; via paintings of stars in a museum; via just thinking about stars . . . etc. The point is that 'star' isn't umpteen ways ambiguous; these different routes *do not determine correspondingly different semantic values for 'star.'* On the contrary, what determines the semantic value of 'star' is precisely what all these routes have *in common*; viz., the fact that they connect 'stars' with stars. The moral is that *the route doesn't matter (much)*; what makes 'star' mean *star* is *that* the two are connected, not *how* the two are connected. It's the covariance that counts.

Similarly for concepts, of course. It may be that my concept of water is, from time to time, connected to water via my concept of cat: I believe that water is what cats like; I find that my cat likes this stuff; I infer that this stuff is water. But it's not being connected to water via CAT that makes my concept of water a water concept. What makes it a water concept is that its tokenings covary with water instances—under appropriate circumstances—by whatever route the covariance may be achieved. That theories mediate the semantically relevant concept-to-world connections does *not* imply Meaning Holism. For we get meaning by *quantifying over* the routes from a symbol to its denotation.

Summary

Just a word to recapitulate the architecture of the discussion that we've been pursuing. We started with the Crude idea that a plausible sufficient condition for 'A's to express A is that it's nomologically necessary that (1) every instance of A causes a token of 'A'; and (2) only instances of A cause tokens of 'A.'

The Slightly Less Crude Causal Theory of Content offers the following two friendly amendments: for (2) read: 'If non-A's cause 'A's, then their doing so is asymmetrically dependent upon A's causing 'A's. For (1) read: 'All instances of A's cause 'A's when (i) the A's are causally responsible for psychophysical traces to which (ii) the organism stands in a psychophysically optimal relation.

What's claimed for SLCCTC is that it does what metaphysical skeptics about intentionality doubt *can* be done: it provides a sufficient condition for one part of the world to be semantically related to another part (specifically, for a certain mental representation to express a certain property); it does so in nonintentional, nonsemantical, nonteleological, and, in general, non–question-begging vocabulary; and it's reasonably plausible—it isn't crazy to suppose that at least some mental symbols have the content that they do because they stand in the sort of relation to the world that SLCCTC prescribes.

I do, however, admit to two checks still outstanding. I've helped myself to the notion of an intact organism; and I've helped myself to the notion of one event being the cause of another. I have therefore to claim that, whatever the right unpacking of these concepts may be, it doesn't smuggle in intentional/semantic notions (perhaps, in the latter case, via the—alleged; Granny and I don't believe it for a minute—'interest relativity' of explanation).

Obligation noted. On the other hand, there is nothing in this line of thought to comfort a skeptic; for if INTACT ORGANISM and THE CAUSE OF AN EVENT are indeed covertly intentional/semantic, then it looks as though belief/desire psychology isn't, after all, the only science whose practice presupposes that intentional/semantic categories are metaphysically kosher. That the organism is (relevantly) intact is part of the background idealization of practically all biological theorizing; and (so I believe) we need to distinguish between the cause of an event and its causally necessary conditions *whenever* we do the kind of science that's concerned with the explanation of particular happenings (cf. the formation of the great Siberian Crater, the extinction of the dinosaur, and the like).

So if INTACT ORGANISM and THE CAUSE are indeed intentional/semantic, then there is nothing special about belief/desire psychology after all. The availability of intentional apparatus would then be quite widely presupposed in the special sciences, so its deployment by psychologists for the explanation of behavior would require no special justification. In which case, I've just wasted a lot of time that I could have put in sailing.

Ah well!

Epilogue
Creation Myth

In principle, functionalists assure us, you can make intelligence out of almost anything. In practice, however, the situation is a little more complicated.

For example: A material substrate capable of sustaining so much as a rudimentary intelligence is likely to be quite remarkably complex in its physical constitution. Given the very nature of matter, such complex systems are invariably unstable. They come apart in what seems, when viewed under the aspect of Eternity, to be a ridiculously short time. This means that the totality of experience that any biologically feasible embodied mind has time to acquire is really quite trivial. And yet, acquired experience is surely a key to the higher forms of mentation; if experience without intelligence is blind, intelligence without experience is empty.

Bernard Shaw suggested that the best way to get a lot smarter would be to live a lot longer; he thought that one might do this simply by deciding to. But as a matter of fact—more precisely, as a fact of matter—one hasn't got the option. Embodiment implies mortality, and mortality constrains the amount of information that a mind can come to have. How, then, is embodied intelligence possible? We might call this the 'EI problem.'

The birds of the air and the beasts of the field never solved it; considered as experiments in EI, they are a dead end. The trouble with these lower forms of creation is that the cognitive achievements of their species don't accumulate. Because learned adaptations are not communicated, each individual is forced to recapitulate the intellectual history of its kind. Correspondingly, what is required for the higher manifestations of intelligence is the capacity to pool experience. Shakespeare wouldn't have gotten around to writing *Hamlet* if he had had first to rediscover fire and reinvent the wheel. What's wanted is that each new generation should somehow inherit the accumulated wisdom of its predecessors. Ideally, each *individual* should be the beneficiary of the learned adaptations of *all* of its conspecifics, cohorts, and predecessors alike.

What makes the EI problem especially interesting from an engineering point of view is that the obvious—Lamarckian—solution proves to be unfeasible. A natural way to pool the experience of conspecifics would be to allow it to affect the transmission of traits from one generation to the next. But this turns out not to be biochemically possible (and, on balance, not to be ethologically desirable either: substantial insulation of genetic material is required to maintain the genotypic stability of a species). So if, in short, the engineering problem is to design a kind of embodied intelligence that will, in the fullness of time, write *Hamlet,* then the practical bottleneck is to devise a non-Lamarckian mechanism for the transmission of acquired traits; one that is capable of preserving and communicating cognitive achievements, to put the matter in a nutshell.

Homo sapiens implements the best solution to this problem that has thus far been proposed. Given language (and other cultural artifacts), each generation can record and transmit what it has learned; and each succeeding generation can assimilate the information that is so recorded and transmitted. It turns out that this process can rapidly and cumulatively modify the characteristic behavioral phenotype of a species without resort to Lamarckian modifications of its genotype. Moreover, the same linguistic vehicle that permits *Homo sapiens* to transmit acquired information between generations also serves to effect its diffusion among contemporaries. Specialization of labor—and with it the development of expertise—follows as the night the day.

The implications of all this for EI have turned out to be positively startling. Early skepticism to the contrary notwithstanding, some biologically embodied intelligences are now able to play very decent games of chess (quite a few of them can beat computers). And, against all odds, a biologically embodied intelligence actually has written *Hamlet.* (Philosophers at Berkeley deny, however, that these initial successes will be sustained. The point out, for example, that no biologically embodied intelligence has yet succeeded in writing *Matilda,* a play that is said to be much better than *Hamlet.* Why, they ask, should we believe that a biologically embodied intelligence ever will? I stand neutral on such questions. Further research is required; speculation is premature.)

As just remarked, if *Homo sapiens* achieves moderately respectable manifestations of EI, that is largely because of the availability of linguistic and cultural mechanisms for the pooling of learned adaptations. This is, of course, an ethological commonplace and will surprise no one. But it has some implications that are less widely advertised and well worth considering.

EI presupposes a culture; and a culture presupposes a social animal, one that is capable of integrating its own behavior with the behaviors of others of its kind. But how are such integrations to be achieved? This problem has the form of a dilemma. On the one hand: The more intelligent the animal, the more it needs to be a social creature; and the more social the animal, the more it needs to coordinate its behaviors with those of conspecifics. But also: The more intelligent the animal, the more intricate its behavioral capacities; and the more intricate the behavioral capacities, the harder the problem of coordinating conspecific behaviors is going to be. You do not want to have to spend your life reinventing the wheel. But neither do you want to have to spend it learning enough about your neighbor's psychology to permit you to exploit his expertise (more generally, to permit a division of labor to be worked out between you). In short, socialization will not solve the EI problem unless a feasible solution to the coordination problem is also somehow achieved.

We are not, of course, the only species for which the coordination problem arises; every animal that moves—certainly every animal that reproduces sexually—is more or less social, so mechanisms to effect behavioral coordinations have often been evolved before. But they are typically—to borrow the inelegant AI expression—kludges; their very feasibility presupposes the stupidity of the organism that employs them.

Male sticklebacks, for example, establish territories which they defend against the encroachments of other males. The result is a solution of the ecological problem of segregating breeding pairs. In order for this solution to work, however, each male must be able to determine which of the objects in its environment is a potential rival. This is a bare minimum sort of coordination problem, and it is solved in a bare minimum sort of way. Sexually active males (but not females) develop characteristic red markings; and, reciprocally, a red marking in the perceptual environment of a sexually active male prompts a display of its territorial behavior. Since this coupling of a fixed releasing stimulus with a correspondingly fixed released response is innate, male sticklebacks don't have to waste time learning how to detect rivals or what to do about the rivals that they detect. They can instead proceed directly to the important business of generating more sticklebacks.

The point to notice, however, is that this solution works only because the ecology of sticklebacks is so impoverished. Male sticklebacks don't get around much; they breed and have their being in a world in which de facto the only things that display red patches are rival sticklebacks. The stupidity of the whole arrangement is immediately manifest when an experimenter introduces an arbitrary red object into the scene. It turns out that practically anything red elicits the territorial display; a breeding stickleback male will take Santa Claus for a rival.

Kludges work as solutions to coordination problems, but only when the behavioral repertoires to be coordinated are exiguous and stereotyped, and only when the environments in which the behaviors are exhibited are relatively static. Whereas: If social coordination is to lead to higher forms of embodied intelligence, it must be achieved across *very rich* behavioral repertoires, and across environments that keep changing as a consequence of the behavior of the very organisms that inhabit them. Moreover, the conditions for accurate coordination must be achieved *rapidly* compared to the length of an individual life. There is, as previously suggested, no use designing a social organism with a long prematurity if most of its apprentice years have to be spent learning the commonsense psychology of its species.

Here is what I would have done if I had been faced with this problem in designing *Homo sapiens*. I would have made a knowledge of commonsense *Homo sapiens* psychology *innate;* that way nobody would have to spend time learning it. And I would have made this innately apprehended commonsense psychology (at least approximately) *true,* so that the behavioral coordinations that it mediates would not depend on rigidly constraining the human behavioral repertoire or on accidental stabilities in the human ecology. Perhaps not *very much* would have to be innate and true to do the job; given the rudiments of commonsense Intentional Realism as a head start, you could maybe bootstrap the rest.

The empirical evidence that God did it the way I would have isn't, in fact, unimpressive (though, for the present speculative purposes, I don't propose to harp on it). Suffice it that: (1) Acceptance of some form of intentional explanation appears to be a cultural universal. There is, so far as I know, no human group that doesn't explain behavior by imputing beliefs and desires to the behavior. (And if an anthropologist claimed to have found such a group, I wouldn't believe him.) (2) At least in our culture, much of the apparatus of mentalistic explanation is apparently operative quite early. Developmental psychologists now admit that at least "a rudimentary awareness of the existence of the mental world is present in toddlers and preschoolers [viz., by age 2.5]" (Wellman, *CTM*, 176), and the trend—in these increasingly nativistic times—is clearly toward revising downwards the estimated age of the child's earliest displays of this sort of cognitive sophistication. The recent history of developmental psychologists' second thoughts on this matter is quite strikingly similar to what's been happening in developmental psycholinguistics: as our experimental techniques get better, infants seem to get smarter. The more we learn about how to ask the questions, the more of the answers infants seem to know. (3) I take the lack of a rival hypothesis to be a kind of empirical evidence; and there are, thus far, precisely no suggestions about how a child might acquire the apparatus of intentional explanation 'from experience.' (Unless by 'introspection'?!) Wellman (CTM) remarks that "language acquisition must be an enormous source of information: there are mental verbs to be learned such as *remember, believe, know, expect, and guess.*" How, precisely, a child who had no idea of what remembering *is* would go about learning that 'remember' is the verb that means *remember*, we are not, however, informed.

The advantage of making a theory innate is that what is innate does not have to be acquired. The advantage of making an innate theory true is that, quite generally, true theories license more reliable predictions than false theories do. God gave the male stickleback the idea that whatever is red is a rival. Because this idea is *false*, the stickleback's innate psychological theory mediates only stereotyped behavioral coordinations, and those only while adventitious ecological regularities obtain. God gave us such—rather more complicated— ideas as that if x wants that P, and x believes that not-P unless Q, and x believes that x can bring it about that Q, then ceteris paribus x tries to bring it about that Q. Because this idea is *true*, our innate psychological theory mediates vastly more flexible behavioral coordinations than the stickleback's, and will continue to do so as long as human nature doesn't change. That is one reason why we wrote *Hamlet* and the stickleback didn't.

Homo sapiens is, no doubt, uniquely the talking animal. But it is also, I suspect, uniquely the species that is born knowing its own mind.

Appendix
Why There Still Has to Be a Language of Thought

"But why", Aunty asks with perceptible asperity, "does it have to be a *language?*" Aunty speaks with the voice of the Establishment, and her intransigence is something awful. She is, however, prepared to make certain concessions in the present case. First, she concedes that there are beliefs and desires and that there is a matter of fact about their intentional contents; there's a matter of fact, that is to say, about which proposition the intentional object of a belief or a desire is. Second, Aunty accepts the coherence of physicalism. It may be that believing and desiring will prove to be states of the brain, and if they do that's OK with Aunty. Third, she is prepared to concede that beliefs and desires have causal roles and that overt behavior is typically the effect of complex interactions among these mental causes. (That Aunty was raised as a strict behaviorist goes without saying. But she hasn't been quite the same since the sixties. Which of us has?) In short, Aunty recognizes that psychological explanations need to postulate a network of causally related intentional states. "But why," she asks with perceptible asperity, "does it have to be a *language?*" Or, to put it more succinctly than Aunty often does, what—over and above mere Intentional Realism—does the Language of Thought Hypothesis buy? That is what this discussion is about.[1]

A prior question: What—over and above mere Intentional Realism—does the language of Thought Hypothesis *claim?* Here, I think, the situation is reasonably clear. To begin with, LOT wants to construe propositional-attitude tokens as relations to symbol tokens. According to standard formulations, to believe that *P* is to bear a certain relation to a token of a symbol which means that *P*. (It is generally assumed that tokens of the symbols in question are neural objects, but this assumption won't be urgent in the present discussion.) Now, symbols have intentional contents and their tokens are physical in all the known cases. And—qua physical—symbol tokens are the right sorts of things to exhibit causal roles. So there doesn't seem to be anything that LOT wants to claim *so far* that Aunty needs to feel uptight about. What, then, exactly is the issue?

Here's a way to put it. Practically everybody thinks that the *objects* of intentional states are in some way complex: for example, that what you believe when you believe that John is late for dinner is something composite whose elements are—as it might be—the concept of John and the concept of being late for dinner (or—as it might be—John himself and the property of being late for dinner). And, similarly, what you believe when you believe that *P & Q* is also something composite, whose elements are—as it might be—the proposition that *P* and the proposition that *Q*.

But the (putative) complexity of the *intentional object* of a mental state does not, of course, entail the complexity of the mental state itself. It's here that LOT ventures beyond mere Intentional Realism, and it's here that Aunty proposes to get off the bus. LOT claims that *mental states—and not just their propositional objects—typically have constituent structure.* So far as I can see, this is the *only* real difference between LOT and the sorts of Intentional Realism that even Aunty admits to be respectable. So a defense of LOT has to be an argument that believing and desiring are typically structured states.

Consider a schematic formulation of LOT that's owing to Steven Schiffer. There is, in your head, a certain mechanism, an *intention box.* To make the exposition easier, I'll assume that every intention is the intention to make some proposition true. So then, here's how it goes in your head, according to this version of LOT, when you intend to make it true that *P.* What you do is, you put into the intention box a token of a mental symbol that *means* that *P.* And what the box does is, it churns and gurgles and computes and causes and the outcome is that you behave in a way that (ceteris paribus) makes it true that *P.*

So, for example, suppose I intend to raise my left hand (I intend to make true the proposition that I raise my left hand). Then what I do is, I put in my intention box a token of a mental symbol that means 'I raise my left hand.' And then, after suitable churning and gurgling and computing and causing, my left hand goes up. (Or it doesn't, in which case the ceteris paribus condition must somehow not have been satisfied.) Much the same story would go for my intending to become the next king of France, only in that case the gurgling and churning would continue appreciably longer.

Now, it's important to see that although this is *going* to be a Language of Thought story, it's not a Language of Thought story yet. For so far all we have is what Intentional Realists qua Intentional Realists (including Aunty qua Aunty) are prepared to admit: viz., that there are mental states that have associated intentional objects (for example, the state of having a symbol that means 'I raise my left hand' in my intention box) and that these mental states that have associated intentional objects also have causal roles (for example, my being in one of these states causes my left hand to rise). What makes the story a Language of Thought story, and not just an Intentional Realist story, is the idea that these mental states that have content also have syntactic structure—constituent structure in particular—that's appropriate to the content that they have. For example, it's compatible with the story I told above that what I put in the intention box when I intend to raise my left hand is a *rock*; so long as it's a rock that's semantically evaluable. Whereas according to the LOT story, what I put in the intention box has to be something like a *sentence*; in the present case, it has to be a formula which contains, inter alia, an expression that denotes me and an expression that denotes my left hand.

Similarly, on the merely Intentional Realist story, what I put in the intention box when I intend to make it true that I raise my left hand and hop on my right foot might also be a rock (though not, of course, the same rock, since the intention to raise one's left hand is not the same as the intention to raise one's left hand and hop on one's right foot). Whereas according to the LOT story, if I intend to raise my left hand and hop on my right foot, I must put into the intention box a formula which contains, inter alia, a subexpression that means *I raise my left hand* and a subexpression that means *I hop on my right foot*.

So then, according to the LOT story, these semantically evaluable formulas that get put into intention boxes typically contain semantically evaluable subformulas as constituents; moreover, they can *share* the constituents that they contain, since, presumably, the subexpression that denotes 'foot' in 'I raise my left foot' is a token of the same type as the subexpression that denotes 'foot' in 'I raise my right foot.' (Similarly, mutatis mutandis, the '*P*' that expresses the proposition *P* in the formula '*P*' is a token of the same type as the '*P*' that expresses the proposition *P* in the formula '*P* & *Q*'.) If we wanted to be slightly more precise, we could say that the LOT story amounts to the claims that (1) (some) mental formulas have mental formulas as parts; and (2) the parts are 'transportable': the same parts can appear in *lots* of mental formulas.

It's important to see—indeed, it generates the issue that this discussion is about—that Intentional Realism doesn't logically require the LOT story; it's no sort of *necessary* truth that only formulas—only things that have syntactic structure—are semantically evaluable. No doubt it's puzzling how a rock (or the state of having a rock in your intention box) could have a propositional object; but then, it's no less puzzling how a formula (or the state of having a formula in your intention box) could have a propositional object. It is, in fact, approximately equally puzzling how *anything* could have a propositional object, which is to say that it's puzzling how Intentional Realism could be true. For better or for worse, however, Aunty and I are both assuming that Intentional Realism *is* true. The question we're arguing about isn't, then, whether mental states have a semantics. Roughly, it's whether they have a syntax. Or, if you prefer, it's whether they have a *combinatorial* semantics: the kind of semantics in which there are (relatively) complex expressions whose content is determined, in some regular way, by the content of their (relatively) simple parts.

So here, to recapitulate, is what the argument is about: Everybody thinks that mental states have intentional objects; everybody thinks that the intentional objects of mental states are characteristically complex—in effect, that propositions have parts; everybody thinks that mental states have causal roles; and, for present purposes at least, everybody is a functionalist, which is to say that we all hold that mental states are individuated, at least in part, by reference to their causal powers. (This is, of course, implicit in the talk about 'intention boxes' and the like: To be—metaphorically speaking—in the state of having such and such a rock in your intention box is just to be— literally speaking—in a state that is the normal cause of certain sorts of effects and/or the normal effect of certain sorts of causes.) What's at issue, however, is the internal structure of these functionally individuated states. Aunty thinks they have none; only the *intentional objects* of mental states are complex. I think they constitute a language; roughly, the syntactic structure of mental states mirrors the semantic relations among their intentional objects. If it seems to you that this dispute among Intentional Realists is just a domestic squabble, I agree with you. But so was the Trojan War.

In fact, the significance of the issue comes out quite clearly when Aunty turns her hand to cognitive architecture; specifically to the question 'What sorts of relations among mental states should a psychological theory recognize?' It is quite natural, given Aunty's philosophical views, for her to think of the mind as a sort of directed graph; the nodes correspond to semantically evaluable mental states, and the paths correspond to the causal connections among these states. To intend, for example, that $P \& Q$ is to be in a state that has a certain pattern of (dispositional) causal relations to the state of intending that P and to the state of intending that Q. (E.g., being in the first state is normally causally sufficient for being in the second and third.) We could diagram this relation in the familiar way illustrated in figure 1.

N.B.: In this sort of architecture, the relation between—as it might be—intending that $P \& Q$ and intending that P is a matter of *connectiv-*

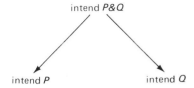

Figure 1

ity rather than *constituency*. You can see this instantly when you compare what's involved in intending that $P \& Q$ on the LOT story. On the LOT story, intending that $P \& Q$ requires having a sentence in your intention box—or, if you like, in a register or on a tape—one of whose parts is a token of the very same type that's in the intention box when you intend that P, and another of whose parts is a token of the very same type that's in the intention box when you intend that Q.

So, it turns out that the philosophical disagreement about whether there's a Language of Thought corresponds quite closely to the disagreement, current among cognitive scientists, about the appropriate architecture for mental models. If propositional attitudes have internal structure, then we need to acknowledge constituency—as well as causal connectivity—as a fundamental relation among mental states. Analogously, arguments that suggest that mental states have constituent structure ipso facto favor Turing/Von Neumann architectures, which can compute in a language whose formulas have transportable parts, as against associative networks, which by definition cannot. It turns out that dear Aunty is, of all things, a New Connectionist Groupie. If she's in trouble, so are they, and for much the same reasons.[2]

In what follows I propose to sketch three reasons for believing that cognitive states—and not just their intentional objects—typically have constituent structure. I don't suppose that these arguments are knockdown; but I do think that, taken together, they ought to convince any Aunty who hasn't a *parti pris*.

First, however, I'd better 'fess up to a metaphysical prejudice that all three arguments assume. I don't believe that there are intentional mechanisms. That is, I don't believe that contents per se determine causal roles. In consequence, it's got to be possible to tell the whole story about mental causation (the whole story about the implementation of the generalizations that belief/desire psychologies articulate) *without referring to the intentional properties of the mental states that such generalizations subsume.* Suppose, in particular, that there is something about their causal roles that requires token mental states to be com-

Figure 2

plex. Then I'm assuming that it does *not* suffice to satisfy this requirement that these mental states should have *complex intentional objects*.

This is not, by the way, any sort of epiphenomenalism; or if it is, it's patently a harmless sort. There are plenty of cases in the respectable sciences where a law connects a pair of properties, but where the properties that the law connects *don't figure in the story about how the law is implemented*. So, for example, it's a law, more or less, that tall parents have tall children. And there's a pretty neat story about the mechanisms that implement that law. But the property of *being tall* doesn't figure in the story about the implementation; all that figures in that story is *genetic* properties. You get something that looks like figure 2, where the arrows indicate routes of causation.

The moral is that even though it's true that psychological laws generally pick out the mental states that they apply to by specifying the intentional contents of the states, it *doesn't* follow that intentional properties figure in psychological mechanisms.[3] And while I'm prepared to sign on for counterfactual-supporting intentional generalizations, I balk at intentional causation. There are two reasons I can offer to sustain this prejudice (though I suspect that the prejudice goes deeper than the reasons). One of them is technical and the other is metaphysical.

Technical reason: If thoughts have their causal roles in virtue of their contents per se, then two thoughts with identical contents ought to be identical in their causal roles. And we know that this is wrong; we know that causal roles *slice things thinner* than contents do. The thought that $--P$, for example, has the same content as the thought that P on any notion of content that I can imagine defending; but the effects of entertaining these thoughts are nevertheless not guaranteed to be the same. Take a mental life in which the thought that $P \& (P \rightarrow Q)$ immediately and spontaneously gives rise to the thought that Q; there is *no* guarantee that the thought that $--P \& (P \rightarrow Q)$ immediately and spontaneously gives rise to the thought that Q in that mental life.

Metaphysical reason: It looks as though intentional properties essentially involve relations between mental states and *merely possible* contingencies. For example, it's plausible that for a thought to have the content THAT SNOW IS BLACK is for that thought to be related, in a certain way, to the possible (but nonactual) state of affairs in which snow is black; viz., it's for the thought to be true just in case that state of affairs obtains. Correspondingly, what distinguishes the content of the thought that snow is black from the content of the thought that grass is blue is differences among the truth values that these thoughts have in possible but nonactual worlds.

Now, the following metaphysical principle strikes me as plausible: the causal powers of a thing are not affected by its relations to merely possible entities; only relations to *actual* entities affect causal powers. It is, for example, a determinant of my causal powers that I am standing on the brink of a high cliff. But it is *not* a determinant of my causal powers that I am standing on the brink of a possible-but-nonactual high cliff; I can't throw myself off one of *those,* however hard I try.[4]

Well, if this metaphysical principle is right, and if it's right that intentional properties essentially involve relations to nonactual objects, then it would follow that intentional properties are not per se determinants of causal powers, hence that there are no intentional mechanisms. I admit, however, that that is a fair number of ifs to hang an intuition on.

OK, now for the arguments that mental states, and not just their intentional objects, are structured entities.

1. A Methodological Argument

I don't, generally speaking, much like methodological arguments; who wants to win by a TKO? But in the present case, it seems to me that Aunty is being a little unreasonable even by her own lights. Here is a plausible rule of nondemonstrative inference that I take her to be at risk of breaking:

> Principle P: Suppose there is a kind of event c_1 of which the normal effect is a kind of event e_1; and a kind of event c_2 of which the normal effect is a kind of event e_2; and a kind of event c_3 of which the normal effect is a complex event e_1 & e_2. Viz.:
>
> $c_1 \rightarrow e_1$
> $c_2 \rightarrow e_2$
> $c_3 \rightarrow e_1$ & e_2
>
> Then, ceteris paribus, it is reasonable to infer that c_3 is a complex event whose constituents include c_1 and c_2.

So, for example, suppose there is a kind of event of which the normal effect is a bang and a kind of event of which the normal effect is a stink, and a kind of event of which the normal effect is that kind of a bang and that kind of a stink. Then, according to P, it is ceteris paribus reasonable to infer that the third kind of event consists (inter alia) of the co-occurrence of events of the first two kinds.

You may think that this rule is arbitrary, but I think that it isn't; P is just a special case of a general principle which untendentiously requires us to prefer theories that *minimize accidents*. For, if the etiology of events that are e1 and e2 does not somehow include the etiology of events that are e1 but not e2, then it must be that there are *two* ways of producing e1 events; and the convergence of these (ex hypothesi) distinct etiologies upon events of type e1 is, thus far, unexplained. (It won't do, of course, to reply that the convergence of two etiologies is only a very *little* accident. For in principle, the embarrassment *iterates*. Thus, you can imagine a kind of event c4, of which the normal effect is a complex event e1 & e6 & e7; and a kind of event c5, of which the normal effect is a complex event e1 & e10 & e12 . . . etc. And now, if P is flouted, we'll have to tolerate a *four*-way accident. That is, barring P—and all else being equal—we'll have to allow that theories which postulate four kinds of causal histories for e1 events are just as good as theories which postulate only one kind of causal history for e1 events. It is, to put it mildly, hard to square this with the idea that we value our theories for the generalizations they articulate.

Well, the moral seems clear enough. Let c1 be intending to raise your left hand, and e1 be raising your left hand; let c2 be intending to hop on your right foot, and e2 be hopping on your right foot; let c3 be intending to raise your left hand and hop on your right foot, and e3 be raising your left hand and hopping on your right foot. Then the choices are: *either* we respect P and hold that events of the c3 type are complexes which have events of type c1 as constituents, *or* we flout P and posit two etiologies for e1 events, the convergence of these etiologies being, thus far, accidental. I repeat that what's at issue here is the complexity of mental events and not merely the complexity of the propositions that are their intentional objects. P is a principle that constrains etiological inferences, and—according to the prejudice previously confessed to—the intentional properties of mental states are ipso facto *not* etiological.

But we're not home yet. There's a way out that Aunty has devised; she is, for all her faults, a devious old dear. Aunty could accept P but deny that (for example) raising your left hand counts as *the same sort of* event on occasions when you *just* raise your left hand as it does on occasions when you raise your left hand while you hop on your right foot. In effect, Aunty can avoid admitting that *intentions* have constituent structure if she's prepared to deny that *behavior* has constituent structure. A principle like P, which governs the assignment of etiologies to complex events, will be vacuously satisfied in psychology if no behaviors are going to count as complex.

But Aunty's back is to the wall; she is, for once, constrained by vulgar fact. Behavior does—very often—exhibit constituent structure, and that it does is vital to its explanation, at least as far as anybody knows. Verbal behavior is the paradigm, of course; everything in linguistics, from phonetics to semantics, depends on the fact that verbal forms are put together from recurrent elements; that, for example, [oon] occurs in both 'Moon' and 'June.' But it's not just verbal behavior for whose segmental analysis we have pretty conclusive evidence; indeed, it's not just *human* behavior. It turns out, for one example in a plethora, that bird song is a tidy system of recurrent phrases; we lose 'syntactic' generalizations of some elegance if we refuse to so describe it.

To put the point quite generally, psychologists have a use for the distinction between segmented behaviors and what they call "synergisms." (Synergisms are cases where what appear to be behavioral elements are in fact 'fused' to one another, so that the whole business functions as a unit; as when a well-practiced pianist plays a fluent arpeggio.) Since it's empirically quite clear that not all behavior is synergistic, it follows that Aunty may not, in aid of her philosophical prejudices, simply help herself to the contrary assumption.

Now we *are* home. If, as a matter of fact, behavior is often segmented, then principle P requires us to prefer the theory that the causes of behavior are complex over the theory that they aren't, all else being equal. And all else *is* equal to the best of my knowledge. For if Aunty has any *positive* evidence against the LOT story, she has been keeping it very quiet. Which wouldn't be at all like Aunty, I assure you.[5]

Argument 2. Psychological Processes (Why Aunty Can't Have Them for Free)

In the cognitive sciences mental symbols are the rage. Psycholinguists, in particular, often talk in ways that make Aunty simply livid. For example, they say things like this: "When you understand an utterance of a sentence, what you do is construct a *mental representation* [sic; emphasis mine] of the sentence that is being uttered. To a first approximation, such a representation is a parsing tree; and this parsing tree specifies the constituent structure of the sentence you're hearing, together with the categories to which its constituents belong. Parsing trees are constructed left to right, bottom to top, with re-

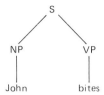

Figure 3

stricted look ahead . . ." and so forth, depending on the details of the psycholinguist's story. Much the same sort of examples could be culled from the theory of vision (where mental operations are routinely identified with transformations of structural descriptions of scenes) or, indeed, from any other area of recent perceptual psychology.

Philosophical attention is hereby directed to the logical form of such theories. They certainly look to be quantifying over a specified class of mental objects: in the present case, over parsing trees. The usual apparatus of ontological commitment—existential quantifiers, bound variables, and such—is abundantly in evidence. So you might think that Aunty would argue like this: "When I was a girl, ontology was thought to be an a priori science; but now I'm told that view is out of fashion. If, therefore, psychologists say that there are mental representations, then I suppose that there probably are. I therefore subscribe to the Language of Thought hypothesis." That is not, however, the way that Aunty actually does argue. Far from it.

Instead, Aunty regards Cognitive Science in much the same light as Sodom, Gomorrah, and Los Angeles. If there is one thing that Aunty believes in in her bones, it is the ontological promiscuity of psychologists. So in the present case, although psycholinguists may *talk as though* they were professionally committed to mental representations, Aunty takes that to be *loose* talk. Strictly speaking, she explains, the offending passages can be translated out with no loss to the explanatory/predictive power of psychological theories. Thus, an ontologically profligate psycholinguist may speak of perceptual processes that construct a parsing tree; say, one that represents a certain utterance as consisting of a noun phrase followed by a verb phrase, as in figure 3.

But Aunty recognizes no such processes and quantifies over no such trees. What she admits instead are (1) the utterance under perceptual analysis (the 'distal' utterance, as I'll henceforth call it) and (2) a mental process which eventuates in the distal utterance being *heard as* consisting of a noun phrase followed by a verb phrase. Notice that this ontologically purified account, though it recognizes mental states

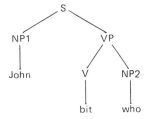

Figure 4

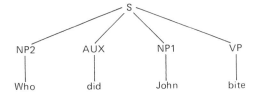

Figure 5

with their intentional contents, does not recognize mental representations. Indeed, the point of the proposal is precisely to emphasize as live for Intentional Realists the option of postulating representational mental states and then crying halt. If the translations go through, then the facts which psychologists take to argue for mental representations don't actually do so; and if those facts don't, then maybe nothing does.

Well, but *do* the translations go through? On my view, the answer is that some do and others don't, and that the ones that don't make the case for a Language of Thought. This will take some sorting out.

Mental representations do two jobs in theories that employ them. First, they provide a canonical notation for specifying the intentional contents of mental states. But second, mental symbols constitute domains over which *mental processes* are defined. If you think of a mental process—extensionally, as it were—as a sequence of mental states each specified with reference to its intentional content, then mental representations provide a mechanism for the construction of these sequences; they allow you to get, in a mechanical way, from one such state to the next *by performing operations on the representations.*

Suppose, for example, that this is how it goes with English wh-questions: Such sentences have two constituent structures, one in which the questioned phrase is in the object position, as per figure 4, and one in which the questioned phrase is in the subject position, as per figure 5. And suppose that the psycholinguistic story is that the perceptual analysis of utterances of such sentences requires the assignment of these constituent structures in, as it might be, reverse order. Well, Aunty can tell *that* story *without* postulating mental representations; a fortiori without postulating mental representations that have constituent structure. She does so by talking about *the intentional contents of the hearer's mental states* rather than the mental representations he constructs. "The hearer," Aunty says, "starts out by representing the distal utterance as having 'John' in the subject position and a questioned NP in the object position; and he ends up by representing the distal utterance as having these NPs in the reverse configuration. Thus we see that when it's *properly* construed, claims about 'perceiving as' are all that talk about mental representation ever really comes to." Says Aunty.

But in saying this, it seems to me that Aunty goes too fast. For what *doesn't* paraphrase out this way is the idea that the hearer gets from one of these representational states to the other *by moving a piece of the parsing tree* (e.g., by moving the piece that represents 'who' as a constituent of the type NP2). This untranslated part of the story isn't, notice, about what intentional contents the hearer entertains or the order in which he entertains them. Rather, it's about the mechanisms that mediate the transitions among his intentional states. Roughly, the story says that the mechanism of mental state transitions is *computational;* and if the story's true, then (a) there must *be* parsing trees to define the computations over, and (b) these parsing trees need to have a kind of structure that will sustain talk of moving part of a tree while leaving the rest of it alone. In effect, they need to have constituent structure.

I must now report a quirk of Aunty's that I do not fully understand: she refuses to take seriously the ontological commitments of computational theories of mental processes. This is all the more puzzling because Aunty is usually content to play by the following rule: Given a well-evidenced empirical theory, either you endorse the entities that it's committed to or you find a paraphrase that preserves the theory while dispensing with the commitments. Aunty holds that this is simply good deportment for a philosopher; and I, for once, agree with her completely. So, as we've seen, Aunty has a proposal for deontologizing the computational story about which state understanding a sentence is: she proposes to translate talk about trees in the head into talk about hearing utterances under descriptions, and that seems to be all right as far as it goes. But it doesn't go far enough, because the ontological commitments of psychological theories are inherited not just from their account of mental states but also from their account of mental processes; and the computational account of mental processes would appear to be *ineliminably* committed to mental representations construed as structured objects.

The moral, I suppose, is that if Aunty won't bite the bullet, she will have to pay the piper. As things stand now, the cost of not having a Language of Thought is not having a theory of thinking. It's a striking fact about the philosophy of mind that we've indulged for the last fifty years or so that it's been quite content to pony up this price. Thus, while an eighteenth-century Empiricist—Hume, say—took it for granted that a theory of cognitive *processes* (specifically, Associationism) would have to be the cornerstone of psychology, modern philosophers—like Wittgenstein and Ryle and Gibson and Aunty—*have* no theory of thought to speak of. I do think this is appalling; how can you seriously hope for a good account of belief if you have no account of belief *fixation?* But I don't think it's entirely surprising. Modern philosophers who haven't been overt behaviorists have quite generally been covert behaviorists. And while a behaviorist can recognize mental states—which he identifies with behavioral dispositions—he has literally no use for cognitive processes such as causal trains of thought. The last thing a behaviorist wants is mental causes ontologically distinct from their behavioral effects.

It may be that Aunty has not quite outgrown the behaviorist legacy of her early training (it's painfully obvious that Wittgenstein, Ryle, and Gibson never did). Anyhow, if you ask her what she's prepared to recognize in place of computational mental processes, she unblushingly replies (I quote): "Unknown Neurological Mechanisms." (I think she may have gotten that from John Searle, whose theory of thinking it closely resembles.) If you then ask her whether it's not sort of unreasonable to prefer no psychology of thought to a computational psychology of thought, she affects a glacial silence. Ah well, there's nothing can be done with Aunty when she stands upon her dignity and strikes an Anglo-Saxon attitude—except to try a different line of argument.

Argument 3. Productivity and Systematicity

The classical argument that mental states are complex adverts to the productivity of the attitudes. There is a (potentially) infinite set of—for example—belief-state types, each with its distinctive intentional object and its distinctive causal role. This is immediately explicable on the assumption that belief states have combinatorial structure; that they are somehow built up out of elements and that the intentional object and causal role of each such state depends on what elements it contains and how they are put together. The LOT story is, of course, a paradigm of this sort of explanation, since it takes believing to involve a relation to a syntactically structured object for which a compositional semantics is assumed.

There is, however, a notorious problem with productivity arguments. The facts of mortality being what they are, not more than a finite part of any mental capacity ever actually gets exploited. So it requires idealization to secure the crucial premise that mental capacities really *are* productive. It is, for example, quite possible to deny the *productivity* of thought even while admitting that people are forever thinking new things. You can imagine a story—vaguely Gibsonian in spirit—according to which cognitive capacity involves a sort of 'tuning' of the brain. What happens, on this view, is that you have whatever experiences engender such capacities, and the experiences have Unknown Neurological Effects (these Unknown Neurological Effects being mediated, it goes without saying, by the corresponding Unknown Neurological Mechanisms), and the upshot is that you come to have a very large—but finite—number of, as it were, *independent* mental dispositions. E.g., the disposition to think that the cat is on the mat on some occasions; and the disposition to think that 3 is prime on other occasions; and the disposition to think that secondary qualities are epiphenomenal on other occasions . . . and so forth. New occasions might thus provoke novel thoughts; and yet the capacity to think wouldn't have to be productive. In principle it could turn out, after a lot of thinking, that your experience catches up with your cognitive capacities so that you actually succeed in thinking everything that you are able to. It's no good saying that you take this consequence to be absurd; I agree with you, but Aunty doesn't.

In short, it needs productivity to establish that thoughts have combinatorial structure, and it needs idealization to establish productivity; so it's open to Somebody who doesn't want to admit productivity (because, for example, She doesn't like LOT) simply to refuse to idealize. This is, no doubt, an empirical issue in the very long run. Scientific idealization is demonstrably appropriate if it eventually leads to theories that are independently well confirmed. But vindication in the very long run is a species of cold comfort; perhaps there's a way to get the goodness out of productivity arguments *without* relying on idealizations that are plausibly viewed as tendentious.

Here's how I propose to argue:

(a) There's a certain property that linguistic capacities have in virtue of the fact that natural languages have a combinatorial semantics.
(b) Thought has this property too.
(c) So thought too must have a combinatorial semantics.

Aunty, reading over my shoulder, remarks that this has the form of affirmation of the consequent. So be it; one man's affirmation of the consequent is another man's inference to the best explanation.

The property of linguistic capacities that I have in mind is one that inheres in the ability to understand and produce sentences. That ability is—as I shall say—*systematic:* by which I mean that the ability to produce/understand some of the sentences is *intrinsically* connected to the ability to produce/understand many of the others. You can see the force of this if you compare learning a language the way we really do learn them with learning a language by memorizing an enormous phrase book. The present point isn't that phrase books are finite and can therefore exhaustively describe only nonproductive languages; that's true, but I've sworn off productivity arguments for the duration of this discussion, as explained above. The point that I'm now pushing is that you can learn *any part* of a phrase book *without learning the rest*. Hence, on the phrase book model, it would be perfectly possible to learn that uttering the form of words 'Granny's cat is on Uncle Arthur's mat' is the way to say that Granny's cat is on Uncle Arthur's mat, and yet have no idea how to say that it's raining (or, for that matter, how to say that Uncle Arthur's cat is on Granny's mat). I pause to rub this point in. I know—to a first approximation—how to say 'Who does his mother love very much?' in Korean; viz., *ki-iy emma-ka nuku-lil mewu saranna-ci?* But since I did get this from a phrase book, it helps me not at all with saying anything else in Korean. In fact, I don't know how to say anything else in Korean; I have just shot my bolt.

Perhaps it's self-evident that the phrase book story must be wrong about language acquisition because a speaker's knowledge of his native language is never like that. You don't, for example, find native speakers who know how to say in English that John loves Mary but don't know how to say in English that Mary loves John. If you did find someone in such a fix, you'd take that as presumptive evidence that he's not a native English speaker but some sort of a tourist. (This is one important reason why it is so misleading to speak of the block/slab game that Wittgenstein describes in paragraph 2 of the *Investigations* as a "complete primitive language"; to think of languages that way is precisely to miss the systematicity of linguistic capacities—to say nothing of their productivity.)

Notice, by the way, that systematicity (again like productivity) is a property of sentences but not of words. The phrase book model really *does* fit what it's like to learn the *vocabulary* of English, since when you learn English vocabulary you acquire a lot of basically *independent* dispositions. So you might perfectly well learn that using the form of words 'cat' is the way to refer to cats and yet have no idea that using the form of words 'deciduous conifer' is the way to refer to deciduous conifers. My linguist friends tell me that there are languages—unlike English—in which the lexicon, as well as the syntax, is productive. It's candy from babies to predict that a native speaker's mastery of the vocabulary of such a language is always systematic. Productivity and systematicity run together; if you postulate mechanisms adequate to account for the one, then—assuming you're prepared to idealize— you get the other automatically.

What sort of mechanisms? Well, the alternative to the phrase book story about acquisition depends on the idea, more or less standard in the field since Frege, that the sentences of a natural language have a combinatorial semantics (and, mutatis mutandis, that the lexicon does in languages where the lexicon is productive). On this view, learning a language is learning a perfectly general procedure for de- termining the meaning of a sentence from a specification of its syn- tactic structure together with the meanings of its lexical elements. Linguistic capacities *can't help but* be systematic on this account, be- cause, give or take a bit, the very same combinatorial mechanisms that determine the meaning of any of the sentences determine the meaning of all of the rest.

Notice two things:

First, you can make these points about the systematicity of lan- guage without idealizing to astronomical computational capacities. *Productivity* is involved with our ability to understand sentences that are a billion trillion zillion words long. But *systematicity* involves facts that are much nearer home: such facts as the one we mentioned above, that no native speaker comes to understand the form of words 'John loves Mary' except as he *also* comes to understand the form of words 'Mary loves John.' Insofar as there are 'theory neutral' data to constrain our speculations about language, this surely ought to count as one of them.

Second, if the systematicity of linguistic capacities turns on sen- tences having a combinatorial semantics, the fact that sentences have a combinatorial semantics turns on their having constituent structure. You can't construct the meaning of an object out of the meanings of its constituents unless it *has* constituents. The sentences of English wouldn't have a combinatorial semantics if they weren't made out of recurrent words and phrases.

OK, so here's the argument: Linguistic capacities are systematic, and that's because sentences have constituent structure. But cogni- tive capacities are systematic too, and that must be because *thoughts* have constituent structure. But if thoughts have constituent structure, then LOT is true. So I win and Aunty loses. Goody!

I take it that what needs defending here is the idea that cognitive capacities are systematic, *not* the idea that the systematicity of cognitive capacities implies the combinatorial structure of thoughts. I get the second claim for free for want of an alternative account. So then, how do we know that cognitive capacities are systematic?

A fast argument is that cognitive capacities must be *at least* as systematic as linguistic capacities, since the function of language is to express thought. To understand a sentence is to grasp the thought that its utterance standardly conveys; so it wouldn't be possible that everyone who understands the sentence 'John loves Mary' also understands the sentence 'Mary loves John' if it weren't that everyone who can *think the thought* that John loves Mary can also think the thought that Mary loves John. You can't have it that language expresses thought *and* that language is systematic unless you also have it that thought is as systematic as language is.

And that is quite sufficiently systematic to embarrass Aunty. For, of course, the systematicity of thought does *not* follow from what Aunty is prepared to concede: viz., from mere Intentional Realism. If having the thought that John loves Mary is just being in one Unknown But Semantically Evaluable Neurological Condition, and having the thought that Mary loves John is just being in another Unknown But Semantically Evaluable Neurological Condition, then it is—to put it mildly—not obviously why God couldn't have made a creature that's capable of being in one of these Semantically Evaluable Neurological conditions but not in the other, hence a creature that's capable of thinking one of these thoughts but not the other. But if it's compatible with Intentional Realism that God could have made such a creature, then Intentional Realism doesn't explain the systematicity of thought; as we've seen, Intentional Realism is exhausted by the claim that there *are* Semantically Evaluable Neurological Conditions.

To put it in a nutshell, what you need to explain the systematicity of thought appears to be Intentional Realism *plus LOT*. LOT says that having a thought is being related to a structured array of representations; and, presumably, to have the thought that John loves Mary is ipso facto to have access to the same representations, and the same representational structures, that you need to have the thought that Mary loves John. So *of course* anybody who is in a position to have one of these thoughts is ipso facto in a position to have the other. LOT explains the systematicity of thought; mere Intentional Realism doesn't (and neither, for *exactly* the same reasons, does Connectionism). Thus I refute Aunty and her friends!

Four remarks to tidy up:

First, this argument takes it for granted that systematicity is *at least sometimes* a contingent feature of thought; that there are *at least some cases* in which it is logically possible for a creature to be able to entertain one but not the other of two content-related propositions.

I want to remain neutral, however, on the question whether systematicity is *always* a contingent feature of thought. For example, a philosopher who is committed to a strong 'inferential role' theory of the individuation of the logical concepts might hold that you can't, in principle, think the thought that (*P* or *Q*) unless you are able to think the thought that *P*. (The argument might be that the ability to infer (*P* or *Q*) from *P* is *constitutive of having* the concept of disjunction.) If this claim is right, then—to that extent—you don't need LOT to explain the systematicity of thoughts which contain the concept OR; it simply *follows from* the fact that you can think that '*P* or *Q*' that you can also think that *P*.

Aunty is, of course, at liberty to try to explain *all* the facts about the systematicity of thought in this sort of way. I wish her joy of it. It seems to me perfectly clear that there could be creatures whose mental capacities constitute a proper subset of our own; creatures whose mental lives—viewed from our perspective—appear to contain gaps. If inferential role semantics denies this, then so much the worse for inferential role semantics.

Second: It is, as always, essential not to confuse the properties of the attitudes with the properties of their objects. I suppose that it *is* necessarily true that the *propositions* are 'systematic'; i.e., that if there is the proposition that John loves Mary, then there is also the proposition that Mary loves John. But that necessity is no use to Aunty, since it doesn't explain the systematicity of our capacity to *grasp* the propositions. What LOT explains—and, to repeat, mere Intentional Realism does not—is a piece of our empirical psychology: the de facto, contingent connection between our ability to think one thought and our ability to think another.

Third: Many of Aunty's best friends hold that there is something very special about language; that it is only when we come to explaining linguistic capacities that we need the theoretical apparatus that LOT provides. But in fact, we can kick the ladder away: we don't need the systematicity of language to argue for the systematicity of thought. All we need is that it is on the one hand true, and on the other hand not a *necessary* truth, that whoever is able to think that John loves Mary is ipso facto able to think that Mary loves John.

Of course, Aunty has the option of arguing the *empirical* hypothesis that thought is systematic only for creatures that speak a language.

But think what it would mean for this to be so. It would have to be quite usual to find, for example, animals capable of learning to respond selectively to a situation such that *a R b*, but quite unable to learn to respond selectively to a situation such that *b R a* (so that you could teach the beast to choose the picture with the square larger than the triangle, but you couldn't for the life of you teach it to choose the picture with the triangle larger than the square). I am not into rats and pigeons, but I once had a course in Comp Psych, and I'm prepared to assure you that animal minds aren't, in general, like that.

It may be partly a matter of taste whether you take it that the minds of animals are *productive;* but it's about as empirical as anything can be whether they are systematic. And—by and large—they are.

Fourth: Just a little systematicity of thought will do to make things hard for Aunty, since, as previously remarked, mere Intentional Realism is compatible with there being no systematicity of thought at all. And this is just as well, because although we can be sure that thought is somewhat systematic, we can't, perhaps, be sure of just how systematic it is. The point is that if we are unable to think the thought that *P,* then I suppose we must also be unable to think the thought that we are unable to think the thought that *P.* So it's at least arguable that to the extent that our cognitive capacities are *not* systematic, the fact that they aren't is bound to escape our attention. No doubt this opens up some rather spooky epistemic possibilities; but, as I say, it doesn't matter for the polemical purposes at hand. The fact that there are *any* contingent connections between our capacities for entertaining propositions is remarkable when rightly considered. I know of no account of this fact that isn't tantamount to LOT. And neither does Aunty.

So we've found at least three reasons for preferring LOT to mere Intentional Realism, and three reasons ought to be enough for anybody's Aunty. But is there any general moral to discern? Maybe there's this one:

If you look at the mind from what has recently become the philosopher's favorite point of view, it's the semantic evaluability of mental states that looms large. What's puzzling about the mind is that anything *physical* could have satisfaction conditions, and the polemics that center around Intentional Realism are the ones that this puzzle generates. On the other hand, if you look at the mind from the cognitive psychologist's viewpoint, the main problems are the ones about mental processes. What puzzles psychologists is belief fixation—and, more generally, the contingent, causal relations that hold among states of mind. The characteristic doctrines of modern cognitive psychology (including, notably, the idea that mental processes are computational) are thus largely motivated by problems about mental causation. Not surprisingly, given this divergence of main concerns, it looks to philosophers as though the computational theory of mind is mostly responsive to technical worries about mechanism and implementation; and it looks to psychologists as though Intentional Realism is mostly responsive to metaphysical and ontological worries about the place of content in the natural order. So, deep down, what philosophers and psychologists really want to say to one another is, "Why do you care so much about *that?"*

Now as Uncle Hegel used to enjoy pointing out, the trouble with perspectives is that they are, by definition, *partial* points of view; the Real problems are appreciated only when, in the course of the development of the World Spirit, the limits of perspective come to be transcended. Or, to put it less technically, it helps to be able to see the whole elephant. In the present case, I think the whole elephant looks like this: The key to the nature of cognition is that mental processes preserve semantic properties of mental states; trains of thought, for example, are generally truth preserving, so if you start your thinking with true assumptions you will generally arrive at conclusions that are also true. The central problem about the cognitive mind is to understand how this is so. And my point is that neither the metaphysical concerns that motivate Intentional Realists nor the problems about implementation that motivate cognitive psychologists suffice to frame this issue. To see this issue, you have to look at the problems about content and the problems about process *at the same time.* Thus far has the World Spirit progressed.

If Aunty's said it once, she's said it a hundred times: Children should play nicely together and respect each other's points of view. I do think Aunty's right about that.

Notes

Chapter 1

1. Perhaps there are laws that relate the *brain states* of organisms to their motions. But then again, perhaps there aren't, since it seems entirely possible that the lawful connections should hold between brain states and *actions* where, as usual, actions cross-classify movements. This is, perhaps, what you would predict upon reflection. Would you really expect the same brain state that causes the utterance of 'dog' in tokens of 'dog' to be the one that causes it in tokens of 'dogmatic'? How about utterances of (the phonetic sequence) [empedokliz lipt] when you're talking English and when you're talking German?

2. The trouble with transcendental arguments being, however, that it's not obvious why a theory couldn't be both indispensable and *false*. I wouldn't want to buy a transcendental deduction of the attitudes if operationalism were the price I had to pay for it.

3. Denying the etiological involvement of mental states was really what behaviorism was about; it's what 'logical' behaviorists and 'eliminativists' had in common. Thus, for example, to hold—as Ryle did, more or less—that mental states are species of dispositions is to refuse to certify as literally causal such psychological explanations as "He did it with the intention of pleasing her," or, for that matter, "His headache made him groan," to say nothing of "The mere thought of giving a lecture makes him ill." (For discussion, see Fodor, *SSA*.)

4. Some philosophers feel very strongly about enforcing an object/state (or maybe object/event) distinction here, so that what have *causal powers* are tokenings of mental state types (e.g., Hamlet's *believing* that Claudius killed his father), but what have *semantic values* are *propositions* (e.g., the proposition that Claudius killed Hamlet's father). The point is that it sounds odd to say that Hamlet's *believing* that *P* is true but all right to say that Hamlet's *belief* that *P* is.

   I'm not convinced that this distinction is one that I will care about in the long run, since sounding odd is the least of my problems and in the long run I expect I want to do without propositions altogether. However, if you are squeamish about ontology, that's all right with me. In that case, the point in the text should be: Belief/desire psychology attributes causal properties to the very same things (viz., tokenings of certain mental state types) to which it attributes propositional objects. It is thus true of Hamlet's believing that Claudius killed his father both that it is implicated in the etiology of his behavior Gertrudeward and that it has as its object a certain belief, viz., the proposition that Claudius killed his father. If we then speak of Hamlet's *state* of believing that Claudius killed his father (or of the event which consists of the tokening of that state) as semantically evaluable, we can take that as an abbreviation for a more precise way of talking: The state *S* has the semantic value *V* iff *S* has as its object a proposition whose value is *V*.

It goes without saying that none of this ontological fooling around makes the slightest progress toward removing the puzzles about intentionality. If (on my way of talking) it's metaphysically worrying that beliefs and desires are semantically evaluable though trees, rocks, and prime numbers aren't, it's equally metaphysically worrying (on the orthodox way of talking) that believings have propositional objects though trees, rocks, and prime numbers don't.

5. *Any* nomic property of symbol tokens, however—any property in virtue of the posession of which they satisfy causal laws—would, in principle, do just as well. (So, for example, syntactic structure could be realized by relations among electromagnetic states rather than relations among shapes; as, indeed, it is in real computers.) This is the point of the Functionalist doctrine that, in principle, you can make a mind out of almost anything.

6. Which is not to deny that there are (ahem!) certain residual technical difficulties. (See, for example, part 4 of Fodor, *MOM.*) A theory of rationality (i.e., a theory of *our* rationality) has to account not merely for the 'semantic coherence' of thought processes in the abstract but for our ability to pull off the very sorts of rational inferences that we do. (It has to account for our ability to make science, for example.) No such theory will be available by this time next week.

7. Because I don't want to worry about the ontology of mind, I've avoided stating RTM as an identity thesis. But you could do if you were so inclined.

8. Like Dennett, I'm assuming for purposes of argument that the machine *has* thoughts and mental processes; nothing hangs on this, since we could, of course, have had the same discussion about people.

9. We can now see what to say about the philosophical chestnut about Kepler's Law. The allegation is that intentionalist methodology permits the inference from 'x's behavior complies with rule R' to 'R is a rule that x explicitly represents.' The embarrassment is supposed to be that this allows the inference from 'The movements of the planets comply with Kepler's Law' to some astronomical version of LOT.

But in fact no such principle of inference is assumed. What warrants the hypothesis that R is explicitly represented is not mere behavior in compliance with R; it's an etiology according to which R figures as the content of one of the intentional states whose tokenings are causally responsible for x's behavior. And, of course, it's *not* part of the etiological story about the motions of the planets that Kepler's Law occurs to them as they proceed upon their occasions.

Chapter 2

1. If, however, Loar (*SCPC*) is right, then the commonsense taxonomy actually fits pattern B; i.e., common sense and psychology both individuate the attitudes narrowly and both respect supervenience.

So far as I know, nobody has explicitly endorsed the fourth logically possible option—viz., that commonsense taxonomy is narrow and psychological taxonomy relational—though I suppose Skinner and his followers may implicitly hold some such view.

2. Notice that taking this line wouldn't commit Burge to a violation of *physicalism;* the differences between the attitudes of Twins and Oscars supervene on the (inter alia, physical) differences between their worlds. Or rather, they do assuming that the relevant differences between the linguistic practices in Oscar's speech community and Oscar2's are physicalistically specifiable. (I owe this caveat to James Higgenbotham.)

3. No need to dogmatize, however, There may be scientific enterprises that are not—
   or not primarily—interested in causal explanation; natural history, for example.
   And in these sciences it is perhaps not identity and difference of causal powers that
   provide the criterion for taxonomic identity. But either propositional-attitude psychology is in the business of causal explanation or it is out of work.
       To put it at a minimum, if there is so much as a presumption of scientific utility in
   favor of a taxonomy by causal powers, then if—as I'm arguing—the causal powers
   of the mental states of Twins are ipso facto identical, then there is a corresponding
   presumption in favor of the utility of narrow individuation in psychology.

4. The implication is that commonsense attitude attributions aren't—or rather, aren't
   solely—in aid of causal explanation; and this appears to be true. One reason why
   you might want to know what Psmith believes is in order to predict how he will
   behave. But another reason is that beliefs are often true, so if you know what
   Psmith believes, you have some basis for inferring how the world is. The relevant
   property of Psmith's beliefs for this latter purpose, however, is not their causal
   powers but something like *what information they transmit* (see Dretske, *KFI*). And,
   quite generally, what information a thing transmits depends on relational properties of the thing which may not affect its causal powers. My utterance 'water is wet'
   has, let's say, the same causal powers as my Twin's; but—assuming that both
   utterances are true—one transmits the information that H_2O is wet and the other
   transmits the information that XYZ is.
       It is, I think, the fact that attitude ascriptions serve both masters that is at the
   bottom of many of their logical peculiarities; of the pervasiveness of opacity/
   transparency ambiguities, for example.

5. Since all brisket2 is brisket (though not vice versa), every brisket2 purchase is a
   brisket purchase. This, however, is a consideration not profoundly relevant to the
   point at issue.

6. This is a little unfair—but, I think, *only* a little. There is, after all, *no causal relation at
   all* between my coin and the particles on Alpha Centauri whose causal powers its
   orientation is alleged to affect. Whereas, by contrast, there is supposed to be a
   causal relation between my Twin's 'water'-thoughts and XYZ puddles (mutatis
   mutandis, between my water-thoughts and H_2O puddles) in virtue of which the
   thoughts refer to the stuff that they do. Similarly, it might be supposed that the
   semantic effects of linguistic coaffiliation require causal relations among the members of the language community so affected. (Though maybe not; it's sometimes
   suggested that the mere existence of experts in my language community shapes the
   contents of my mental states, whether or not there's a causal chain that connects
   us.)
       But this hardly seems enough to meet the present worry, which isn't that my
   coin affects particles 'at a distance,' but that such relations as there are between the
   coin and the particles *aren't the right kind* to affect the causal powers of the latter.
   The point is that just specifying that *some causal relation or other* obtains isn't enough
   to plug this hole. Effects on causal powers require mediation by laws and/or mechanisms; and, in the Twin cases, there are no such mechanisms and no such laws.
       If you are inclined to doubt this, notice that for any causal relation that holds
   between my mental states and the local water puddles, there must be a corresponding relation that holds between my *neurological* states and the local water
   puddles; a sort of causal relation into which, by assumption, my Twin's neurological states do not enter. Despite which, the intuition persists that my neurological
   states and my Twin's are taxonomically identical. Why? Because the difference in
   the causal *histories* of our brain states is not of the right sort to effect a difference in

the causal *powers* of our brains. And qua scientific, neurological taxonomy groups *by* causal powers.

Parallelism of argument surely requires us to hold that the differences between the causal histories of the mental states of Twins are not of the right sort to effect differences in the causal powers of their minds. And, qua scientific, *psychological* taxonomy groups by causal powers too.

7. Burge points out (personal communication) that the Oscars' food preferences *don't* differ if you individuate *de re;* i.e., that brisket and gruel are such that *both* Oscars prefer the former to the latter (a fact that Psyche could establish by testing them on samples). But I don't see that this helps, since it seems to me thoroughly implausible that linguistic affiliation per se determines food preferences de dicto.

If it does, that opens up new vistas in nonintrusive therapy. For example, it looks as though we can relieve Oscar's unnatural craving for brisket just by changing the linguistic background—viz., by getting his colinguals to talk English2 instead of English. Whereas it used to seem that we'd be required to operate on *Oscar:* desensitization training, depth therapy, Lord knows what all else.

Psyche and I find this sort of consequence preposterous, but no doubt intuitions differ. That's why it's nice to have a principle or two to hone them on.

8. More precisely, methodological solipsism is a doctrine not about individuation in psychology at large but about individuation in aid of the psychology of mental processes. Methodological solipsism constrains the ways mental processes can specify their ranges and domains: They can't apply differently to mental states just in virtue of the truth or falsity of the propositions that the mental states express. And they can't apply differently to concepts depending on whether or not the concepts denote. (See Fodor, MS.) This is, however, a nicety that is almost always ignored in the literature, and I shan't bother about it here.

9. In published commnents on an earlier version of this chapter, Martin Davies (*EPENC*) remarks that what I say about being a planet "seems to be in tension with the insistence that causal powers must be compared across contexts or environments. For it cannot be the case *both* that a planet has characteristic causal powers and not merely those of a physically similar chunk of matter that is not a planet, *and* that causal powers have to be compared across contexts or environments quite generally." But—to put it roughly—this confuses the question whether *being a planet* is taxonomic (which it is; two things that differ in *that* property ipso facto differ in their effects in many contexts) with the question whether *being this piece of rock* is taxonomic (which it isn't; two things that differ in *that* property do not thereby differ in their effects in *any* context).

Once again: A difference between properties P and P1 can affect causal powers (can be taxonomic) only when there is a situation S such that the instantiation of P in S has, ipso facto, different effects from the instantiation of P1 in S. By this criterion, the difference between *being a planet* and *not being a planet* affects causal powers because there are situations in which something that's a planet has, ipso facto, different effects from something that isn't. By contrast, the difference (in content) between the thought that water is wet and the thought that water2 is wet does *not* affect the causal powers of tokens of these thoughts: there are *no* situations in which one thought has, ipso facto, different effects than the other. So, in particular, if I am transported to Twin Earth, all else being left unchanged, then if I have the thought that water is wet in a situation where my Twin's thought that water2 is wet has consequence C, then my thought has consequence C in that situation too. (Compare a real—taxonomically relevant—difference in content; e.g., the difference between my thought that water is toxic and your thought that it's potable. Tokens of these thoughts differ in their consequences in *all sorts* of situations.)

10. It is, however, worth echoing an important point that Burge makes; the differences between the way that these taxonomies carve things up only show in funny cases. In practically all the cases that anybody actually encounters outside philosophical fantasies, the states that one is tempted to count as token beliefs that *P* share not just the causal powers that psychologists care about but also the relational background to which the commonsense taxonomy is sensitive. This enormous de facto coextension is part of the argument that the psychologist's story really is a vindication of the commonsense belief/desire theory.

11. Since you buy the narrow content construct at the cost of acknowledging a certain amount of inexpressibility, it may be some consolation that *not* buying the narrow content construct also has a certain cost in inexpressibility (though for quite a different sort of reason, to be sure). So, suppose you think that Twin-Earth shows that content doesn't determine extension and/or that content doesn't supervene on physiology. So, you have no use for narrow content. Still there's the following question: When my Twin thinks 'water2 is wet,' how do you say, in English, what he is thinking? Not by saying 'water2 is wet,' for that's a sentence of Tw-English; and not by saying 'water is wet,' since, on the present assumptions, whatever 'water2' means, it's something different from what 'water' means; not by saying 'XYZ is wet,' since my Twin will presumably take 'water2 is XYZ' to say something informative; something, indeed, which he might wish to deny. And not, for sure, by saying 'H$_2$O is wet,' since there isn't any H$_2$O on Twin-Earth, and my Twin has never so much as heard of the stuff. It looks like the meaning of 'water2 is wet' is *inexpressible* in English. And of course, the same thing goes—only the other way 'round—for expressing the meaning of 'water' in Tw-English.

12. Much the same treatment of Twin examples as the one I propose here was independently suggested by White, in *PCLT*.

My indebtedness to the spirit of David Kaplan's treatment of demonstratives will be clear to readers familiar with his work. However, the current proposal is *not* that kind terms and the like are indexicals. You have to relativize narrow contents to contexts—roughly, to a world—to get *anything* that's semantically evaluable. But in the case of true indexicals you require a *further* relativization—roughly, to an occasion of utterance. So, according to this analysis, "water" isn't an indexical, but "I" and the like are. Which is just as it should be.

Chapter 3

1. Strictly speaking, Stich claims only that Mrs. T's case demonstrates the holism of content *ascription;* and, of course, it does do that. But clearly something stronger is needed if the facts about Mrs. T are to argue for Meaning Holism. Barring verificationism, nothing *semantic* follows from the fact that we take evidence of someone's not knowing what assassination is, who McKinley was, and so forth, as evidence that he doesn't believe that McKinley was assassinated. Stich is a little inclined to waffle on this point; but by the time we get to page 85—where the slippery slope half of the argument is set out—the inference from holism of belief *ascription* to holism of belief *content* (viz., to Meaning Holism) is pretty explicit. See such passages as: "At what point *would we be prepared to say* that Paul and the future scientists first have identical beliefs? Well, at no *point*. Their beliefs *simply become more and more identical in content.*" (First and third emphases added.) Here we slide from the epistemic doctrine to the semantic one almost in adjacent sentences.

2. Putnam must have in mind a passage from "Two Dogmas" that goes: "The statement, rather than the term, came with Frege to be recognized as the unit accountable to an empiricist critique. But what I am now urging is that even in taking the statement as the unit we have drawn our grid too finely. The unit of empirical significance is the whole of science" (p. 42). But it looks to be Confirmation Holism rather than Semantic Holism that Quine is espousing here. God knows what it is to be "accountable to an empiricist critique," but in this context "empirical significance" is surely more plausibly paraphrased as 'testability' than as 'intentional content.'

3. This argument assumes, of course, that the confirmation of 'data sentences' is itself nonholistic. Behind this assumption lay the Positivistic idea that whereas you evaluate theory sentences indirectly via the evaluation of the data sentences they entail, you evaluate data sentences directly by comparing them with the world (or with experience, or whatever). The doctrine that the epistemic difference between data sentences and theory sentences is principled is the second of the two 'dogmas' of Empiricism that Quine considers and rejects.

4. In some cases mental states fall under psychological generalizations in virtue of the *logical form* of their intentional objects (if you believe *Fa*, then probably you believe $\exists x(Fx)$ and so forth.) Here too the observation applies that the counterfactual-supporting psychological generalizations abstract from the intentional content of the attitudes that they subsume.

There are, however, real counterexamples. Consider such generalizations as that 'the cat is on the mat' is the form of words that English speakers standardly use to express the belief that a contextually relevant cat is on a contextually relevant mat. It's plausible that learning English involves learning a recursive specification of such generalizations, and, in this case, quantifying over content won't do. Precisely what the speaker has to learn is *which* belief content goes with which verbal form. So a functionalist could argue that these sorts of generalizations supply the basis for content distinctions among mental states that are, at a minimum, as fine grained as English can express. But this leaves content ascription perilously dependent upon the ascribee's ability to talk. What do you do about infants and animals?

5. Concepts, properties, symbols, and the relations between them will loom large from here on; we'd better have an orthographic convention.

Whenever it matters, names of concepts will appear in caps; names of properties in italic; and names of words—as usual—in quotes. From time to time, I use quoted English formulas to refer to the corresponding expressions of Mentalese, leaving it to context and the reader's perspicacity to disambiguate. Thus *red* is a property (the one that red things qua red things share); RED is the concept which denotes (or expresses) *red;* and 'red' is a term (either of English or Mentalese) that encodes that concept. (Since, however, RTM has it that concepts just *are* expressions of Mentalese, it turns out that the two formulas 'the concept RED' and 'the Mentalese expression "red" ' are coreferential. My usage relies on this from time to time.)

6. Begging this question is a nasty habit of "use theories" of meaning. For example, the Wittgenstein of the early pages of the *Investigations* appears to hold that the fact that a word has the meaning that it does *reduces to* the fact that we use it the way we do. (For example, the fact that my imperative utterance of 'Slab' has the compliance conditions that it does reduces to the fact that people regularly bring slabs when tokens of that type are uttered.) One wonders how, precisely—or how even roughly—this reduction is supposed to go.

7. A possible line would be that functional roles somehow give rise to (not satisfaction

conditions but) conditions of putative *warrant*. (On this view, Oedipus's problem was that what he took to warrant the belief that he was marrying J he failed to take to warrant the belief that he was marrying Mother.) But the old worry recurs; two-factor theory now has no way of ensuring that the conditions under which a belief is warranted have *anything* to do with the conditions under which that belief is true. Imagine somebody who has a belief that is warranted just in case he has good evidence that Wagner was a German but that is true or false depending on whether Canton is in China. What on Earth would be the content of such a belief? (Equivalently preposterous, and for the same reasons: What would a sentence mean that was assertable just in the first of these conditions and true just in the second?)

I don't, myself, hold with the notion that warrant is a semantic category. But if I did, I'd make sure to be the traditional one-factor sort of warrant theorist who gets rid of satisfaction as an independent meaning component by, for example, identifying truth with warrant-in-the-long-run.

8. This looks like implying that you can have the concept FATHER even though you don't have the concept PARENT; which, of course, you can't, since the concept FATHER *is* the concept MALE PARENT, and surely you can't have the concept MALE PARENT unless you have the concept PARENT.

What's needed to avoid this embarrassment is a distinction between having a concept "free" and having it "bound." The claim about WATER and H_2O is that having the latter concept requires having the concept H "free"; i.e., it requires that you have some thoughts in which H occurs in contexts other than $..._2O$ (and similarly for O and 2). By contrast, it seems plausible that although you can't have the concept FATHER without having the concept MALE PARENT, you can perfectly well have FATHER without having either MALE or PARENT free; i.e., as constituents of any *other* concepts. On this view, there's an ambiguity in the claim that someone has the concept MALE PARENT, depending on whether he has it with the constituent concepts free or bound. Hence the claim that having the concept FATHER is having the concept MALE PARENT is also ambiguous, and there is a possible state of mind that's correctly described as having the one concept but not the other.

I think this consequence is acceptable; in fact, I think it's true. Children know about fathers long before they know about males and parents. So either they don't have the concept FATHER when they seem to, or you can have the concept MALE PARENT without having access to its internal structure; viz., by having the concept FATHER. Of these alternatives, the last seems best.

9. It wouldn't follow that *believing* that three is a prime number could constitute an entire mental life; believing is a functional state. See above.

10. Stich has, however, another use for Mrs. T which, though it doesn't bear directly on issues of Meaning Holism, is nonetheless worth discussing.

His point can be put in the form of a dilemma. It's agreed on all hands that Mrs. T, at the end, lacked the belief that McKinley was assassinated. It follows, therefore, that she failed to be subsumed by any psychological generalization that applies to subjects in virtue of their holding that belief. Yet Mrs. T was not, we may assume, irrational. For example, she was prepared to accept such arguments as 'if McKinley was assassinated in Ohio, then McKinley was assassinated'; in effect, she subscribed to the argument scheme 'if Fx and Gx, then Fx.' At very least— whatever the case may actually have been with Mrs. T—it seems conceptually possible that someone should be in a condition of radically impaired memory combined with intact ratiocination.

The moral Stich draws from this possibility is that we lose a generalization about the argument schemes that people accept if we insist that psychological laws apply in virtue of a subject's intentional states. For, on the one hand, Mrs. T accepts simplification of conjunction; and, on the other, her mental state has no intentional content that we can specify; we can't say what, if anything, it is that she believes about McKinley's death. Stich has similar remarks to make about children and cultural exotics. When the subject's "doxastic surround" is sufficiently different from ours, "there is simply no saying" what intentional state he's in. Yet many of the laws of psychology presumably hold for these populations. The moral is that since the ascription of intentional content is, as it were, more parochial than the ascription of psychological law, *we lose predictive/explanatory power if we identify the domains of such laws by reference to intentional states.* So perhaps we'd better identify these domains *syntactically* instead; so Stich's argument goes.

Now, of course, it may be that Mrs. T really wasn't, in the relevant respects, an intentional system; that she really didn't believe *anything* about McKinley, and that her apparent rationality consisted in no more than a commitment to a principle of (logical) syntax (so that if she found herself asserting anything of the form '*Fx* and *Gx*,' then she knew she'd better also be prepared to assert something of the form '*Fx*' even if there was nothing in particular that she took herself to mean by asserting either formula). But that story is surely implausible for the children and exotics. It's as true of them as it is of Mrs. T that we can't say what intentional states they're in. But surely they *are* intentional systems; surely they're in some intentional states or other. For children and exotics, then, we're not at all inclined to infer from '*we can't say* what it is that they believe' to '*there isn't* anything that they believe.' How, after all, *could* such an inference go through? How *could* what we can say constrain what they can believe?

What licenses the inference for Stich is a certain analysis of belief ascription. On Stich's account, "What we are saying when we say '*S* believes that *P*' [is roughly:] '*P*. *S* is in a belief state similar to the one which would play the typical causal role if my utterance of that had had a typical causal history.' The 'that' . . . is a demonstrative, referring to the play-acting utterance of '*P*' that preceded" (*FFPCS*, p. 88).

On this analysis, it presumably makes no sense to suppose that someone might entertain a belief whose content one is oneself unable to express. Notice that this is much stronger than the truism that if you can't say *such and such* then you can't attribute a belief that such and such by using an expression of the form '. . . believes that such and such.' Stich is claiming that given what belief ascriptions mean, they involve implicit reference to the expressive capacities of the ascriber. More particularly, for me to say that Mrs. T believes that such and such is for me to say something about a respect in which her expressive capacities and mine are similar.

But there seems no reason to take this account of belief ascription seriously. It simply isn't part of my concept of belief that people can only believe the things that I can say. To take just one case, we noticed in chapter 2 (note 11) that what my Twin believes when he believes that water2 is wet is inexpressible in English (and, indeed, in any language that I speak). And conversely, my Twin can't say in any language that he speaks what it is that I believe about the wetness of water. I am not, however, remotely tempted to infer that my Twin is not an intentional system. For one thing, it would be churlish of me to do so; and for another, it would invite him to draw the corresponding inference about *me*.

What all this comes to is just that it would be nice to have a canonical language for intentional ascription: one in which we're guaranteed (empirically, of course; not logically) that any belief that we want to attribute can be expressed. Barring that, there's an obvious way to get Mrs. T subsumed by the relevant psychological generalizations; viz., by quantifying over the intentional contents of her attitudes. So long as *identity and difference* are defined for Mrs. T's concepts, we can perfectly well say that she's subsumed by *if you believe that Fx and Gx, then you believe that Fx*, even though we are, by assumption, unable to find an English paraphrase for 'F' or 'G.'

The problem, to put it succinctly, is not with intentional generalization but just with Stich's account of what belief ascriptions mean.

11. The last three paragraphs were prompted by a conversation with Ned Block and Paul Horwich, to both of whom many thanks.

Chapter 4

1. Notice that this is *not* the same question as: 'What is it for a physical system to be an "intentional system"?' Intentional systems have, by definition, propositional attitudes: beliefs, as it might be. And being a belief requires (not just having an intentional object but) having the right sort of functional role. I'm leaving it open that a good reconstruction of intentionality might recognize things that have intentional states but no propositional attitudes; hence, things that have intentional states but are not intentional systems. For example, it doesn't seem to me to count against a theory of intentionality if it entails that the curvature of the bimetalic strip in a thermostat represents the temperature of the ambient air. By contrast, a theory that entails that thermostats are intentional systems—that they have beliefs and desires—would thereby refute itself.

2. No doubt, some questions are begged by assuming that the totality of an organism's mental representations does constitute a language. In particular, I'm taking it for granted that Mentalese has a combinatorial semantics. The arguments for assuming this are set out in the Appendix.

3. Skinner and Quine had, of course, proposed causal accounts of meaning in the '50s. But they assumed the psychological framework of conditioning theory; and Skinner, at least, seems not to have understood the central importance of combinatorial structure in language. Chomsky took critical note of both these flaws, with results that were enormously liberating for both linguistics and psychology. But the impact on semantics was, perhaps, more equivocal; in particular, philosophical interest in causal accounts of meaning was among the casualties of Chomsky's attack and it has only recently begun to recover.

It is, therefore, worth emphasizing that a causal theory of meaning need not assume a behavioristic psychology; and that there is no contradiction between a combinatorial semantics and a causal solution to the naturalization problem. It seems, in retrospect, that the Chomsky landslide may after all have buried something valuable.

4. Any case where false beliefs have greater survival value than the corresponding true ones would, of course, do just as well as repression to point this moral. See Stich (*FFPCS*), where this sort of argument against teleological semantics is pressed; plausibly, in my view.

5. This isn't supposed to be a Paradigm Case Argument: it's perfectly possible to say 'that's a unicorn' falsely even though there aren't any unicorns and no one ever says 'that's a unicorn' truly. But even here the possibility of making false predications depends upon the semantical setup being available for making true ones, if only the world would cooperate by providing some unicorns to make them *of*.

Perhaps what CCT should say about unicorns is that they *would* be nomically sufficient for 'unicorn'-tokenings if there were any. (There can, of course, be a nomic connection between properties one or more of which is de facto uninstantiated.) On the other hand, I suppose that treatment would require unicorns to be at least *nomologically possible;* so Heaven only knows what a causal theory ought to say if they're not. For that matter, Heaven only knows what a causal theory ought to say about *any* symbol which expresses a property that can't be instantiated; perhaps that such a symbol can't be primitive.

6. It needs to be borne in mind, however, that this construal of asymmetric dependence, formulated in terms of causal connections between B's and 'A's (between, say, cows and 'horses'), is short for a more precise version formulated in terms of nomic dependences between higher-order properties (between, say, the property of being an instantiation of *cow* and the property of being a tokening of 'horse'). So, the parade version goes like this:

B-caused 'A' tokens are wild only if the nomic dependence of instantiations of the property of being an 'A' tokening upon instantiations of the property of being a B tokening is itself dependent upon the nomic dependence of the property of being an 'A' tokening upon instantiations of some property other than B.

You can see why I prefer to work with the undress version. Still, the difference between the formulations sometimes matters. One reason why it does is made clear by a puzzle that I owe to Scott Weinstein. Consider:

(*i*)   Small horses cause 'horses.'

(*ii*)   Horses cause 'horses.'

(*iii*)   (*i*) depends on (*ii*) (small horses wouldn't cause 'horses' unless horses did).

(*iv*)   (*ii*) is not dependent on (*i*) (horses would cause 'horses' even if small horses didn't; even if, for example, there were only large horses).

(*v*)   So small-horse-caused 'horse' tokenings are asymmetrically dependent on horse-caused horse tokenings; so small-horse-caused 'horse' tokenings are wild.

This seems to show that asymmetric dependence can't be sufficient for wildness even if it's necessary. One avoids the conclusion, however, by noting that (*Pi*), the parade version of (*i*),

(*Pi*) 'Horse' tokenings are nomically dependent on the instantiation of small horse.

is false; the counterfactual-supporting connection is between 'horse' tokenings and *horse* instantiation, not between 'horse' tokenings and *small horse* instantiation. Notice how the subjunctives go: this (recently denoted) small horse would have caused a 'horse' tokening *even if it had been larger;* to a first approximation, horses cause 'horse' tokenings regardless of their size.

7. I'm indebted for this case to Georges Rey, Barry Loewer, and Ron McClamrock.

8. To deny that it's *even* necessary, you must accept the following as a possible case: We apply 'horse' to cows, and we would continue to do so even if we didn't apply 'horse' to horses; yet 'horse' means *horse,* and applications of 'horse' to cows are ipso facto false.

This doesn't look like a possible case to me. What on earth would *make* 'horse' mean *horse* in such a case? What would stop it from meaning *cow?*

9. A number of people have suggested to me that the extensions of concepts with prototype structure would exhibit a sort of asymmetric dependence: the non-prototypic members wouldn't be in the extension unless the prototypic ones were, but the prototypic ones would be in even if the others weren't.

But I think this is wrong. Sparrows are prototypical birds. But suppose they turned out to be reptiles, hence not birds at all (in the way that whales turned out to be mammals, hence not fish at all). It wouldn't follow that we would stop calling penguins and parrots 'birds'; that would depend on whether they turned out to be reptiles too. You don't destroy a category by showing that its prototype is incoherent (in the way that you *do* destroy a category by showing that its *definition* is incoherent).

This suggests what's independently plausible; viz., that prototype structure has nothing much to do with *meaning*. (What then *does* it have to do with? Well might one wonder.)

10. Terminology in this area is a bit unstable. What I'm calling 'observation' vocabulary (and what often does get called that in epistemological theorizing) is more or less the same as what gets called 'sensory' vocabulary in traditional philosophical psychology. The intuition that there is an important distinction in this area is wider spread than consensus on what to call it or how to draw it.

11. Even the claim that there are circumstances under which psychophysics guarantees the contents of the occurs-to-me box is a little less drastic than it may seem at first: In the sort of psychology I'm assuming, an organism need not be conscious of the thoughts that occur to it. On the other hand, it's a good deal more than vacuous, since, given functionalism, what's in the occurs-to-me box (or any other box, for that matter) is ipso facto guaranteed to modify the flow of mental processing actually or potentially.

12. It is, however, perfectly possible to imagine creatures for which WATER *is* a psychophysical concept; creatures that have transducers for H_2O so that, in particular, their sensory mechanisms respond differently to samples of water than they do to samples of XYZ. If we were creatures, Putnam would have had to choose a different example.

This by way of emphasizing that if 'observation concept' means 'psychophysical concept,' then which concepts *are* observational can't be determined a priori.

13. This means more than 'Dobbin's being a horse is *causally necessary* for Dobbin's having that horsy look'; but I don't know how much more. I take it, however, that it's OK for an astronomer to say 'a meteor was the cause of the Great Siberian Crater,' knowing that he means more by this than 'no meteor, no crater.' Well, if he can help himself to 'the cause' without further analysis, so can I. I propose to.

It is *simply unreasonable* to require that a solution to the naturalization problem for semantics should also provide an account of causal explanation. Semantics is respectable if it can make do with the same metaphysical apparatus that the rest of the empirical sciences require; it doesn't *also* have to incorporate a theory of that apparatus.

14. More precisely, what's required is of the form: It's nomologically necessary that protons affect the belief box if . . . . We want the modal operator to insure against vacuous or accidental satisfactions of the conditional.

15. And, of course, the causation of 'horse's by nonhorses has to be asymmetrically dependent upon the causation of 'horse's by horses, as per the first half of this chapter.

16. At this level of psychological unsophistication, intertranslation between the association story and the belief-box story is trivial and not worth the bother of spelling out. I emphasize, however, that I am *not*, by any conceivable stretch of the imagination, endorsing an associative theory of the mind. My point is just that the role of internalized theories *in fixing the semantic contents of concepts* is so merely mechanical that even an Associationist can reconstruct it.

Appendix

1. Aunty's not the only one who'd like to know; much the same question has been raised by Noam Chomsky, John Searle, Brian Loar, David Israel, Jon Barwise and John Perry, and Tyler Burge, to name just a few. Aunty and I are grateful to all of the above for conversations which led to the present reflections. Also to Ned Block for characteristically perceptive comments on an earlier draft.

2. Do not be misled by the fact that the *node labels* in associative networks are composed of transportable constituents; the labels play no part in the theory. Cf. Fodor, *IA*, where this point is made twelve thousand eight hundred and fifteen times.

   By the way, it isn't the *associative* part of 'associative network' that's at issue here. Classical Associationists—Hume, say—held that mental representations have transportable constituents and, I suppose, a combinatorial semantics: the mental image of a house contains, as proper parts, mental images of proper parts of houses. Hume is therefore on my side of the argument as against Aunty and the New Connectionists. The heart of the issue—to repeat the text—is whether you need *both* constituency *and* connectivity as basic relations among the semantically evaluated mental objects, or whether you can make do with connectivity alone.

3. In *From Folk Psychology to Cognitive Science*, Stich wrings his hands a lot about how I could hold that the counterfactual-supporting generalizations of psychology are uniformly intentional *and also* hold the 'solipsistic' principle that mental operations are computational (viz., formal/syntactic). "How is it possible for Fodor to have it both ways, for him to urge *both* that cognitive generalizations apply to mental states in virtue of their content and that 'only *non*-semantic properties of mental representations can figure in determining which mental operations apply to them'?" (*FFPCS*, 188).

   But there's no contradiction. The vocabulary required to articulate the characteristic laws of a special science is—almost invariably—different from the vocabulary required to articulate the mechanisms by which these laws are sustained, the theory of the mechanisms being pitched—to put it crudely—one level down. So the typical *laws* of psychology are intentional, and the typical *operations* of psychological mechanisms are computational, and everything's fine except that Stich has missed a distinction.

4. Notice—by contrast—that relations to nonactual entities can perfectly well be *constitutive of* causal powers: the solubility of this salt consists in such facts as that if there *were* water here, the salt would dissolve in it. The point in the text, then, is that though relations to nonactual objects can figure in the analysis of a causal power, they can't be among its causal determinants. Nothing—causal powers included—can be an effect of a merely possible cause. (I'm grateful to Georges Rey for helping me to get this sorted out.)

5. It remains open to Aunty to argue in the following relatively subtle sort of way: "All right, so principle P requires that the causes of complex behaviors should themselves be complex. But that still doesn't show that there's a Language of Thought, because the required complex causal objects could be the *propositional attitude states themselves* rather than the (putative) formulas of this (putative) mental language. *Believing that P & Q is itself a complex state* of which the simple parts are the state of believing that P and the state of believing that Q." In effect, Aunty could try conceding that propositional attitudes are *complex* but denying that they are, in the relevant respect, *relational*.

   This, however, will not do. Believing that P is *not* a constituent of, for example, believing that P or Q (or of believing that if P then Q . . . etc.); for it is perfectly possible to believe that P or Q (or that if P then Q) and not to believe that P. For similar reasons the required notion of constituency can't be defined over the *causal roles* of the attitudes, either. Thus, the causal role of believing that P is not a constituent of the causal role of believing that P or Q since, for example, the effects of believing that it will snow in August are categorically different from—and are not included among—the effects of believing that either it will snow in August or it won't.

See Fodor, *R*, circa p. 30, and Fodor, *RBL*, where these sorts of observations are parlayed into yet another argument fot LOT. (I do wish that Aunty would read my stuff occasionally!)

References

Barwise, J., and Perry, J. (*SA*). *Situations and Attitudes*. Cambridge, Mass.: MIT Press, 1981.

Block, N. (*RB*). "Reply to Burge." MS, Massachusetts Institute of Technology, 1984.

Block, N. (*ASP*). "Advertisement for a Semantics for Psychology." In French, P., Euhling, T., and Wettstein, H. (eds.), *Studies in the Philosophy of Mind*. Vol. 10, *Midwest Studies in Philosophy*. Minneapolis: University of Minnesota Press, 1986.

Burge, T. (*IM*). "Individualism and the Mental." In French, P., Euhling, T., and Wettstein, H. (eds.), *Studies in Epistemology*. Vol. 4, *Midwest Studies in Philosophy*. Minneapolis: University of Minnesota Press, 1979.

Burge, T. (*IP*). "Individualism and Psychology." *Philosophical Review* 95 (January 1986): 1, 3–45.

Carroll, L. (*WTSA*). "What the Tortoise Said to Achilles." *Mind* 4 (1895).

Chomsky, N. (*RVB*). "Review of B. F. Skinner's *Verbal Behavior*." *Language* 35 (1959): 16–58.

Churchland, P. M. (*EMPA*). "Eliminative Materialism and Propositional Attitudes." *Journal of Philosophy* 78, no. 2 (1981).

Cummins, R. (*IMM*). "The Internal Manual Model of Psychological Explanation." *Cognition and Brain Theory* 5, no. 3 (1982).

Davidson, D. (*PAP*). "Psychology as Philosophy." In Brown, S. (ed.), *Philosophy of Psychology*. New York: Macmillan and Barnes, Noble, 1974.

Davidson, D. (*MM*). "The Material Mind." In Suppes, P., Henkin, L., Moisil, G., and Joja, A. (eds.), *Proceedings of the 4th International Congress for Logic, Methodology, and Philosophy of Science*. Bucharest: North Holland Publishing Company, 1973.

Davies, M. (*EPENC*). "Externality, Psychological Explanation and Narrow Content, Reply to Jerry Fodor's 'Individualism and Supervenience.' " Paper delivered to the Joint Session of the Aristotelian Society and the Mind Association, July 1986.

Demopoulos, W., and Matthews, R. (*HGMR*). "On the Hypothesis That Grammars Are Mentally Represented." *Behavioral and Brain Sciences* 3 (1983).

Dennett, D. (*CCC*). "A Cure for the Common Code?" In *Brainstorms*. Cambridge, Mass.: MIT Press, 1981.

Dennett, D. (*IS*). "Intentional Systems." Reprinted in *Brainstorms*. Vermont: Bradford Books, 1978.

Dretske, F. (*KFI*). *Knowledge and the Flow of Information. Cambridge, Mass.: MIT Press, 1981*.

Field, H. (*MR*). "Mental Representation." *Erkenntnis* 13, no. 1 (1978).

Fodor, J. (*ATK*). "The Appeal to Tacit Knowledge in Psychological Explanation." *Journal of Philosophy* 65, no. 20 (1968). (Reprinted in Fodor, J., *Representations*, q.v.)

Fodor, J. (*SS*). "Special Sciences." *Synthese* 28 (1974). (Reprinted in Fodor, J., *Representations*, q.v.)

Fodor, J. (*LOT*). *The Language of Thought*. New York: Thomas Y. Crowell, 1975.

Fodor, J. (*PA*). "Propositional Attitudes." *The Monist* 64, no. 4 (1978). (Reprinted in Fodor, J., *Representations*, q.v.)

Fodor, J. (*MS*). "Methodological Solipsism Considered as a Research Strategy in Cognitive Science." *Behavioral and Brain Sciences*, 1980. (Reprinted in Fodor, J., *Representations*, q.v.)

Fodor, J. (*R*). *Representations*. Cambridge, Mass.: MIT Press, 1981.

Fodor, J. (*SSA*). "Something on the State of the Art." Introduction to Fodor, J., *Representations*, q.v.

Fodor, J. (*MOM*). *The Modularity of Mind*. Cambridge, Mass.: MIT Press, 1983.

Fodor, J. (*RBL*). "Reply to Brian Loar's 'Must Beliefs Be Sentences.' " In Asquith, P., and Nickles, T. (eds.), *Proceedings of the Philosophy of Science Association for 1982*. East Lansing, Michigan, 1983.

Fodor, J. (*P*). "Psychosemantics." MS, Massachusetts Institute of Technology, 1984.

Fodor, J. (*NCMH*). "Narrow Content and Meaning Holism." MS, Massachusetts Institute of Technology, 1985.

Fodor, J. (*BD*). "Banish DisContent." In Butterfield, J. (ed.), *Language, Mind, and Logic*. Cambridge: Cambridge University Press, 1986.

Fodor, J. (*IA*). "Information and Association." *Notre Dame Journal of Formal Logic*, in press.

Grice, H. P. (*LC*). "Logic and Conversation." In Harman, G., and Davidson, D. (eds.), *Semantics of Natural Languages*. Dordrecht: Reidel, 1972.

Jubien, M. (*OPPT*). "On Properties and Property Theory." MS, University of Massachusetts at Amherst, 1986.

Kaplan, D. (*D*). "Demonstratives." MS, 1977.

Lewis, D. (*C*). *Counterfactuals*. Oxford: Blackwell, 1973.

Loar, B. (*SCPC*). "Social Content and Psychological Content." MS, 1985.

Loar, B. (*MAM*). *Mind and Meaning*. Cambridge: Cambridge University Press, 1982.

Lycan, W. (*TB*). "Tacit Belief." In Bogdan, R. (ed.), *Belief*. Oxford: Oxford University Press, forthcoming.

McClamrock, R. (*IC*). *Intentionality and Cognitivism*. Doctoral dissertation, Massachusetts Institute of Technology, 1984.

McGinn, C. (*SC*). "The Structure of Content." In Woodfield, A. (ed.), *Thought and Object*. Oxford: Clarendon Press, 1982.

Matthews, R. (*TWR*). "Troubles with Representationalism." *Social Research* 51, no. 4 (1984).

Putnam, H. (*MM*). "The Meaning of 'Meaning.' " In Gunderson, K. (ed.), *Language, Mind, and Knowledge*. Vol. 7, *Minnesota Studies in the Philosophy of Science*. Minneapolis: University of Minnesota Press, 1979.

Putnam, H. (*MH*). "Meaning Holism." MS, Harvard University.

Putnam, H. (*CPIT*). "Computational Psychology and Interpretation Theory." In *Realism and Reason*. Vol. 3, *Philosophical Papers*. Cambridge: Cambridge University Press, 1983.

Quine, W. V. (*TDE*). "Two Dogmas of Empiricism." Reprinted in *From a Logical Point of View*. 2d ed. Cambridge, Mass.: Harvard University Press, 1961.

Quine, W. V. (*WO*). *Word and Object*. Cambridge, Mass. MIT Press, 1960.

Ryle, G. (*COM*). *The Concept of Mind*. New York: Barnes and Noble, 1949.

Schiffer, S. (*TTC*). "Truth and the Theory of Content." In Parret, H., and Bouvaresse, J. (eds.), *Meaning and Understanding*. Berlin: Walter de Gruyter, 1981.

Skinner, B. F. (*VB*). *Verbal Behavior*. New York: Appleton Century Crofts, 1957.

Stabler, E. (*HAGR*). "How Are Grammars Represented?" Behavioral and Brain Sciences 3 (1983).

Stampe, D. (*TCTLR*). "Towards a Causal Theory of Linguistic Representation." In French, P., Euhling, T., and Wettstein, H. (eds.), vol. 2, *Midwest Studies in Philosophy*. Minneapolis: University of Minnesota Press, 1977.

Stich, S. (*FFPCS*). *From Folk Psychology to Cognitive Science*. Cambridge, Mass.: MIT Press, 1983.

Ullman, S. (*IVM*). *The Interpretation of Visual Motion*. Cambridge, Mass.: MIT Press, 1979.

Wellman, H. (*CTM*). "The Child's Theory of Mind: The Development of Conceptions of Cognition." In Yussen, S. (ed.), *The Growth of Reflection*. San Diego: Academic Press, 1985.

White, S. (*PCLT*). "Partial Character and the Language of Thought." *Pacific Philosophical Quarterly* 63 (1982): 347–365.

Author Index

Barwise, J., 85, 166
Block, N., 40, 75, 81, 87, 163
Burge, T., 28, 29, 30–32, 36, 37, 40–42, 44, 156, 158
Carroll, L., 23
Chomsky, N., 163, 166
Churchland, P., 20
Cummins, R., 23
Davidson, D., 5
Davies, M., 158
Demopoulos, W., 21
Dennett, D., 21–23, 24, 89, 156
Dretske, F., 85, 102–104, 157
Duhem, P., 90
Field, H., 16
Fodor, J., 5, 16, 18, 24, 63, 104, 116, 156, 158, 166
Frege, G., 64, 89, 150, 160
Freud, S., 15
Gibson, J., 116, 147, 148
Grice, P., 50, 100
Hegel, G., 154
Higgenbotham, J., 156
Horwich, P., 163
Hume, D., 9, 117
Israel, D., 166
Joyce, J., 18
Jubien, M., 92
Kant, I., 9, 123
Kaplan, D., 159
Kripke, S., 85
Kuhn, T., 88
Lewis, D., 108
Loar, B., 29, 79, 81, 156, 166
Lower, B., 164
Lycan, W., 22
McClamrock, R., 59, 64
McGinn, C., 81
Matthews, R., 102

Perry, J., 85, 166
Putnam, H., 27, 28, 31, 36, 37, 44, 46, 48, 50, 53, 64–66, 89, 93–94
Quine, W., 63–66, 122, 160, 163
Rey, G., 147, 155, 164, 166
Schiffer, S., 17
Searle, J., 147, 166
Shakespeare, W., 2
Shaw, G., 129
Skinner, B., 163
Slezak, P., 111
Stabler, E., 21
Stampe, D., 104
Stich, S., 20, 53, 61–62, 159, 161–163, 166
Turing, A., 23
Wellman, H., 132–133
White, S., 159
Wittgenstein, L., 147, 149, 160